Pragmatism, Democracy, *and the* Necessity of Rhetoric

Studies in Rhetoric/Communication
Thomas W. Benson, Series Editor

Pragmatism, Democracy, *and the* Necessity of Rhetoric

Robert Danisch

The University of South Carolina Press

Published by the University of South Carolina Press
Columbia, South Carolina 29208

www.sc.edu/uscpress

Manufactured in the United States of America

16 15 14 13 12 11 10 09 08 07 10 9 8 7 6 5 4 3 2 1

Library of Congress Cataloging-in-Publication Data

Danisch, Robert, 1976–
Pragmatism, democracy, and the necessity of rhetoric / Robert Danisch.
p. cm. — (Studies in rhetoric/communication)
Includes bibliographical references and index.
ISBN-13: 978-1-57003-690-3 (cloth : alk. paper)
ISBN-10: 1-57003-690-X (cloth : alk. paper)
1. Pragmatism. 2. Rhetoric—Philosophy. 3. Rhetoric—United States
4. Democracy—United States. I. Title.
B832.D36 2007
144'.30973—dc22

2007007320

This book was printed on Glatfelter Natures, a recycled paper with 50 percent postconsumer waste content.

For Jess

Contents

Series Editor's Preface

In *Pragmatism, Democracy, and the Necessity of Rhetoric,* Robert Danisch explores how the philosophy of American pragmatism developed by William James and John Dewey suggests the possibility for theorizing and enacting new versions of classical rhetoric suitable for the needs of American democracy. Danisch argues that the commitments of American pragmatism mirror those of classical rhetoric—belief in uncertainty, epistemological anthropocentrism, pluralism, interest in the relations of individual and community, and the search for tools and methods of thought and action. But classical rhetoric was developed to suit the practical discursive needs of a different time and place, and the American pragmatists did not fully develop the rhetorical thinking that was implicit in their work. Danisch proposes to re-energize the project of developing rhetorical theories suggested by the association of pragmatic philosophy and classical rhetorical theory.

Professor Danisch explores the philosophical writings of James and Dewey as resources for the development of rhetorical theorizing, and he examines the discourse of American rhetorical practitioners who were themselves imbued with the spirit of pragmatism and whose persuasion at least implicitly demonstrates its tools and methods. Danisch insists, in the spirit of the philosophy itself, that pragmatism is best thought of as productive of multiple lines of rhetorical theorizing, rather than as foundational of some single doctrine of rhetoric. He concludes his work with suggestive illustrations of the pragmatic strain in rhetorical theorists Kenneth Burke, Wayne Booth, Stephen Toulmin, Stanley Fish, and others.

Pragmatism, Democracy, and the Necessity of Rhetoric is a lively and compelling rethinking of the resources for American democratic rhetoric in the spirit of pragmatic philosophy, suggesting many lines of further inquiry into the theory, criticism, and practice of rhetoric.

Thomas W. Benson
Series Editor, Studies in Rhetoric/Communication

Acknowledgments

This book has benefited from the assistance of many people. John Poulakos's insightful guidance helped develop one simple, muted, and unclear idea into something far more substantive. His generosity and willingness to listen profoundly to someone struggling to find a voice were matched only by his intellectual standards and expectations. To the extent this book is able to get at large ideas clearly and convincingly, it is a product of provocative and inspiring conversations with John Poulakos, who is a master of the art.

Pete Simonson's thoughtful criticisms and thorough command of American intellectual history, along with his encouragement, helped me immeasurably. I owe a great deal to Pete's ability to get right to the most essential questions and to recommend brilliant methods for answering those questions—I cannot imagine a better person with whom to work. Jonathan Sterne provided more support, kindness, and insight than I could have ever expected. He is proof that someone who is highly intelligent can be a tremendous help regardless of whether his expertise coincides with yours. He pushed me to make clearer and better arguments than I would have otherwise.

I owe a great deal to Allan Megill. As my undergraduate adviser, he was a model of scholarly excellence, and his influence still lingers over all my writing and research. I have yet to experience a better learning environment than the classes he taught. I am a far better writer and thinker because of the time he spent correcting my work for those four years. The University of Virginia was a remarkable place to begin an academic career.

I also wish to thank Thomas Benson, who is the editor of this series, for his suggestions and encouragement, and I owe much to Ed Schiappa for his review of the manuscript. Barry Blose at the University of South Carolina Press was a great help, and working with the rest of the staff there has been a terrific experience.

Books are not merely products of scholars or writers. They are also deeply personal. It is too easy and too much of an understatement to say that this would not have been possible without Jessica Mudry, my best friend and the love of my life. Without her support and faith I am not sure I would have finished my doctorate, let alone gone on to produce this book. She has given me more happiness, more confidence, more hope—in fact more of everything than I could ever have possibly imagined. I thank her for her wit, intelligence, copyediting, conversation, good humor, kindness, and vivaciousness. I thank her especially for carrying our "raisin." I dedicate this book, and everything else, for that matter, to her.

Pragmatism, Democracy, *and the* Necessity of Rhetoric

Introduction

The Consequences of Pragmatist Thought

On December 7, 1941, hours after the Japanese attacked Pearl Harbor, John Dewey lectured to hundreds of people at Cooper Union in New York City.[1] The lecture had been planned months before, and Dewey was expected to speak on "Lessons from the War in Philosophy." The title of the lecture referred to the First World War, not the battles raging in Europe or the Japanese aggression in the Pacific, which was in the minds of the audience. This situation was a great test for Dewey's pragmatism. A philosophy that sought to address the pressing problems of the moment should have had something to say on the matter of war on that particular evening. However, Dewey told the audience, "I have nothing, had nothing, and have nothing now, to say directly about the war" (Diggins 1994, 1). In an effort to explain his reticence, Dewey argued that "[p]hilosophy, intellectual operations, in general, are likely to come after events. This is a sort of *ex post facto* enterprise and very often by the time philosophy is formed, events have changed so much that there isn't much for ideas to lay hold of" (2). Given an instrumental approach to knowledge and a promise to help people deliberate when challenged by difficult situations, Dewey's lecture may seem to have been a momentary failure of pragmatism. Also it may seem as if Dewey were not living up to many of his bold claims about the task of philosophy. John Patrick Diggins suggests just this in his introduction to *The Promise of Pragmatism.*

An alternative explanation of Dewey's lecture on December 7, 1941, is possible. Such an occasion exemplifies the importance of the art of rhetoric in human affairs. A rhetor, through an act of public speech, can offer counsel, define problems, suggest solutions, provide meaning when all appears confused and uncertain, or persuade an audience to believe or to act in a fitting and timely manner. In this case, Dewey failed as a rhetor. By building a case on moments such as these, Diggins makes a broader claim—that pragmatism, in general, failed to fulfill its promise as a public-oriented, instrumental philosophy. What is most significant about Dewey's lecture, though, was his inability to find the words necessary to articulate a response to the attack on Pearl Harbor. Although pragmatism demands that its practitioners seek practical arts grounded on knowledge and experience to solve problems, it does not prescribe specific linguistic practices. In this instance, Dewey remained beholden to the tradition of philosophy and its pursuit of knowledge. His failure, then, was not a failure of the principles of pragmatism; it was a sign of pragmatism's inability to develop a suitable rhetoric embedded in its own principles. His failure as a rhetor also suggests the need to develop an American rhetoric guided by the intellectual commitments of pragmatism. This book begins that task.

This work advances a reading of pragmatism grounded in the belief that Dewey's own intellectual aspirations were guided by the attempt to make philosophy more rhetorical. In fact, I argue that pragmatism can be defined by its search for rhetorical practices that use knowledge to guide deliberation and judgment. Dewey's lecture illustrates his inability to master the art of rhetoric despite the fact that his public performances indicated his own interest in such a task. If, in that moment, pragmatism did not fulfill all of its promise, this is not because its principles are faulty. It is, rather, because those principles hint at the possibility and necessity of rhetoric for American democracy but do not fully articulate that rhetoric. Such a reading issues from a deep similarity between pragmatism and classical rhetoric. Classical rhetoric and pragmatism share a specific orientation to the world, an orientation that informs the beliefs and practices of each. By virtue of an interest in the problems of the moment; a commitment to plurality, uncertainty, and contingency; a desire to find practical arts to guide deliberation and judgment; and a belief in the power of individuals and communities to influence the course of social and political affairs, pragmatism reiterates many of the intellectual commitments of classical rhetoric in new variations.

Accordingly, pragmatism can be read in the light of the rhetorical tradition. Specifically I argue that pragmatism opens the possibility for a search for contemporary, American rhetorics, with roots in classical rhetorical theory but with the determination to respond to contemporary irresolutions. This argument associates American pragmatism with an alternative but significant tradition—a tradition often overlooked. The corollary to this argument is that classical rhetoric can suggest ways to improve pragmatism. In the search for practical methods to use knowledge effectively, rhetoric can prove an indispensable art and a useful tool, particularly in a democratic society. Stated another way, classical rhetoric can be a helpful and fitting resource for rethinking, reshaping, and extending the variety of contemporary pragmatisms. Conversely pragmatism can be a useful resource for rethinking, reshaping, and extending rhetoric's varied roles in human affairs. Pointing to the similarities between pragmatism and classical rhetoric highlights the need to find appropriate rhetorics for American democracy and to articulate the intellectual conditions for the realization of such rhetorics.

Dewey's lecture on December 7, 1941, points to the significance of such a reading. If Dewey had had access to the rhetorical tradition, if he had practiced the art of public address in response to pressing problems, or if he had had a specific set of practices available for use at the moment, he might have been able to offer intelligent insight into the situation. Classical rhetoric offers specific recommendations for pragmatism to be made more useful and more effective. Such recommendations would work in line with the basic principles of pragmatism, thus fulfilling some of its promise, which Diggins claims goes unfulfilled.[2] Moreover, pragmatism's own situation as a product of, and a force in, American culture recommends the use of specific practical arts. These practical arts provide important suggestions for the effective use of rhetoric in American society. The principles of pragmatism are the grounds for such suggestions.

The argument that pragmatism shares an orientation to the world with classical rhetoric and opens the possibility for the development of possible American rhetorics rests on three claims. First, by rejecting the speculative concerns of traditional philosophy and searching for a philosophy of action, William James and John Dewey imply that philosophy is tied inextricably to rhetoric. Second, by doing so they attend to the need for practical methods designed to improve American life and create responsible agents of change. Such a project resembles the historical experience of classical Athens and illustrates the importance of rhetoric for a democratic society. Third, by focusing on concrete communicative practices instead of abstract ideas, the pragmatists were persistently hinting at, and searching for, rhetorical strategies for binding communities together and granting individuals a voice in the affairs of those communities. While James and Dewey worked within philosophy departments to craft this orientation to the world, other pragmatists extended these beliefs through specific, concrete practices. Jane Addams as a political activist, Alain Locke as a cultural critic, and Oliver Wendell Holmes as a lawyer and judge are three such examples.

Exploring the connections between pragmatism and classical rhetoric begs two fundamental and challenging questions. The first concerns the meaning of "pragmatism," while the second concerns the meaning of "rhetoric." Both terms evoke a variety of possible definitions, writers, and ideas. This variety may, in fact, include discordant features or personalities. What is important, however, is that both pragmatism and rhetoric resist easy definitions because both are multifaceted and broad-ranging intellectual enterprises. The rhetorical tradition encompasses thinkers as discordant as Gorgias, St. Augustine, and George

Campbell and it is founded on Aristotle's claim that "rhetoric is not bound up with any single set of subjects, but is as universal as dialectic" (*Rhetoric* 1355b5). Likewise, pragmatism implicates thinkers as various as F. C. S. Schiller, Reinhold Niebuhr, and Richard Rorty. The first task, then, is to identify the meanings of both "pragmatism" and "rhetoric."

Pragmatism as an Orientation to the World

In the preface to *The Metaphysical Club,* Louis Menand offers one account of the general features of pragmatism: "They [Holmes, James, Peirce, and Dewey] all believed that ideas are not 'out there' waiting to be discovered, but are tools—like forks and knives and 'microchips'—that people devise to cope with the world in which they find themselves. They believed that ideas are produced not by individuals, but by groups of individuals—that ideas are social. They believed that ideas do not develop according to some inner logic of their own, but are entirely dependent, like germs, on their human carriers and the environment. And they believed that since ideas are provisional responses to particular and unpredictable circumstances, their survival depends not on their immutability but on their adaptability" (Menand 2001, xi–xii). According to Menand, it is this "attitude toward ideas" that united an otherwise disparate group of thinkers. Such an attitude was, in part, the result of the Civil War and the advent of "modern life" in America. By believing that ideas are useful and adaptable social tools, the pragmatists implicitly rejected dogma, moral certainty, and the quest for absolute truth.

Two important implications result from Menand's description of this "attitude toward ideas." First, pragmatism cannot be defined by a set of first principles or axiomatic truths, as is the tendency in most traditional philosophies. Menand replaces axioms or dogmas with the notion of "attitude." An "attitude" implies a position, or a stance, and a set of beliefs that influence the way one interacts with others. Attitudes can change, and social interaction is often what causes that change. For the purposes here, Menand's notion of "attitude" is built on through a description of pragmatism as an orientation to the world. An orientation to the world points to interactions and experiences with social and natural surroundings, as well as the role of the individual in interpreting those interactions and experiences. Second, by claiming that ideas are tools used to respond to specific situations, Menand points to the pragmatic belief that philosophy is best understood as a method for using knowledge to respond to pressing problems in their particularity. Understood as a tool, philosophy can be judged by the work it does, the problems it can solve, or the influence it is able to have.

Given Menand's claim that pragmatism is grounded on the notion that ideas are social, his "story of ideas in America" accounts for the intellectual, political, and social contexts that made the pragmatic "attitude" possible. The consequences of the Civil War provide the primary contextual instigation. The Civil War was a horrifying and traumatic experience that permanently altered the social and political fabric of the United States. For Menand, the war, by mobilizing people under the banner of moral certitude based on the delusion of timeless truths, embodied the spirit against which pragmatism emerged. Both the abolitionists and the proslavery South used absolute moral claims to justify the deaths of millions of people. In response to this violence, pragmatism sought to replace timeless truths with local, functional truths subject to revision. Menand ends his book by claiming that "pragmatism was designed to make it harder for people to be driven to violence by their beliefs" (2001, 440).[3] Beyond the rejection of moral certitude and timeless truths learned from the Civil War, several other important factors inspired pragmatism.

Charles Darwin's *Origin of the Species* (first published in 1859) describes a world filled with unique species that change over time by a natural process guided only by chance.[4] Darwin used a massive amount of material evidence to suggest the mutability of the natural world, including human beings. Menand argues that one of the fundamental insights of *The Origin of the Species* is that "among groups of sexually reproducing organisms, the variations are much more important than the similarities" (2001, 122). Thus any science that appeals only to general types that are fixed, determinate, and uniform fails to account adequately for the world that Darwin describes as "characterized by chance, change, and difference" (123).[5] *The Origin of the Species* represented "a completely different method of scientific thought" (124). It showed that science, through collecting material data, is not a project with a definitive end that describes a final set of truths, but rather a process of using theories to explain the changes in the natural world.[6] This scientific outlook had a significant impact on pragmatist thought, reinforcing the belief that the world is plural, uncertain, and determined by individual, human perspectives. It also underscored the role of chance in human affairs and helped show that changes to the sociopolitical world could happen suddenly and by unpredictable causes.

Beyond Darwin's theory of evolution, William James and John Dewey played roles in the burgeoning science of psychology. They were both influenced by Wilhelm Wundt's "experimental psychology."[7] In the 1860s Wundt began to do experiments on the "personal equation" in astronomy—"the measurement of differences between individual observers in their determinations of the position of a star" (Menand 2001, 269). Wundt learned that minds are not just passive receivers of stimuli but active participants in attending to specific aspects of their experiences. The study of the brain, the faculty of attention, experience, and perception became critical areas of inquiry for psychology with Wundt's influence. Although James and Dewey reacted against many aspects of "experimental psychology," they attended closely to issues of experience, perception, and cognition—arguing that individual consciousness plays an active role in perception and experience. This position further demonstrated a belief in scientific work as illustrating an uncertain, plural, and subjective world, not as establishing immutable and certain truths.

These immediate intellectual influences were compounded both by personal experiences and by the general social context of late nineteenth-century American society. James's pragmatism, with its faith in making self-generated convictions, clearly grew out of his long bouts with depression.[8] The city of Chicago influenced Jane Addams and John Dewey, particularly its rapidly expanding immigrant populations, its industrial economy, and its corrupt political institutions.[9] The chaos and confusion of city life brought both Addams and Dewey to reconsider the meaning of their lifeworks and encouraged both to pursue particular kinds of intellectual investigation—Chicago became a center for pragmatist thought. Progressive Party politics and labor-union activism also influenced Dewey and Addams, as well as Holmes's decisions as a judge.[10] By virtue of his experiences in the military, Holmes was also profoundly influenced by the Civil War, and his work as a judge reveals the residual impact of the violence he saw firsthand.[11] Alain Locke constantly confronted issues of race that remained a vital part of the social fabric after the Civil War, and ultimately played a critical part in the Harlem Renaissance.[12] My task, however, is not to outline these influences (as important as they may be) but to define the pragmatic orientation to the world that grew out of these influences.

As an orientation to the world, American pragmatism is characterized by five central commitments. First, pragmatists believe that the world is uncertain and contingent. Building on scientific advances that pointed to the critical role of chance and change, the pragmatists asserted that uncertainty and contingency are basic characteristics of the natural and the social worlds. Second, given such uncertainty, pragmatism advances an epistemological anthropocentrism. Human interests (taken either collectively or individually) become the measure of what constitutes knowledge. Third, if knowledge is a function of human interests, then, as William James says at the beginning of *The Will to Believe,* "the world is a pluralism" (1897, viii). Philosophically, pluralism is the view that the world consists of independent things whose relations depend on individuals. This notion of pluralism has cultural and political ramifications as well. It highlights the critical role individual experience plays in making meaning, and it suggests that final determinations regarding human affairs are impossible. Fourth, even though the world is manifold, an individual's relationship to the community is a central preoccupation of pragmatism. How communities influence individuals and how individuals maintain and express themselves through communities are key questions that lead to questions about democracy, as a community with a plural citizenry. Maintaining, organizing, and fostering communities in the face of pluralism, uncertainty, and human interests are key tasks for pragmatism. Fifth, negotiating the social and natural worlds requires a set of methods or tools for use by individuals and communities. In an effort to integrate theory and practice, pragmatism tries to invent methods for negotiating uncertainty, generating knowledge, expressing individualism, and building communities. Pragmatism pays constant attention to practical and productive arts capable of these tasks.

Underlying these five commitments is the basic directive to look toward the consequences of actions and ideas to test their validity. Defining pragmatism as an orientation to the world is meant to highlight the interactions between people and between individuals and the natural and social worlds. By constantly attending to interactions between people, ideas, and the material world, pragmatism tries to attend to the consequences of actions or words. Such attention to consequences also points to the idea that the world is constantly in the process of changing and being made and remade by different people. The consequences of our actions are part of this process of making; they issue from the commitments to uncertainty, epistemological anthropocentrism, pluralism, community, and the search for practical arts.

These themes can be expanded to present a picture of pragmatism as an intellectual movement. These major themes unite the different, individual pragmatists. Even though different pragmatists may put more or less emphasis on any one of the characteristics identified above, the varying emphases give depth and richness to the meaning of pragmatism as a whole. Many others have expanded and extended these commitments in a variety of fruitful and fascinating ways. Contemporary figures such as Richard Bernstein, Richard Posner, and Jürgen Habermas are examples of scholars working out the implications of pragmatism. This work focuses explicitly on the earliest pragmatists and their positions in American culture between 1890 and 1940. Clearly this account is limited as it does not include other important figures such as C. S. Peirce, George Herbert Mead, or F. C. S. Schiller. Even so, I argue that the people discussed are representative of the spirit of pragmatism as embodied in the general characteristics outlined.

The Significance of Classical Rhetoric

Classical rhetoric is particularly important for pragmatism because it poses enduring questions about the relationship between individuals and communities and continues to animate questions about the promise and danger of communication, all in addition to its attention to issues of composition, arrangement, style, and delivery. For example, what role does language play in regulating and defining relationships between people? How does the process of persuasion work, and how can language be used as a mechanism for persuasion? How does rhetoric contribute to the creation of democratic societies? What is the power of eloquence? How can rhetoric help us use knowledge for the practical benefit of the community? In response to these questions I outline an orientation to the world that places rhetoric at the center of human affairs and that issues from three distinct and formidable strands of rhetorical theory authored by the sophists, Isocrates, and Aristotle respectively. Certain key themes underlie the diverse perspectives of the sophists, Isocrates, and Aristotle—themes that have continued to serve as the grounds for rhetorical theory and to pose enduring questions about the nature, function, and scope of rhetoric.

The study and practice of rhetoric in Greece in the fifth century B.C.E. coincided with the advent of the democratic city-state. In part, rhetorical theory and practice helped establish and strengthen the city-state by providing a practical art capable of organizing human societies, shaping social and political sensibilities, and providing communities with direction and meaning.[13] Moreover, rhetoric came to be regarded as an essential aspect of public deliberation, and mastery of it represented the highest achievement of a well-educated citizen. One standard story of rhetoric's origins identifies Corax and Tisias as its first teachers. In 467 B.C.E. the sudden development of democracy in Syracuse, Sicily, led to the need for political leadership based on the skill of public speaking. Corax and Tisias responded to this need by inventing simple techniques for effective presentation and argumentation—including the theory of argument from probability. In the mid-fifth century sophists such as Protagoras taught similar skills in Athens and began to develop a political theory founded on the necessity of rhetoric. According to Cynthia Farrar, "Protagoras was, so far as we know, the first democratic political theorist in the history of the world" (1988, 77). His theory suggests that "the very process that enables every citizen to *be* a citizen" requires "positive participation in furthering the aims of the *polis* by contributing as best one can to the process of socialization and enlightenment in the interests of harmony and rational purposefulness" (95). The practice of rhetoric was an integral part of this form of participation and ultimately provided the grounds for a citizen's "personal excellence" and for the full success of the community.

Underlying these theoretical stipulations is the assumption that *all* citizens have something to contribute to the discussion of moral and political questions. However, all opinions and all pieces of advice are not of equal value. According to G. B. Kerferd, "in a Protagorean democracy the operative principle concerning advice will be 'from each according to his capacity,' and somehow or other it will be necessary for the community to *choose* between conflicting advice" (1981, 144). This capacity that Kerferd refers to involves the effective use of language: "For Protagoras, *logos* was the means through which citizens deliberated and came to collective judgments. Protagoras contributed to the theoretical defense of consensual decision making, and he may have been the first to provide rules to facilitate the orderly conduct of debate and discussion" (Schiappa 2003b, 199).

Gorgias, another sophist, developed a similar perspective on the relationship between language, rhetoric, and a democratic community. Scott Consigny argues that "Gorgias is a conventionalist who sees individuals as being fashioned through participation in the institutions and customs of their community" (2001, 119). The relationship between community and individual is again regulated by logos: "Gorgias construes language as an array of maneuvers or tropes that people use in various socially sanctioned agons or games." In addition, Gorgias "characterizes inquiry as a debate between rival rhetors in sanctioned agons of the culture," and he "depicts truth as a label of endorsement, a prize awarded by the audience or community to the accounts they find most persuasive" (60). These are arguments for understanding "the rhetoricity of *logos,*" according to Consigny, and for understanding the capacity of rhetoric to shape communities and individuals.

In the light of Protagoras's and Gorgias's positions, it is clear that the democratic city-state was supported by assumptions about language. Specifically, the sophists consistently pointed to the power of language to influence political and legal decisions—thus indicating that all people are capable of and subject to persuasive speech acts. This assumption is grounded in the recognition that the human mind has the power to alter reality through words and images (Consigny 2001, 60–92). Most important, Greek citizens believed that human beings could direct their own lives as conscious agents of change, instead of acting out predetermined fates decided by the gods. Essentially, they acknowledged the power of individuals to know themselves through interactions with others and not through the determinations of higher authorities.

In addition to these claims about language and community, the sophists argued that man is the measure of all things. This pithy statement articulates an agnostic, anthropocentric orientation to the world, an orientation that conditioned the possibility and potential of rhetoric as a dynamic force in sociopolitical affairs.[14] The sophists also argued that knowledge is grounded in human perception and is dependent on the knower, not just the thing known. Kerferd identifies this view as "sophistic relativism," which conditions a specific understanding of the function of rhetoric: "if all perceptions and moral judgments are to be accepted as equally true how is it possible for any one logos giving expression to perceptual and moral judgments ever to be described as superior to another logos?" (1981, 101) The persuasive character of a particular view determines the superior perspective. Persuasion, then, "consists in making one view appear preferable to another" given a particular occasion and context (102).

Hence the sophistic attention to developing a doctrine of persuasion that attends to the use of language.

Sophistic relativism was further grounded on the claim that words and things are separate and have no natural relationship beyond the one invented by language users. Such a view implies that words do not give access to some fixed and determinate reality. This view also implies the power of words to shape perceptions and ultimately leads to the basic assumption that people are capable of and subject to persuasion. If persuasion plays such a key role in determining human affairs, then social and political arrangements are functions of collective agreements brought about through the practice of rhetoric. Timely, appropriate, and creative messages could invent, build, or destroy the relationships that defined social and political arrangements. Linguistic acts, if they are timely, appropriate, and creative, can determine the character of an individual and that of an entire community.

Like the sophists, Isocrates was a prominent teacher of rhetoric. Also like the sophists, he emphasized the power of appropriate and timely messages in directing the affairs of the state (Schiappa 2003b, 72–73). However, he departed from the sophistic perspective by emphasizing the importance of practical knowledge in building and maintaining communities. His school in Athens was designed explicitly to train political leaders. Less interested in theorizing about the nature of language and knowledge, he taught his students how to use knowledge to make decisions under difficult circumstances—decisions that were in the community's best interests. According to Takis Poulakos, "Isocrates borrowed Gorgias' notion of rhetoric as the power to create meaning and applied it to the public task of constituting the polis as an integrated community" (1997, 105). Rhetoric, therefore, meant the "process of discerning and advocating the common welfare, and rhetoric could be rearticulated as the art of deliberating publicly the good and possible for the polis." Thus, rhetorical discourse was judged by its ability to bring benefits to those who listened. Such a belief was founded on the assumption that final determinations regarding political affairs are impossible because individuals have access to only partial knowledge limited by opinions and imperfect choices (78–80). The goal of political deliberation was not absolute certainty but useful suggestions based on practical, available evidence —suggestions that could be revised at some point. Thus, Isocrates cultivated a form of "practical wisdom" in his students by teaching them how to use available, imperfect knowledge for the betterment of the community.[15]

Aristotle systematized much of the practical advice offered by Isocrates and the sophists, and he ultimately produced a handbook theorizing the available means of persuasion.[16] The *Rhetoric* prescribes specific tools and practices for the persuasive use of language in any given circumstance. In offering practical tools for use, Aristotle also argues that the contingent, the uncertain, and the probable are rhetoric's proper arena (1357a, 1359a–b). In other words, experiential and symbolic ambiguities make rhetoric possible, and thus ambiguity and uncertainty are the grounds for a variety of rhetorical strategies (1377b). This makes all rhetorical discourse situated and contingent. Consequently, the significance of the practical suggestions that Aristotle makes for finding the available means of persuasion issues from the contingency of human affairs.[17] In trying to accommodate and systematize the various perspectives on rhetoric and the variety of available persuasive practices, Aristotle attempts to control and order the power of rhetoric to guide decision making.

At the center of the *Rhetoric* is Aristotle's division of rhetorical discourse into the deliberative, forensic, and epideictic genres. This system of classification is predicated on his claim that rhetoric is determined by the audience it addresses, the place in which it happens, and the purposes it serves. Thus rhetoric in the Athenian Assembly is different from rhetoric in the courts or at a festival. As such, an orator must say things appropriate to the audience being addressed, and precedent can serve an important function in determining what to say. His system of classification issues from the belief that such precedents are established by the regularity and reliability of the sociopolitical world, the recurrence of human situations within it, and the cognitive character of emotions. In other words, Aristotle's is a "rhetoric that seeks to tame chance by working out a taxonomy based on probability and by providing a blueprint for political stability, societal coherence, and intellectual order" (J. Poulakos 1995, 181). For those reasons, the *Rhetoric* attends to the inventive potential of the topics; the argumentative power of ethos, pathos, and logos as modes of proof; and the role of the enthymeme in persuasion. In prescribing tools for the invention of arguments, the organization of discourse, and the understanding of an audience, Aristotle presents rhetoric as a practical and productive art with the capacity to guide decision making and public judgment given recurrent situations marked by uncertainty, particularity, and ambiguity.

These three perspectives on rhetoric form the foundation for a particular way of understanding an individual's relationship to the world. Thus, like pragmatism, rhetoric can be understood as an orientation to the world. Mark Backman offers a compelling description of such a perspective: "Rhetoric takes its starting point in crisis, uncertainty, and opinion and is successful if it leads to a semblance of order. Consequently, although it lacks the metaphysical features found in philosophy and psychology, rhetoric is an epistemological art of the highest degree. It apprehends, defines, shapes, preserves, embodies and transmits the most fundamental kind of knowledge, that of the consequences of action exercised to some end. It is not concerned with collecting facts about the natural world but with assembling and disposing opinions that animate the social world. Rhetoric deals with the artificial structures of reality that in their compound complexities constitute what we call culture" (1991, 18). Backman demonstrates that classical rhetorical theory implies both a philosophical position and the need to find practical tools for use given a specific description of the human predicament. I interpret this to mean that the study and practice of rhetoric in Greek antiquity issued from a particular orientation to the world. In addition, the variety of rhetorical theories developed in Athens demonstrates the different possibilities of using, developing, and coping with this orientation to the world.[18]

I use the term "rhetoric" to refer to the Greek tradition briefly outlined here. Specifically, the sophists, Isocrates, and Aristotle articulate a collective view of rhetoric inspired by five central themes. First, as Backman points out, uncertainty and ambiguity characterize human affairs. Multiple, idiosyncratic perspectives derived from human experience and the particularities of new situations create contingent circumstances subject to change. Thus, rhetoric is formed in response to uncertainty and ambiguity. Second, democracy requires general participation in public decision making by the citizens who make up the polis. In such cases rhetoric is a mechanism for guiding democratic deliberation, expressing individual perspectives, and binding communities together. Third, the eloquent and persuasive use of language is one way to distinguish between competing voices or multiple perspectives. In other words, the ability to use language eloquently and persuasively is an integral part in deciding the best course of action for the community. Fourth, rhetoric can be understood as a *techné,* or a body of rules, derived from experience and that may be known or applied through the exercise of reason. These rules are not a representational body of knowledge but instead useful tools for the application of knowledge in difficult circumstances. Fifth, rhetoric can also be understood as a *dynamis,* or a powerful capacity for doing.[19] The notion of *dynamis* points to rhetoric's ability to construct the world through language, invent possibilities for the future, and influence the course of human affairs. In the classical tradition, rhetoric is deeply associated with uncertainty and ambiguity, democratic decision making, the persuasive use of language, a system of rules for speech making, and a force in the dynamic construction of the social world.

Building on these five themes presents a picture of the capacities of rhetoric in ancient Greece in order to compare a classical orientation to the world with that of pragmatism. Pragmatism may not place rhetoric at the center of human affairs as classical Greek intellectuals did. However, by emphasizing uncertainty, contingency, plurality, community, and the consequences of ideas and actions, pragmatism, I argue, shares a basic theoretical orientation with classical rhetoric.

Rhetorical Processes and the Pragmatic Method

American pragmatism and classical rhetoric are related by a shared outlook on the human predicament and the search for practical methods to cope with that predicament. An initial comparison between the pragmatic method and rhetorical processes will help draw out this similarity and illustrate its significance. According to Menand, "pragmatism is an account of the way people think—the way they come up with ideas, form beliefs, and reach decisions" and tries to answer the question "What makes us decide one thing when we might do another thing instead?" (2001, 351). Oftentimes while engaged in the process of deciding on a particular course of action, we may ask ourselves what the "right decision" is in the given circumstance. The first lesson of pragmatism is that when we try to make decisions we do not consult first principles, logical reasons, scientific laws, or religious dogmas to determine what is "right." Thinking, choosing, and acting are processes, the results of which lead to first principles, logic, scientific laws, religious dogmas, and some notion of "rightness." Prior to thinking and acting, all of those things are indeterminate, but this does not mean that our choices are arbitrary or merely self-serving: "When we are happy with a decision, it doesn't feel arbitrary; it feels like the decision we *had* to reach. And this is so because its inevitability is a function of its 'fit' with the whole inchoate set of assumptions of our self-understanding and of the social world we inhabit, the assumptions that give the moral weight—much greater moral weight than logic or taste could ever give—to every judgment we make. This is why, so often, we know we're right before we know *why* we're right. First we decide, then we deduce" (353). For those reasons the pragmatists teach us to look toward the consequences of our actions to evaluate their worth.

Oliver Wendell Holmes used to invite his fellow justices, during deliberations, to name any legal principle they liked, and he would use that principle to decide the case under consideration *either way* (Menand 2001, 340). This is a perfect instantiation of *dissoi logoi,* and the sophists used such exercises to help train their students in the art of rhetoric. Holmes was also fond of arguing that a judge first decides a case and then crafts a justification for that decision. As a judge, then, Holmes did not simply advance his own interests; instead he attempted to design methods to judge the best possible outcome for the democratic community to which he belonged—knowing that his decisions would have consequences. In this case it is clear that pragmatism makes the process of public decision making a rhetorical process. Why? First, because the pragmatists see decision making as a situated and strategic social act and consequently as an instrument in coordinating social action. Second, because decisions are not generated by first principles but instead are the results of competing persuasive claims subject to questions of appropriate fit and the best interests of the community. Both rhetoric and pragmatism judge decisions and actions by their consequences. The successful rhetor/pragmatist must be skilled in negotiating the difficulties of public decision making to secure the best possible outcomes. The pragmatists tried to invent a "pragmatic method" capable of exercising the kind of good judgment that the rhetorician possessed in ancient Athens.

Rhetorical processes are guided by the persuasive use of language. Accordingly, public decision making is subject to the force of eloquence. From the sophists, Isocrates, or Aristotle a student would learn techniques for using language so as to have a persuasive impact on an audience given uncertain, ambiguous, and particular circumstances. Rhetorical processes are situations in which the persuasive use of language makes one opinion prevail over others in the minds of many. The intellectual orientation to the world outlined above creates the conditions of possibility for the practice of rhetoric. In other words, a recognition of uncertainty, ambiguity, and particularity in combination with a commitment to democratic participation, the dynamic capacity of language, and enduring questions about an individual's relationship to the community creates the need for an art of rhetoric to cope with the human predicament. Pragmatism, as an orientation to the world, establishes a similar set of beliefs. By claiming that the world is contingent and uncertain, by adhering to epistemological anthropocentrism and pluralism, and by addressing questions about an individual's relationship to the community, pragmatism is constantly seeking practical methods capable of guiding decision and judgment. I argue that one such set of practical methods is the art of rhetoric. The central claim of this book is that pragmatism implicitly establishes the necessity of rhetoric for American democracy. The similarities pointed out between classical rhetoric and pragmatism are the warrant for this claim. Put another way, pragmatism describes a theoretical commitment to rhetoric and suggests practical conditions for the uses of rhetoric in democratic affairs.

Therefore, when one sees the world as uncertain, plural, ambiguous, and subject to human intervention, one creates the conditions of possibility for seeing rhetoric as a necessary art, an art of guiding decision and judgment. The pragmatic method tries to serve a similar function as rhetoric did in classical Athens. In this book, then, pragmatism is read in the light of classical rhetoric. Such a reading will demonstrate how pragmatism establishes the necessity of rhetoric for American democracy. To this end, the vocabulary and texts of classical rhetoric are used to critically interpret pragmatism as a call for appropriate American rhetorics. Such an argument is primarily theoretical. An attempt is made to explain a certain perspective on the pragmatic method and to predict how pragmatism can be made more useful. This theoretical argument is guided by classical rhetoric as a historical example and is grounded in pragmatism's rejection of the traditional commitments of philosophy.

In light of the above considerations, this book is divided into two parts. The first part discusses the philosophical perspectives of William James and John Dewey. I argue that the manner in which these philosophers establish pragmatism as an orientation to the world draws their project close to classical rhetoric. The theoretical claim is that the intellectual commitments of pragmatism are usefully comparable to the intellectual commitments of classical rhetoric. In drawing this comparison I argue that James and Dewey outline intellectual conditions that, if granted, necessitate the practice of rhetoric in American democracy. Using the classical tradition, I highlight the necessity of rhetoric for democratic affairs and suggest that pragmatism makes a similar argument for that necessity and replaces the word "rhetoric" with "pragmatic method" in James's case or "communication" in Dewey's case.

In the second part Aristotle's tripartite division of rhetoric into the deliberative, epideictic, and forensic is used to interpret how Jane Addams, Alain Locke, and Oliver Wendell Holmes, respectively, can be understood as searching for rhetorical practices for politics, art, and law. In other words, I show how pragmatism outlines the practical conditions that call for the uses of rhetoric in various contexts. In addition, Aristotle's scheme is used to show how the various pragmatists share an intellectual orientation to the world with classical rhetoric *and* how they exceed the boundaries of classical rhetorical theory in such a way that the excess provides a useful resource for rethinking rhetoric's place in our world.

If pragmatism establishes intellectual and practical conditions that necessitate rhetoric, then three critical implications result from this reading. First, pragmatism suggests the possibility of developing rhetorics based on its principles and fit to the problems of contemporary democracy. Although none of the pragmatists understand themselves as rhetoricians, they consistently leave hints at what American rhetorics might look like—it is our task to follow those hints. Second, the themes of classical Greek rhetoric are still around today, albeit with variations. More important, these themes can be useful in renewing and improving contemporary culture if we adapt them to our own circumstances. Classical rhetoric was designed to offer flexible and adaptable tools for use on any occasion, and so mixing the ideas of the sophists, Isocrates, James, Dewey, and others can result in a rich resource for making a better American democracy. Third, philosophies are improved by exploring their relationships to rhetoric, and rhetorics are improved by exploring their intellectual justifications. Pragmatism consistently points to the practical applications of philosophy and in so doing evaluates philosophical beliefs by their ability to influence the problems of the moment. Similarly, we can evaluate rhetorics by investigating the philosophical commitments that underpin them.

Implied in this argument is the claim that classical rhetoric is an appropriate resource for understanding pragmatism. In order to support the claim of appropriateness, I argue that my interpretation, in the spirit of pragmatism, is useful in continuing to extend, develop, and strengthen a public-oriented and instrumental philosophy. However, there are limits to the uses of classical rhetoric. The pragmatists were embedded in a distinct historical moment far removed from ancient Athens. The particularity of pragmatism as an American intellectual phenomenon confines the uses of classical rhetoric as a hermeneutic and explanatory resource. In light of this fact, pragmatism is an appropriate resource for adapting rhetoric to contemporary irresolutions. Because of these shared intellectual commitments, I suggest that new, appropriate American rhetorics can be founded on pragmatist principles. In fact, if pragmatism is to remain a significant philosophy for American intellectual affairs, it must seek appropriate rhetorics, rhetorics that would render it more useful. Before such a project can be attempted, the spirit of pragmatism recommends that the consequences of my argument be tested. In other words, what does my reading of pragmatism do for us, in our contemporary moment? What is the "cash-value," to use James's metaphor, of drawing similarities between pragmatism and classical rhetoric? Why does such an interpretation matter? What usefulness will my reading bring? These are the essential questions for any pragmatic account of pragmatism.

By arguing that classical rhetoric shares an orientation to the world with American pragmatism, I do not mean to imply that the pragmatists were actually rhetorical theorists and did not know it. Instead, I argue that a belief in uncertainty, epistemological anthropocentrism, pluralism, community, and the need for practical arts are the grounds for a philosophy that indicates rhetoric's central place in human affairs. Whether the pragmatists acknowledged or explicitly attended to this fact does not matter—they did not actually make such an argument. In my interpretation of pragmatist thought, however, the intellectual commitments they articulate can be understood as arguments for the necessity of rhetoric. Comparing pragmatism with classical rhetoric will make this argument clear and convincing. Such an argument also indicates that the contemporary study of pragmatism should account for the study and practice of rhetoric—I argue that this is a central implication of a pragmatist orientation to the world. Aside from the work of Stanley Fish and Steven Mailloux, this is a heretical interpretation of classical American pragmatism.

More specifically, based on the intellectual commitments of the pragmatists, I argue that rhetorical practice and a healthy democracy go hand in hand. In other words, reading pragmatism in the light of the rhetorical tradition demonstrates the necessity of rhetoric for democracy. In classical Athens such an argument was embodied in the acts of public address that were a central part of politics, but this argument is obscured in American political affairs with the development of a myriad of forms of democratic participation and communication. Pragmatism explores rhetorical strategies and mechanisms for communication outside of public address and thus reanimates lines of thought that attend to the connections between rhetoric and democracy. The pragmatists face the unique test of finding timely and fitting mechanisms for rhetorical action, and in so doing they suggest the need for expanding classical themes to account for contemporary American irresolutions. Both pragmatism and classical rhetoric show that the practice of rhetoric is necessary for a fully functioning democracy, and my reading brings the relationship between rhetoric and democracy into specific relief.

From the perspective of the rhetorical tradition, this book establishes a particular foundation for rhetorical scholarship consonant with classical rhetoric but also uniquely fit to contemporary American affairs. Pragmatism offers a rich resource for exploring explicitly rhetorical themes and suggests specifically American lines of thought for contemporary rhetorical scholars. Instead of understanding rhetoric as merely a practice or skill, my interpretation illustrates the philosophical commitments that create the most promise and potential for the practice of rhetoric. Such philosophical issues demand the attention of rhetorical scholars and further ground the practice of rhetorical criticism and the practical skills that teachers of rhetoric offer their students. I suggest that pragmatism offers a unique and important perspective on debates about a philosophy of rhetoric and the foundation for rhetorical scholarship. As a corollary, I also suggest that pragmatism offers promising grounds on which to engage in a specifically American version of rhetorical theory and criticism.[20]

Extending this argument, pragmatism also opens the possibility for a decentered rhetorical theory. By attending to rhetorical processes that extend beyond public address and by investigating communicative practices other than oratory, pragmatism supplements rhetorics that focus exclusively on speech by attending to other rhetorical processes—for example, the collective voice of social movements in Jane Addams's case. In these ways pragmatism extends classical rhetorical theory while also suggesting the possibility and necessity of extending the scope of rhetoric to account for a larger variety of practical strategies designed to enhance community life. In other words, pragmatism demands that we think about communication and rhetoric not by focusing on particular speakers or subjects first but by focusing on the myriad ways language and symbol systems influence our thoughts, beliefs, and decisions.

These preliminary consequences of my argument demand further elucidation. This is accomplished through an intellectual portrait of five of the most central first-generation pragmatists: James, Dewey, Addams, Holmes, and Locke. Reading these figures shows the centrality of rhetoric in their various projects. Ultimately, rhetoric waits at the end of pragmatist thought to take up the project of improving and remaking American democracy.

One

William James on Contingency, Plurality, and Belief

Toward a Pragmatist Philosophy of Rhetoric

In May of 1908, at the age of sixty-six, William James delivered the Hibbert Lectures at Manchester College, Oxford.[1] With the audience in the "several hundreds," he addressed "the present situation in philosophy."[2] For such a gifted and popular lecturer, the size of the crowd was not a surprise. During the preceding eighteen years, since the publication of *Principles of Psychology* in 1890, James had become a "public philosopher."[3] His intellectual life was intimately linked to issues of the moment, and he consistently performed in front of a mixed audience extending far beyond professional philosophers. The Hibbert Lectures were eventually published under the title *A Pluralistic Universe,* marking James's commitment to viewing the world as uncertain and multifarious.[4] Both the presentation and the content of these lectures point to one of the central characteristics of James's pragmatism: philosophy ought to become less rationalistic, technical, and professional. Instead, it should focus on experience, belief, and the practical consequences of an active life.

James was an orator-philosopher. He performed a rhetoric that abandoned the technical jargon of professional academics and instead used metaphors that adapted his ideas to a broad audience. Such an approach meant that his philosophy did not seek to express and transmit truth but to create an instrumental and useful set of ideas applicable to a wide array of problems—a pragmatic method. On the one hand, James describes an orientation to the world that demands belief and action in the face of uncertainty. On the other hand, he invites us to use his advice to renew, reconstruct, and improve our own lives. I read these two commitments as an outline for an orientation to the world that requires the practice of rhetoric and as a suggestion for practical methods to use rhetoric. A comparison of a classical philosophy of rhetoric with James's pragmatism demonstrates how James lays the groundwork for theorizing rhetoric's place in American democracy.

The central argument advanced in *A Pluralistic Universe* is that respect for and attention to individual experience must not be ruined by overconceptualization; in essence "individuality outruns all classification" (James 1909, 7). Such an emphasis on individuality shifted attention toward the arbitrary flux of life and away from the arresting and static nature of concepts.[5] The lectures, replete with metaphors and vivid imagery, enact this call away from rationalistic conceptualization by trying to communicate the varied, complex, and uncertain characteristics of the "pluriverse." *A Pluralistic Universe* is one particular case that represents the general trend of James's position as a "public philosopher." In his performances he tried to "make ideas accessible to a general public," and as a philosopher he "addressed the public issues of his day" (Cotkin 1990, 11–12). The pragmatism that emerges from *The Will to Believe* (1897), *Pragmatism* (1907), *A Pluralistic Universe* (1909), *The Meaning of Truth* (1911), and *Some Problems in Philosophy* (1911) (almost all of the material in these books was composed in lecture form first) is a thorough critique of the idea, direction, and presuppositions of philosophy as James understood them at the time.[6] His critique articulates a vision of the world in which philosophy is tied to experience and in which the practical consequence of an idea is the only relevant epistemological test.[7] Given such emphases, his intellectual commitments reiterate, in new variation, the basic tenets of classical rhetoric.

Three key points demonstrate how the intellectual commitments of James's pragmatism share an orientation to the world with classical rhetoric and open the possibility for a new American rhetoric. First, the basic tenets of James's pragmatism—pluralism, an anthropocentric epistemology, and attention to experience and belief—reiterate a classical philosophy of rhetoric. James articulates these basic tenets by critiquing philosophy's obsession with absolutism and the correspondence theory of truth, arguments that are comparable to the sophistic orientation to the world. Second, James's public performances reveal a commitment to language, communication, and argument. However, he does not fully account for the role that language plays in shaping the world, and that is a weakness of his pragmatism.[8] Instead, the pragmatic method relies on empiricism to test and validate experiences. I argue that, from a pragmatist perspective, empirical or scientific investigation works analogously to rhetoric. Combining James's emphasis on scientific empiricism with rhetoric's focus on language and communication can help improve the pragmatic method. Third, the philosophical tenets of James's pragmatism provide the theoretical groundwork for an American philosophy of rhetoric.

Pragmatism and Humanism as Rhetorical Strategy

F. C. S. Schiller, the British philosopher whom James greatly admired, explicitly linked the project of pragmatism to Protagoras's doctrine that humans are the measure of all things.[9] In his introduction to *Humanism,* Schiller argues that pragmatic humanism has "affinities with the great saying of Protagoras, that *Man is the measure of all things.* Fairly interpreted, this is the truest and most important thing that any thinker has ever propounded" (1903, xvii). In a later work, *Studies in Humanism,* he shows how the political situation in Greece in the fifth century B.C.E. in combination with the theoretical importance of the human-measure principle resulted in "a great development of rhetoric and dialectic" (Schiller 1907, 31–32). Steven Mailloux explicates these connections between Schiller's pragmatic humanism and sophistic thought in his introduction to *Rhetoric, Sophistry, Pragmatism.*[10] Mailloux, by interpreting and extending Schiller's reading of Protagoras, points to the important intellectual and theoretical contributions made by the sophists. Both Mailloux and Schiller focus on the orientation to the world implied by the human-measure principle (an affirmation of the human origin of truth) as the grounds for rhetoric and pragmatism.

James had reservations about the sophist's doctrine. In *The Meaning of Truth* he equates sophistry with "hairsplitting" and refutes the charge, made by Hugo Münsterberg, that his pragmatism reproduces Protagoras's doctrine (263, 297). However, these reservations are tempered by Schiller's recognition of the intellectual significance of Protagoras for pragmatic humanism. In his review of Schiller's essay, James credits Schiller with using Protagoras's doctrine not as a skeptical refutation of the correspondence theory of truth but as a means of locating truth in "the actually felt relations between experiences themselves."[11] Insofar as Schiller relies extensively on Protagoras and the sophists to argue questions of epistemology and to articulate his philosophy of pragmatic humanism, James's praise of Schiller's philosophy implies an acknowledgment of pragmatism's intellectual debt to the sophists.[12] Although James did not make the link to the sophists explicit in his own writings, comparing aspects of the sophists, as well as Isocrates and Aristotle, to his own philosophy can illustrate the significance of rhetoric for pragmatism—a project that James overlooked but Schiller only began.

In *Sophistication,* Mark Backman eloquently describes the sophist's role in constructing a rhetorical worldview. From Backman's perspective, rhetoric is "an art or a method or a form of persuasion," but, more important, it is "an attitude about public expression and the nature of the world" (1991, 11). Given this position, questions about epistemology are not the sole possession of philosophers. In fact, the sophistic conception of rhetoric has its own "radical epistemology": "Knowledge is not based on systematic first principles. Rather, it inheres in the effects it has on circumstances of expression. It is the residue of the mind at work in a setting, not an abstraction of mental processes. . . . Results take priority over premises. Knowledge is functional order imposed for some specific end and rhetoric is the primary instrument for its institution" (17). Backman goes on to claim that the key features of this "radical epistemology" are "probability, opportunity, and relativity," in addition to "crisis, uncertainty, and opinion" (17, 18).[13] Rhetoric's ability to provide structure or order to the world through language, and ultimately to influence the course of events, issues from this radical epistemology. Protagoras, Gorgias, and the other sophists are all key figures in the practice of rhetoric as a method *and* the articulation of an orientation to the world founded on and characterized by probability, relativity, uncertainty, and opinion.

Protagoras's "human-measure" principle is one part of this orientation to the world. Despite James's misgivings about the implications of the word "sophistry," there is a clear affinity between Protagoras's principle and James's pragmatism. The "human-measure" principle succinctly expresses an underlying confidence in human ingenuity and the belief that all perceptions and judgments are relative to the perceiver(s). As early as 1897 in *The Will to Believe,* James described his own version of the "human-measure" principle: "truth cannot be a self-proclaiming set of laws, or an abstract 'moral reason,' but can only exist in act, or in the shape of an opinion held by some thinker" (*WB,* 199). Truthfulness, in this case, resides in an individual's willingness to act on a particular truth-claim. In *Pragmatism,* James reiterates this position by arguing that "truth is *made,* just as health, wealth and strength are made in the course of experience" (*PR,* 84). The creative capacity of the individual, the critical role of opinion and belief, and the subjective experience of the world are linked to the process of making truth for James. Clearly James's epistemology is similar to the sophistic orientation to the world.

Protagoras's "human-measure" doctrine is not the only major intellectual contribution made by the sophists. Gorgias's *On the Nonexistent* remains a rich and provocative statement about the nature of the world. Although James never makes mention of this particular work, Gorgias's intellectual commitments resonate throughout James's pragmatism. *On the Nonexistent* boldly refutes the existence of a world outside of language and human experience. Gorgias advances three main arguments: first, nothing exists; second, even if anything does exist it is unknowable and incomprehensible to man; and third, even if we could know the things that exist, we could not communicate that knowledge to others. These three arguments rest on his belief that the object in itself and the object perceived are two different things. Given this distinction, an individual's perceptual experience of something is subjective and not necessarily shared by others. Language, according to Gorgias, is the result of our perceptual encounters with the world. However, what is made, in language, after a perceptual encounter with the world can never completely and fully represent the world as it actually is outside of an individual's perception. Gorgias's argument that nothing exists actually implies that language (including the word "nothing") refers to perceptual experiences and not to the thing itself. Given such an argument, one must conclude that there are potentially as many different worlds as there are people who perceive the world. Existence, reality, knowledge, and truth are all subjective inventions made through experience and language; the implication of this position is that the world is uncertain and multifarious, not given and fixed.

James was preoccupied with questions of perceptual experience and how they govern an individual's knowledge of the world. *Principles of Psychology* addresses the question of sensation and perception at length. One central argument in James's psychology is that conscious states influence behavior and guide activity by selecting and highlighting some parts of experience and not others. Essentially, he argues that interests (for example, practical, ethical, religious) control an individual's selective attention. According to Charlene Seigfried, the idea that the human mind employs an active and selective interest in experience "forces a radical reconstruction of our beliefs about reality, truth, metaphysics, and ethics" (1990, 78). James's psychology further emphasizes the creative capacity of the individual, the critical role of opinion and belief, and the subjectivity that is inherently part of experience. This is not a refutation of the existence of the real world as is Gorgias's *On the Nonexistent,* but it is a clear statement about the critical role that individual consciousness plays in perceptual encounters.[14] For example, calling an object "real" adds nothing except reference to us since language refers to our perceptual encounters with the world and not to the world itself. Furthermore, our descriptions of the world reveal our own self-interests, our own perspectives, or our own conscious states. In other words, James considers our cognitive access to the world to be neither neutral nor objective but rather affective: "as thinkers with emotional reaction, we give what seems *to us* a still higher degree of reality to whatever things we select and emphasize and turn to with *a will*" (1890, 297).[15]

Ultimately this psychological foundation reinforces the arguments advanced in *A Pluralistic Universe.* In an attempt to refute different versions of absolutism that rest on the assumption that reality is fixed, James locates questions of existence in a language of process, flux, and change: "What really *exists* is not things made but things in the making. . . . Reality *falls* in passing into conceptual analysis; it *mounts* in living its own undivided life—it buds and burgeons, changes and creates" (*PU*, 117–18). Here, James refutes intellectualism, which mistakenly believes that the logical function of breaking reality into concepts is the key feature of comprehending an absolute and fixed reality. It is impossible to achieve a complete and final apprehension of a world that is changing, budding, and burgeoning. Instead, such a world readily lends itself to multiple interpretations affected by the interests of an individual's consciousness.

In *On the Nonexistent,* Gorgias does not offer any clear position on the nature of the world outside of language because perceptual encounters with the world give rise to language and to debates surrounding the nature of reality. James's view seeks to develop the function of perceptual encounters further, but he adds a description of the world as itself growing, changing, and mutating. Gorgias's pluralism derives strictly from many different individuals having different perceptual encounters with the world. James's psychology begins with that premise and proceeds to the claim that the world itself is in flux and hence pluralistic: "Every smallest state of consciousness, concretely taken, overflows its own definition. Only concepts are self-identical; only 'reason' deals with closed equations; nature is but a name for excess; every point in her opens out and runs into the more" (*PU*, 129). By extending pluralism beyond perceptual experience to include the very nature of the world, James believes that he has exceeded the possibilities of language. What he is trying to "describe by concepts and words" exceeds "conceptualization and verbalization." This pluralism is so extreme that "the return to life cannot come about by talking" (131). James means that philosophers cannot turn to language if they want to understand or to live life.[16]

Compared to Gorgias, for whom language and rhetoric are our primary resources in a world of plural, subjective encounters with objects, James's pluralism may seem far more radical if it purports to eschew "talking" for "acting." However, *A Pluralistic Universe* functions as a refutation of the kind of logical and rationalistic philosophy inspired by Socrates and Plato. When James refers to the inadequacies of "talking," he is not referring to the persuasive and practical power of language represented by the rhetorical tradition. According to James, "The ruling tradition in philosophy has always been the Platonic and Aristotelian belief that fixity is a nobler and worthier thing than change. Reality must be one and unalterable. Concepts, being themselves fixities, agree best with this fixed nature of truth, so that for any knowledge of ours to be quite true it must be knowledge by universal concepts rather than by particular experiences, for these notoriously are mutable and corruptible" (*PU*, 106). Unlike the philosophical tradition that James identifies, the rhetorical tradition begins with just those counterassumptions that he tries to advance. Gorgias articulates a view of the human condition, in *On the Nonexistent* and elsewhere, according to which rhetoric and language are necessary for dealing with uncertainty, plurality, and change.[17] James critiques the philosophical tradition that began by searching for absolutes as an attempt to reject the sophistic worldview, but he does not fully explore the rhetorical tradition's competing perspective. Whereas Schiller uses the rhetorical tradition, specifically the sophists, to argue philosophical issues, James does not move beyond the basic philosophical orientations to the world instigated by Socrates, Plato, and Aristotle and carried forward by the rationalist and intellectualist tradition.[18]

James's pluralism, therefore, rejects the kind of talking inspired by rationalistic, conceptual thought that expects language to represent the real and the absolute: "Intellectualism in the vicious sense began when Socrates and Plato taught that what a thing really is, is told us by its *definition.* Ever since Socrates we have been taught that reality consists of essences, not of appearances, and that the essences of things are known whenever we know their definitions. So first we identify the thing with a concept and then we identify the concept with a definition, and only then, inasmuch as the thing *is* whatever the definition expresses, are we sure of apprehending the real essence of it or the full truth about it" (*PU,* 99). The philosophical urge to access the fixed, real essence of the world is precisely the position that James's pragmatism works to refute. What James calls "intellectualism," however, is also the understanding of language and experience that Gorgias refutes in *On the Nonexistent.* Concepts and definitions do not reveal essences; instead "logos arises from external things impinging upon us, that is, from perceptible things." In other words, "logos is not evocative of the external, but the external becomes the revealer of logos" (85–86). The radical implication, for Gorgias, is that what we reveal in communication with others is not substances or existing things but only language, which is proof that the concept of existence issues only from language and perceptual encounters with the world and not from some actual, fixed reality.

James seems intent on pointing out the problem with Plato's reversal of sophistic thought, and in doing so he articulates Gorgias's position in a new variation. However, James does not go so far as to offer a full-blown alternative to Plato's position. According to Edward Schiappa's *Defining Reality,* however, twentieth-century philosophy has generally dismissed the absolutist position that definitions reveal fixed essences in favor of the position that meaning in language is a matter of how words are used (2003a, 42). Schiappa claims that James's arguments against essentialism are one of the sources of this change (40). In an attempt to move beyond realist, or absolutist, arguments over definitions, Schiappa claims that definitions constitute rhetorically induced social knowledge. In other words, such a perspective recommends that definitions should not be treated as "philosophical or scientific questions of 'is'" but rather "as sociopolitical and pragmatic questions of 'ought'" (3). Schiappa's intention is to open questions of definition to rhetorical analysis, and he employs an explicitly pragmatist approach to accomplish this task. *Defining Reality* is an example of how the implications of James's pragmatism can be developed into a more complete rhetorical theory.

Instead of focusing on language, James attends to the process of perceptual experience, the mind, and how the latter comes to believe in one reality rather than in other possible realities. Such a preoccupation with experience betrays a concern with the effects of the world on an individual and an individual's ability to affect a world through conscious choices. This is precisely what the sophists identify as the primary function of language. According to Gorgias, "The effect of speech upon the condition of the soul [mind] is comparable to the power of drugs over the nature of bodies. For just as different drugs dispel different secretions from the body, and some bring an end to disease and others to life, so also in the case of speeches, some distress, others delight, some cause fear, others make the hearer bold, and some drug and bewitch the soul [mind] with a kind of evil persuasion" (*Encomium of Helen* 14). Gorgias's *Encomium of Helen* gives a clear account of the way in which rhetoric can make one opinion prevail over others and influence the outcome of human events. Although James does not assign language the same function that Gorgias does, both his psychology and his philosophy are attempts to understand how experiences are given meaning and how some opinions become beliefs that individuals are willing to act upon. Logos (or rhetoric), for the sophists, is the means by which one individual can inspire, convince, or move another to believe and to act. For James, the connections between belief, experience, and action are more complicated and rely on more factors than just persuasive language. Despite this difference, both Gorgias and James's positions issue from arguments that reject the idea of a fixed and absolute real world accessible by humans in favor of a world of uncertainty, plurality, and change regulated by human experience. Both seek to understand the human tools or mechanisms that cause change and lead to action.

As a philosopher, James sought to repudiate the dualistic view that there is an epistemological and metaphysical gap between the subjective knower and the objective world. By introducing the term "experience," he sought a means of eliminating and moving beyond the philosophical problems associated with this gap between subject and object.[19] In introducing "experience," however, he returned to the basic position advanced by Gorgias in *On the Nonexistent*. Gorgias's proof that nothing exists rests on the belief that we cannot know or even postulate a world prior to experience and language. James reiterates and moves beyond this form of anthropocentrism throughout his work, relying on the assumption that the world does not stand fixed outside of human perception.[20]

He suggests that since we are most intimately acquainted with our own experiences, these experiences should guide our understanding of the world.

For James, then, the exercise of the human capacity for action, the novel additions of individuals, and the psychological process of perception all play a part in the continuing process of determining our understanding of the world. For the sophists, Isocrates, and their students, these same activities required the use of rhetoric. Rhetoric was *the* tool par excellence used in determining one's perspective on reality and the outcome of human affairs in classical Athens.[21] In addition, for both rhetoric and pragmatism, experience and perception open the possibility for the creation of opinion, belief, and truth. The rhetoricians focused on the ways that language can translate experience into belief, opinion, and possibly truth, while James focused on the psychological link between experience, belief, and opinion.

Protagoras's notion of *dissoi logoi,* the idea that on every issue there are at least two sides opposing one another, ensures the same kind of pluralism that James advocates. *Dissoi logoi* also requires the practice of rhetoric to make one perspective prevail over others in the minds of many. Without a resource such as rhetoric to draw from, the question of how an opinion becomes a belief or a truth haunted James throughout his life. However, he did acknowledge the existence of a continuous process in which one opinion prevailed over others to become true—just the process initiated by Protagoras's concept of *dissoi logoi.* James carefully distinguishes his notion of opinion from "insulated and unmotivated abstractions" by referring to "opinions in the flesh, as they have really formed themselves, opinions surrounded by their causes and the influences they obey and exert, and along with the whole environment of social communication [of] which they are a part and out of which they take their rise" (*MT,* 269). In other words, he stipulates that opinions are contextually located and communicatively produced.

In addition to this position, however, James adds the "independent something" called "experience." The benefit of experience is that "The more of it a man has, the better position he stands in, in respect of truth; that some men, having had more experience, are therefore better authorities than others . . . that the more systematically and thoroughly such comparison and weighing of opinions is pursued, the truer the opinions that survive are likely to be. *When the pragmatist talks of opinions, it is opinions as they thus concretely and livingly and interactingly and correlatively exist that he has in mind*" (*MT,* 270).[22] If we consider Protagoras's human-measure doctrine in the light of this statement, it is clear that James, while agreeing with the anthropocentric implications of Protagoras's doctrine, shifts the focus to the process of measurement. In and through a person's experiences of the world, opinions are acquired; but in and through the careful measurement of those experiences, one can produce more truthful claims. James concedes that all people have opinions and that "their opinions are self-willed." The corollary to this assumption is that truth is formed "out of the life of opinion," and thus truth "does indeed consist of nothing but opinions." However, James's pragmatism holds some opinions to be more truthful than others based on their verifiability in experience not based on their eloquence.

The nature of truth and opinion are not the primary concern of the pragmatist. In fact, truth and opinion are important only if they have "cash-value" or if they are useful: "A new opinion counts as 'true' just in proportion as it gratifies the individual's desire to assimilate the novel in his experience to his beliefs in stock. It must both lean on old truth and grasp new fact; and its success . . . in doing this, is a matter of the individual's appreciation. When old truth grows, then by new truth's addition, it is for subjective reasons. . . . That new idea is truest which performs most felicitously. . . . It makes itself true, gets itself classed as true, by the way it works" (*PR*, 25). This is one of the basic beliefs of pragmatism, and it is a belief shared by rhetoricians. By rejecting an external world outside of human perception, the sophists acknowledged the necessity of acting on opinion. Opinions could be judged in relation to one another based on their usefulness or their ability to persuade an audience successfully. In other words, opinions become true by virtue of their consequences.

Isocrates' *Antidosis* illustrates a similar understanding of truth and philosophy as related to use. In describing the educational program of the philosopher, Isocrates requires his students to develop an ability to judge the uses of knowledge. This position rests on the belief that "it is not in the nature of man to attain a science by the possession of which we can know positively [certainly]" what is true in itself. In addition, we cannot know how to act in any given situation with absolute certainty. To replace such a false hope in certainty, Isocrates turns to wisdom as "the powers of conjecture to arrive generally at the best course" of action (*Antidosis* 271). He defines a philosopher as someone who is able to know how best to use available information in the service of useful action. When describing his program for education, Isocrates relies on the cultivation of judgment to secure such wisdom—judgment that comes from experience. Learning philosophy involves practice and exercise in the use of knowledge. Such exercises were designed to test the consequences of an idea and determine its usefulness. In general, this was precisely the kind of test to which James tried to subject philosophical propositions. For Isocrates, oratory—usually political oratory—was the means for testing the usefulness of an idea. Although James does not test his philosophical positions in political affairs, the basic presupposition of pragmatism is that ideas should be useful in whatever arena one chooses to participate. This is central to the Isocratean program for education in oratory and philosophy: truth is inextricably tied to action, specifically political action for the betterment of the community.[23]

Opinion, truth, and action are tied together in James's complex understanding of belief. In his doctrine of "the will to believe," James rejects the accepted canons of epistemological reasonableness. He argues that there are occasions in which it is more reasonable for a person to follow emotional or spiritual motives for holding a belief—for the sake of fulfilling one's hopes, desires, aims, needs, for example—than to believe on more narrowly "rational" grounds. He is willing to grant that objectivity, impartiality, and the judicious assessment of evidence have an important place in human life. Still, his point is that human interests and commitments extend beyond the limits of a disinterested intellect, and he holds that justification of belief must take into account the total context in which beliefs are formulated and in which they work.

Although James's argument that people could be moved to believe and to act without logical or reasonable cause may strike some philosophers as odd, that position has been a hallmark of rhetorical theory and practice since Aristotle's *Rhetoric.* According to Aristotle, there are three modes of persuasion: reasoning logically; appealing to the personal character of the speaker; and putting the audience in the right frame of mind and utilizing their emotions (1356a). A well-trained rhetorician knows that the best way to influence an audience or to stir an audience to action is by appealing to all three modes of persuasion and that in some instances logical reasoning will not work. In the rhetorical tradition belief, action, and leading people toward truth have generally been the results of more than logical reasoning—character and emotion often play a big part. In addition, a rhetorician could test the beliefs of an audience by the actions of that audience. Whether casting a vote at the Ekklesia or at a trial, or inspiring an army to fight, a speaker tested an audience's beliefs by their actions. James's "will to believe" reiterates this position in a new variation. He defines a belief as that which an individual is willing to act on in the future. For a rhetorician, the inspiration for that action is eloquent language that appeals to ethos, pathos, *and* logos. For James, the will to believe is based in experience and can issue from a variety of claims. For example, *The Varieties of Religious Experience* explains the power of religious belief in categories extending beyond logical argument. James shows that different people come to their religious beliefs based on a variety of claims that may seem to have little basis in rational or logical thought. People are led to believe and to act for many reasons—emotional, spiritual, or logical; both pragmatism and rhetoric assert and explain this phenomenon.

As a philosopher and a scientist, James was caught within two traditions that held the practice of rhetoric in contempt and emphasized the search for logical, rational, and timeless truths. In critiquing these traditions from within, James never connected his pragmatism to classical rhetorical theory. According to my reading, however, the underlying themes of James's pragmatism are provocatively similar to the themes articulated by the first theorists of logos. James's blooming and buzzing "pluriverse" is open to a variety of experiences. His epistemology rests on opinionated individuals willing to experience the world around them while using and acting on their beliefs. Such an epistemology ensures further plurality, a process of correction and accommodation, and the search for a method to test truth. As a thinker James is committed to seeing the world as a process in which experience can cause changes in beliefs, opinions, and truths. Perhaps what is more important is that James stipulates that the world is in the process of being determined, which implies "the possibility that things may get better" (*PR*, 46).

In such a world a "genuine pragmatist" is "willing to live on a scheme of uncertified possibilities which he trusts; willing to pay with his own person, if need be, for the realization of the ideals which he frames" (*PR*, 115). In dealing with a "world of influences," making and realizing ideals requires the "wisdom" to know what is appropriate "at the appropriate moment"—a clear reiteration of Gorgias's conception of *kairos* (53). This is also Isocrates' vision for philosophy. The goal of oratory and philosophy was the improvement of life in Athens, which could be accomplished through the wise and timely use of knowledge. James's writings bear an unmistakable trace of key rhetorical themes: possibility, opportunity, opinion, belief, plurality, experience, and consequences. His metaphysics relies on the same themes that grounded rhetorical theory, and he extends those themes through his attention to science, psychology, and religious studies. What is perhaps most telling, however, is that James's metaphysics requires a complementary method, just as any rhetoric inspires an active method for persuasion.

Method and Performance in James's Pragmatism

James states clearly that pragmatism "is a method." It is a method that turns toward "concreteness and adequacy, towards facts, towards action and towards power"; that lives in the "the open air and possibilities of nature"; and that rejects "dogma, artificiality and the pretence of finality in truth" (*PR*, 20). Given such an orientation to the world, "theories" are "instruments," philosophy is a practice, and interests (practical, ethical, religious, for example) guide empirical investigation (21). The first and primary use of the pragmatic method is that "of settling metaphysical disputes that otherwise might be interminable" (18). James provides several examples, including the one versus the many, free will versus determinism, and mind versus matter, to name several. The way to reconcile such disputes is to trace the respective practical consequences of each idea. In other words, "what difference would it practically make if this notion rather than that notion were true?"

By looking toward the consequences of such disputes, James critiques a philosophical problem from a rhetorical perspective. Given the orientation to the world that I outlined, any notion of a fixed, independent truth that is timeless and certain is of no interest to James. The rhetorician, unconcerned with fixed and timeless truths, also looks toward the results of an argument to test its efficacy. Whether an argument gains the assent of the many, whether a speech inspires action, or whether an adversary is persuaded to the other side, rhetorical discourse is tested by the results of its utterance; its truthfulness is upheld or refuted in and through those consequences. By subjecting historically important philosophical issues to such a test, James shifts the grounds of dispute away from traditional methods of argument in philosophy and toward the ways of the rhetorician.

James devotes a whole lecture of his *Pragmatism* to the question of the one and the many. By applying the pragmatic method to this problem, he comes to the following conclusion: "The world is one just so far as its parts hang together by any definite connexion. It is many just so far as any definite connexion fails to obtain. And finally it is growing more and more unified by those systems of connexion at least which human energy keeps framing as time goes by" (*PR,* 60). In other words, from some perspectives the world is one, and from others it is many. The consequences of this problem point to the different contexts in which the world can be considered as one or many.

Making philosophy a matter of context results in a critical position grounded on the sophistic notions of appropriateness and timeliness. The truth of a proposition is dependent on occasion, perspective, purpose, or moment in time, just as the effects of rhetorical discourse are tested by such criteria. However, James goes beyond these notions to test such ideas empirically as well: "pragmatism, pending the final empirical ascertainment of just what the balance of union and disunion among things may be, must obviously range herself upon the pluralistic side" (*PR,* 62). If humans are the measure of all things, empirical measurement is a key factor in judging the consequences of any idea. It is through empirical investigation that James sees the process of verification and of making truth take place. Thus he points to science as a method similar to rhetoric.

Empirical investigation is a method of testing the consequences of ideas, actions, and experiences; as such it is a way of assessing the rhetorical effects of human notions and interests. Science, understood as this kind of empirical investigation, shares the same goals as rhetoric does. By looking toward consequences and effects, both are mechanisms for changing the world, advancing human interests, and solving problems. In other words, both operate from a similar orientation to the world. Although science and rhetoric are clearly different tools, comparing the two suggests that understanding science from a rhetorical perspective can help illustrate how science operates as a persuasive mechanism in human affairs. It also suggests that combining both science and rhetoric as complementary sets of tools can be rewarding on pragmatic grounds—James in his public role as lecturer points to such a possibility.

According to James, in order to bring out the "practical cash-value" of an idea, one must "set it at work within the stream of . . . experience" (*PR*, 21). Once ideas are part of the stream of experience, they become "a program for more work" or "an indication of the ways in which existing realities may be *changed*." In other words, ideas "become true just in so far as they help us to get into satisfactory relation with other parts of our experience" (23). Empirical verification, therefore, becomes a central feature of the process of making truth and working toward change. James ties truth to notions of empirical verification, process, and method in a controversial passage from *Pragmatism*: "*True ideas are those that we can assimilate, validate, corroborate and verify. False ideas are those that we cannot.* That is the practical difference it makes to us to have true ideas; that, therefore, is the meaning of truth, for it is all that truth is known-as. . . . The truth of an idea is not a stagnant property inherent in it. Truth *happens* to an idea. It *becomes* true, is *made* true by events. Its verity *is* in fact an event, a process: the process namely of its verifying itself, its veri-*fication*. Its validity is the process of its own valid-*ation*" (77–78). Not only is pragmatism a method of solving metaphysical disputes (a method of philosophy), but it also describes the method of making truth in general. In a parallel fashion, rhetoric is not only a method of arriving at consensus decisions in politics or in the courts; it also describes the method of making truth from opinion. The difference between pragmatism and rhetoric lies in James's insistence that empirical verification is the primary cause of making truth, while the rhetorician relies on the force of eloquence. However, there are also important similarities between the two.

Paul Schollmeier's essay "The Pragmatic Method and Its Rhetorical Lineage" explicitly traces the genealogical origins of the pragmatic method to rhetorical argument by example. Schollmeier contends that both the pragmatic method and rhetorical argument by example "have the same structure. Both techniques are arguments proceeding from particulars through generalities to other particulars" (Schollmeier 2002, 369). Therefore, "rhetorical theory provides an intellectual perspective explaining why the experimental method has the broad scope that the pragmatists claim for it. Rhetorical theory shows especially why we can employ the experimental method when formulating principles for our conduct or making practical decisions" (379). In other words, the connections between rhetoric and the pragmatic method explain how the scientific or empirical method can be used for decision making in human affairs.

In *The Metaphysical Club*, Louis Menand recounts how James arrived at his understanding of science. The story begins with James's work as a student under Louis Agassiz, the man for whom the Lawrence Scientific School at Harvard was created. Agassiz was a researcher, trained in methods that "may seem the essence of scientific practice," who collected huge volumes of zoological artifacts and data (Menand 2001, 101). His research was characterized by "working with actual things, rather than with prior abstract conceptions about things," and by ignoring "unseen or unverifiable agencies" in favor of "generating testable hypothesis," which on the surface indicate a quintessential scientific objectivity. However, his career exemplified the exact opposite. According to Menand, "Agassiz had concepts and he had preferences. . . . The lesson of his career is that since everything we do we do out of some interest, we had better be clear about what our interests are. This lesson was not lost on William James" (101). Agassiz tried to refute Darwinism and show scientifically that certain races were superior to others; of course, this was a reactionary political agenda that he justified by relying on the persuasive appeal of scientific investigation *and* the pervasive racism in American culture. James accompanied Agassiz on an expedition to Brazil—a mission designed "to gather evidence to disprove the theories of Charles Darwin" (120). On this trip James began to see how science can work as a rhetoric and how a persuasive scientist can collect data based on previously determined political agendas.

James was only twenty-two years old when he joined Agassiz's expedition to Brazil, and on the trip he fluctuated wildly from great admiration to loathing for Agassiz. Later in his career James abandoned Agassiz altogether and his intellectual debt to *The Origin of the Species* would become much clearer and more pronounced. As one of the most influential and controversial works of the nineteenth century, *The Origin of the Species* had various interpreters and interpretations. One of those interpretations suggested that science, as an activity, is independent of individual or social interests and preferences—the same belief that gave Agassiz credibility. James rejected this interpretation. He saw Darwin's ideas as "devices for generating data," devices available for use by a scientist. The great advance of Darwin's theory is that it "opens possibilities for inquiry" in ways that Agassiz's did not. Darwin's empirical investigations led him to the conclusion that "it is in the nature of experience to offer exceptions and eccentricities" (Menand 2001, 141). For James, a theory that anticipates those exceptions—and that is actually predicated on those exceptions—holds the potential to be far more useful than a theory that believes in timeless truths about all living organisms. James learned the importance of collecting data from Agassiz and Darwin. However, he also understood that scientific theories are tools, and in a world that is constantly changing, the search for data can produce surprising results—either because of the individual doing the searching or because of the theory being used.

James's career as a scientist, his interest in Darwin, and his brief time as a naturalist taught him lessons essential to his pragmatism. According to Menand, "James believed that scientific inquiry, like any other form of inquiry, is an activity inspired and informed by our tastes, values, and hopes" (2001, 143). This does not, however, "confer any special authority on the conclusions it reaches."

Instead, such a perspective "obligates us to regard . . . conclusions as provisional and partial." Science, as an authority, can be malleable, just as species were malleable in Darwin's theory. In other words, the method of empirical verification could never produce objective, timeless truths given a changing "pluriverse" and scientific investigations guided by interests, values, and tastes. Science and empirical verification, therefore, "are only tools for decision making, one of the pieces people try to bundle together with other pieces, like moral teachings and selfish interests and specific information, when they need to reach a decision" (145). Menand's reading makes the methods of scientific and empirical verification comparable to the methods of rhetoric.

If we follow pragmatism's conception of the scientific method and Menand's reading of James's experiences, then several general features of science result. Science is a method of coping with uncertainty; a method of making beliefs true for the time being; a method that allows human beings to be active agents of change in the evolving constitution of the universe; a method of choosing beliefs and acting on them; and a way to change the way things are. Most important, science is informed by the scientist's interests. As such it can be mobilized as a set of persuasive arguments whose goal is to achieve some ends. In other words, science becomes a tool for arguing for and supporting one possible way of seeing and understanding the world. From a rhetorical perspective, therefore, science works as a persuasive mechanism for encouraging action and persuading people to believe in a particular vision of the world. Science and empirical verification supplement the persuasive tools offered by classical rhetoric while working toward the same ends. The authentic pragmatist, however, cannot eliminate the possibility that there are other reliable rhetorical resources. James, as a popular lecturer, certainly did not deliver his philosophy in the manner of a scientific report. The fact that he chose lectures as his mechanism for communicating his philosophy to others recommends him to rhetoricians and builds from his perspective on the scientific method as an additional means of influencing public issues.

The practice of public lecturing was still very much alive throughout James's career. His father, Henry James Sr., participated in this culture, as did his friend Oliver Wendell Holmes and some of his important intellectual influences, such as Ralph Waldo Emerson and Agassiz. Although the American lyceum movement, the driving force behind oratory in the antebellum years, declined in significance during James's lifetime, the public lecture remained a principal mode of communication in intellectual affairs.[24] James, in fact, delivered the initial statement of American pragmatism as a lecture in Berkeley, California. James (unlike C. S. Peirce and John Dewey) proved a master at speaking a language capable of communicating to a mixed audience extending beyond professional philosophers in ways that reflected pragmatism's dynamic, sensible, and useful principles. According to Charlene Haddock Seigfried, "William James's use of analogy and metaphor is more than a rhetorical device. It is integral to his hermeneutics and reflects his concrete analysis of human thinking" (1990, 209). Furthermore, she claims that "James was most comfortable using language as a poet does, to create such a compelling interpretation of life that the reader [or listener] can appropriate it as her own, rather than using language as a logician does, to elaborate a consistent system and avoid errors of technique" (210). Creating a compelling interpretation is not only the concern of the poet; it is also the primary concern of the rhetorician—compelling interpretations are persuasive.

In a world of flux and change, a world in which context informs meaning, metaphorical language communicates a sense of pluralism and individualism better than logical or analytic language does. The metaphor works through association by similarity—it is a form of communication that amplifies and builds from what is previously available to our experience. Analytic language, by contrast, attempts to reduce phenomena through precision and abstraction. As a form of communication, the metaphor mirrors a pluralistic world that grows, changes, and builds from what is available and avails itself to multiple interpretations. In *A Pluralistic Universe,* James argues that we continually use analogy in practical life, and he claims that the ability to perceive analogies is actually a sign of genius (*PU,* 71). James used a great deal of metaphors throughout his lectures and his writings. Seigfried claims that "it is not an exaggeration to say that all of James's central concerns are expressed in striking metaphors and analogies" (1990, 214). The potential of the metaphor lies in its being interpreted from a variety of perspectives and for a variety of ends. For those reasons, it is fitting that a philosophy that emphasizes practical consequences should employ a suggestive language designed to provide its audience with tools for use.

One of the most provocative metaphors James uses refers to the "cash-value" of a truthful idea. Associating truth with an economic mode of exchange struck many philosophers as heretical. Such a crude metaphor, they thought, violates the very standards of logical precision that philosophy tries to uphold. However, for James, the force of this metaphor shows the limits of logical language and the possibilities of a language that ties philosophy to the experience of everyday economic activity. Truth becomes a more useful and concrete idea when it is understood in terms of "cash-value" instead of some other abstract function. The goal of this metaphor is to associate philosophy with the concerns of practical experience, and this is precisely what James accomplishes by means of his linguistic choices.

Another goal of using metaphor is to rehabilitate the role of feeling in belief and the role of imagination in philosophy. Sensual or emotional language expresses James's claim that philosophy ought to be tied to experience. In addition, such language embodies the notion that people arrive at beliefs by virtue of more than just logical argument. Metaphors can point to the fact that *we* must interpret reality and that *we* are interactively involved in that process as active agents, not as passive observers. Instead of relying on our conceptual schemes to interpret reality, James emphasizes the concrete role of the individual through metaphor. Having the imagination actively interpret reality requires the ability to think in terms of metaphors, and to feel committed to the unfolding project of making the world, one must feel emotionally *and* intellectually part of that project.

It is instructive to compare a passage from James's work with a passage from Alfred North Whitehead's work. Whitehead was a member of the philosophy department at Harvard from 1924 until 1937, and his principal contributions were in the fields of philosophy of mathematics and science. In a series of lectures delivered at the University of Edinburgh in 1927 (published as *Process and Reality*), he spoke about such issues as "perception," "experience," and "subjectivism," similar concerns to those of pragmatism. He even acknowledged an intellectual debt to James and Dewey in the preface to these lectures (Whitehead 1929, vii.). Consider, however, the following passage, meant to describe an "authentic perceptive feeling": "Such a feeling, by virtue of its modes of origination, has as its datum a proposition whose predicate is in some way realized in the real nexus of its logical subjects. Thus the proposition felt proposes a predicate derived from the real nexus, and not refracted by the prehending subject. . . . For the primary physical feeling of that nexus by the prehending subject may have involved 'transmutation' according to categorical condition IV. In this case, the proposition ascribes to its logical subjects the *physical* enjoyment of a nexus with the definition of its predicate; whereas that predicate may have only been enjoyed *conceptually* by these logical subjects" (401). My concern here is not with the truthfulness or the logical rigor of Whitehead's argument but with his use of language. Clearly he builds his description of "feeling" and "enjoyment" on technical jargon that requires a level of professional competence in order to be evaluated and understood ("nexus," "predicate," "prehending subject"). Whitehead expects his audience to be fluent in this language and demands that they adapt to his style of writing. He turns questions of feeling into questions of logic.

Such a passage can be read in the light of a passage from James's work in which he describes both the act of perception and the ability of the philosopher to understand perceptions. In *The Varieties of Religious Experience,* James says, "There is in the living act of perception always something that glimmers and twinkles and will not be caught, and for which reflection comes too late. No one knows this as well as the philosopher. He must fire his volley of new vocables out of his conceptual shotgun, for his profession condemns him to this industry, but he secretly knows the hollowness and irrelevancy. His formulas are like stereoscopic or Kinetoscopic photographs seen outside the instrument; they lack the depth, the motion, the vitality" (356). This passage responds to Whitehead's claims on two fronts.

First, James argues that philosophers know that they cannot capture all aspects of perception in their conceptual frameworks. Logical or conceptual language lacks the ability to depict the motion and vitality of human experience, the features that James considers most important. Second, the metaphors of the shotgun and the photograph adapt the argument to the language of ordinary experience and thus make the argument accessible to the larger public. Specifically, the shotgun indicates that professional philosophy has a tendency to destroy that which it seeks to capture and take life from it. In addition, the photograph demonstrates how conceptual language arrests that which is in motion. Both metaphors indicate how philosophy acts as a tool for shaping our interactions with the world. If we accept James's position, then reflecting on our philosophical practices will illustrate the role that rhetoric plays in influencing our thoughts, beliefs, and actions—a task that any audience is capable of when thinking in terms of everyday metaphors.

In using metaphors to make philosophy approachable, accessible, and useful, James's work is audience-centered—as any good rhetoric is. In attempting to employ a language with which large audiences could identify, he demonstrates the capacity of philosophical thought to enrich life. Whitehead's parallel example demonstrates only how language can divide the project of philosophy from everyday applications. This juxtaposition lays the groundwork for theorizing rhetoric's role in applying philosophy to life. James's work is an example of the capacity of rhetoric to teach, influence, and improve an audience. His linguistic choices ground his critique of traditional philosophy and his desire to found a useful method of acting intelligently in the world, both of which issue from a concern with rhetoric.

Another provocative metaphor used by James to describe his philosophy of pragmatism is the sculptor: "To bid the man's subjective interests be passive till truth express itself from out of the environment, is to bid the sculptor's chisel be passive till the statue express itself from out of the stone. Operate we must! And the only choice left us is between operating to poor or to rich results" (*WB*, 103). This metaphor nicely expresses one of the key principles of James's pragmatism: we actively partake in the construction of our world. A statue cannot be foreshadowed in the material from which it is made; the hand of the sculptor must be used. It is the sculptor who chooses to make something that is rich or poor (which one could interpret as another economic metaphor). James's search is to find tools for philosophy that could be used as the sculptor uses the chisel, tools to help us construct a better world. His lectures and his metaphorical approach suggest rhetoric as one such possible tool.

The example of the sculptor explains why James's own writings have proved to be an inexhaustible resource for generations of scholars. His metaphorical approach is suggestive, and so we interact with his work as the sculptor interacts with stone—we make from it our own interpretations and use it to set our own work in motion. The impact of the metaphor allows his meaning to overflow in ways that a straightforward, abstract proposition cannot, and through metaphor he is able to reach multiple audiences in his own time and after. His language, therefore, holds the potential to inform the ways we can reconstruct our world, and the language of pragmatism should have the power to avail itself to use by others. In James we find an expression of a pragmatist rhetoric because of the ability of his language to be used as the sculptor uses stone. We also find a tool for reconstructing and improving rhetoric's role in philosophy and in American society.

James does not appear to have reflected self-consciously on his own rhetorical practices, and for that reason he was not a rhetorician. It is remarkable, however, that as a philosopher who was attempting to critique the basic presuppositions of philosophy, he was able to find a language removed from the kind of abstraction that others were using and that he detested. In metaphors he found life, change, experience, and most of all a means to affect audiences profoundly without violating his own metaphysical commitments. His aversion to conceptual and overly rationalistic thought is also an aversion to conceptual and overly rationalistic language. If any philosophy is to be a public, instrumental tool, then it must attend to the language with which it is articulated. We learn this lesson from James, and thus we learn the potential role that rhetoric might play both in pragmatism, specifically, and in philosophy, broadly. Reading James's lectures now, with their rich and provocative metaphors, demonstrates how closely pragmatism, as an intellectual project, is tied to rhetoric. The enduring significance of James's work testifies to such a claim.

From a Philosophy of Pragmatism to a Philosophy of Rhetoric

Measured by its effects on academic philosophy, James's pragmatism was a failure. In *The Rise of American Philosophy,* Bruce Kuklick recounts the history of the philosophy department at Harvard between the turn of the century and World War II. James was an original member of Harvard's department, which also included Josiah Royce and Hugo Münsterberg. The main intellectual preoccupations of that department were the combination of psychology and philosophy and the reconciliation of science and theology. Kuklick claims that James, Royce, and Münsterberg, the members of "the great department," were "personally committed to comprehending man's place in the universe, [and] they conceived of philosophy as the love of wisdom and the guide to practical [cultural] affairs of life" (1977, xx). James was certainly a central inspiration for this vision, but by 1930 Harvard philosophers "mostly abandoned interest in the culture for a preoccupation with technique and with affairs of their discipline," following, instead of James, the work of Alfred North Whitehead (xxiii).

Kuklick traces the transformation of philosophy from a public intellectual activity concerned with the broadest issues of culture to a more esoteric and professional enterprise focusing on technical problems. The logical, rationalistic, and intellectualist traditions triumphed at Harvard and in other philosophy departments by the 1930s. The result of this shift was that "being a philosopher was inconsistent with having a public function" (Kuklick 1977, 532). This was a reversal of the original aspiration of the Harvard department, which was to make philosophy more "suitably rhetorical" so it could have a "broader appeal" (88). James's language of metaphors, his attention to experience and belief, and his preoccupation with practical consequences and an overflowing, plural universe were abandoned as professional philosophical commitments.

In its own time, therefore, pragmatism did not find a home in philosophy departments. James and Dewey, despite spending a good deal of time and energy responding to criticisms in *The Journal of Speculative Philosophy* and elsewhere, were unable to achieve wide acceptance in their discipline for their version of philosophy. However, a set of intellectuals, working in other fields, extended and used pragmatism toward a variety of ends. Jane Addams as a progressive reformer, Alain Locke as a cultural critic, Oliver Wendell Holmes as a lawyer and a judge, Robert Park and C. Wright Mills as sociologists, Lionel Trilling as a literary critic, W. E. B. Du Bois as a cultural critic, and George Mead as a social psychologist all shared and used the pragmatist intellectual orientation to the world. James's pragmatism, then, set an agenda for work in a broad range of fields beyond philosophy, and that is a testament to pragmatism's success on its own terms. James's philosophy of pragmatism is not a philosophy for strict contemplation by philosophers. Rather it is a philosophy for action that lends itself to use by many different intellectual endeavors. Accordingly, James's pragmatism can be broadly construed as a philosophy of rhetoric.[25]

James's attention to method, his performances as a lecturer, and his interest in pluralism, experience, and belief all lay the intellectual and theoretical foundations for understanding rhetoric's role in American culture. In so doing, he suggests critical areas of inquiry for the contemporary study of rhetoric. For example, his particular attention to psychology and science indicates important areas for considering rhetoric's role in shaping both public and private decision making. In *The Varieties of Religious Experience* and *Principles of Psychology,* James shows how the human mind is affected by more than just rational language. In these works he treats the process of persuasion and the roles of belief, opinion, and action as psychological, but still rhetorical, issues. Aristotle's *Rhetoric* makes explicit connections between psychology and rhetoric by demonstrating the cognitive dimension of the emotions. By considering the psychological process of arriving at beliefs and acting on those beliefs, James reopens the connections between rhetoric and psychology made by Aristotle.[26]

By pointing to the role that individual interests play in collecting data and forming hypotheses, by showing how scientific knowledge is itself subject to revision, and by showing how science can be mobilized in decision-making processes, James opens a place for the role of rhetoric in science.[27] Although Protagoras's "human-measure" principle resonates with pragmatism, James focuses on the importance of measurement in that process. By considering how empirical verification orders and gives meaning to the world, he suggests that contemporary science can work in a comparable fashion to rhetoric, and thus he suggests that eloquent language is not the only method for affecting the course of human affairs. Furthermore, combining his focus on science and empirical verification with the capacity for language he displayed in his lectures suggests that combining science and rhetoric can be a practical, beneficial project.

The question for both pragmatism and rhetoric concerns method. Active human agents employ tools and techniques designed to order and influence human affairs; pragmatism and rhetoric share this concern. It is possible, then, to extend the project of pragmatism by connecting it to rhetoric or to extend the functions of rhetoric by connecting it with pragmatism. Further characterizing the attributes of an American rhetoric founded on a philosophy of pragmatism requires a turn to other pragmatist intellectuals. Tracing the way pragmatism was developed in thinkers such as John Dewey, Jane Addams, Oliver Wendell Holmes, and Alain Locke points to further connections between pragmatism and rhetoric and shows the variety of mechanisms of persuasion developed to intervene in the course of American public life.

James asked questions about the interaction between an individual and the world and how these interactions are regulated, controlled, and influenced by a variety of factors. In asking such questions James returned to the intellectual roots of rhetoric's birth in classical Athens. Specifically, he returned to questions of invention, purpose, and consequences. For these reasons Mark Backman can point to William James's "discovery that the mind exists as both product and producer of the stream of consciousness" as "the basic intellectual premises of our present sophistication" (1991, 152). According to this position, pragmatism "transformed how individuals relate to communities" and reintroduced the central theoretical problems of rhetoric as first understood in classical Athens.

Looking to the ways that pragmatism has been extended in various fields and by varying thinkers can help demonstrate the myriad similarities between rhetoric and pragmatism and help theorize rhetoric's place in American democracy. James teaches us that we can no longer afford to see pragmatism as a philosophy whose validity is subject to professional and technical disputes through rational and conceptual language. Such a perspective fails to offer the most useful means of extending pragmatism's ability to contribute to the making of our own culture and does not fairly reflect the metaphysical claims upon which pragmatism is built. According to my interpretation, James's pragmatism can be seen as a philosophy of rhetoric. More important, it establishes the intellectual necessity of rhetoric in human affairs and opens the practical possibility for the development of uniquely American rhetorics.

Two

John Dewey on Communication and the Practical Arts

A History of Philosophy and a Return to Rhetoric

In the summer of 1894 John Dewey rode a train from Michigan to Illinois to begin his new job in the philosophy department at the University of Chicago.[1] On the train he met a union organizer passionately involved with the Pullman Strike that was under way at that time.[2] After talking for "10 or 15 minutes," Dewey's "nerves were more thrilled than they had been for years; [he] felt as if [he] had better resign [his] job teaching and follow [the union organizer] around till [he] got into life."[3] For him, the strike was an intriguing event. The union of people around a common interest, motivated to seek an appropriate solution to the problem before them, pushed Dewey's thought away from Hegelian idealism and toward the "problems of men."[4] Such a visceral response to his conversation and to the larger situation in Chicago pointed toward the central questions of Dewey's intellectual career: How could philosophy be brought to bear on the pressing problems of the moment? How could the practices that inform everyday life and the tools for solving human problems be made more intelligent, more thoughtful, more effective? What could philosophy tell us about the necessary conditions for a successful, vibrant democracy with well-educated citizens and fully functioning communities? Dewey's pragmatism is essentially an attempt to address these questions.

The Pullman Strike was one of many public instances that gave Dewey the opportunity for philosophical reflection and, more important, philosophical action.[5] Although he did not influence the outcome of the strike, Dewey's intellectual legacy is marked by the search for ways to "intellectualize practice," to solve "the problems of men," and to contribute to the health and promise of American democracy.[6] Dewey's pragmatism leaves the realm of speculation in search of sensible responses to difficult and intractable problems such as the Pullman Strike.[7] Specifically, Dewey's pragmatism is grounded on the belief that the discipline of philosophy (understood traditionally as a "quest for certainty") is inadequate and misdirected if it is not concerned with the practice of rhetoric.[8] Although Dewey does not use the term "rhetoric," I use it to explain his effort to craft a philosophy for action. As noted, rhetoric points to the importance of tools, methods, communication, and the "practical arts" for solving pressing problems and making the community better.[9]

Whereas William James developed pragmatism as an orientation to the world, Dewey added to this perspective by providing a historical description of the failures of traditional philosophy. In *The Quest for Certainty* and *Reconstruction in Philosophy,* Dewey articulates a history of philosophy as the disinterested pursuit of knowledge and the concomitant neglect of issues concerning the uses of knowledge. His goal in these works is to show that pragmatism, by virtue of an attention to the "practical arts," can connect theory and practice and avoid the pitfalls that had plagued philosophy until his moment. I argue that his belief in the necessity of the "practical arts" can be understood as an attempt to illustrate the significance of rhetoric for philosophy. Although he does not make explicit connections between his pragmatism and the rhetorical tradition, his historical description of philosophy can be read by drawing out those connections.

In addition to the argument for the necessity of the "practical arts," Dewey's pragmatism connects theory and practice by investigating philosophy's role in democratic affairs. This is most obvious in his belief that philosophy ought to be concerned with pressing, social problems, a belief that anticipates the contemporary preoccupation with the "rhetorical situation." As with his history of philosophy, Dewey does not make any comparison between the rhetorical tradition and his focus on the "problems of men." Even so, I read his commitments as an opportunity for exploring the similarities between the two. In order to solve the "problems of men" and address rhetorical situations most effectively, Dewey, like James, insists that we rely on knowledge invented by science. As a mechanism for ordering, controlling, and arranging human experience, science can be a useful tool. Such a perspective points to the importance of rhetoric for scientific practice. Dewey also addresses communication. Although science has a distinctive method capable of producing knowledge, the communication of that knowledge is critical for solving pressing problems. According to Dewey's pragmatism, philosophy must reconcile scientific knowledge with communication; such a project is essential for social action, democracy, and the health of the community.

Dewey's thought can be read in the light of classical rhetoric in order to demonstrate how pragmatism points to the need for rhetoric in sociopolitical affairs. More specifically, Dewey's history of philosophy outlines the intellectual conditions for theorizing rhetoric's place in human affairs. In addition his attention to science and communication outlines the practical conditions for using rhetoric in American democracy. It follows from this view that pragmatism functions as a locus for the varied and important connections between philosophy and rhetoric. It also follows that rhetoric can be the "practical art" most capable of using knowledge to solve problems, fostering social cooperation, and sustaining a democratic way of life—arguments hinted at in Dewey's texts but never fully developed.

Comparisons can be drawn between Dewey's work and classical rhetorical theory, as was the case with James's work. Isocrates and Cicero articulate pragmatic visions of rhetoric tied to methods of using knowledge and philosophical wisdom. Both Isocrates and Cicero saw rhetoric as an art capable of directing the affairs of the state, improving the life of the community, and combining wisdom or knowledge with action. According to Takis Poulakos and David Depew, Isocrates "recast philosophy *as* rhetoric" in forming a program for civic education that aimed at prudential action (2004, 2). I argue that Dewey attempts a similar move—his pragmatism represents new variations of an interest in *phronesis* (or practical wisdom), wisdom and eloquence, the construction of the best possible community, and the ethical responsibilities of the rhetor. Drawing parallels between Dewey's philosophy and Isocrates and Cicero's rhetoric shows that pragmatism shares an orientation to the world with classical rhetoric. At the same time, it exceeds the classical tradition in provocative ways and thus operates as a suggestive resource for contemporary rhetoric.

In order to elaborate on the implications of Dewey's pragmatism, I address three features of his philosophy that point to the importance of rhetoric. First, a reading of his history of philosophy shows that Dewey comes close to arguing that rhetoric is critically important to philosophy and to establishing the intellectual necessity of rhetoric as a practical art. Second, showing how his pragmatism focuses on the importance of science and communication for rhetorical situations demonstrates that Dewey works within the classical rhetorical tradition to develop practical conditions for the uses of rhetoric in democratic affairs. Third, Dewey's pragmatism can be understood as a search for distinctively American rhetorics.

Dewey's History of Philosophy

In 1916 Dewey claimed that "knowledge of the past is the key to understanding the present. History deals with the past, but this past is the history of the present" (Dewey 1916, 214). What this implied for the historian is that "the true starting point of history is always some present situation with its problems." Following through on this claim, Dewey published *Reconstruction in Philosophy* in 1920 and *The Quest for Certainty* in 1929. Both accounts tell "the story of an inevitably unsuccessful pursuit by philosophers of a therapeutic quest for absolutely certain knowledge of truth, goodness, and beauty in an unavoidably contingent world" (Westbrook 1991, 348). The purpose of these stories was to show that philosophy "must assume a practical nature" and "invent methods of changing the world through action"(*RP,* 121; *QC,* 3). Dewey's own, particular moment made such a historical account important because "the new movements in science and in the industrial and political human conditions" must be "carried to completion" with the help of philosophy. As such, he argues that philosophy "can be nothing less than the work of developing, or forming, or producing . . . the intellectual instrumentalities which will progressively direct inquiry into the deeply and inclusively human . . . facts of the present scene and situation" (*RP,* xxvii). In other words, Dewey insists that we look critically at philosophy's historical preoccupation with absolute certainty so that we can reconstruct philosophy as a practice better suited for understanding and influencing current human affairs.[10]

The first step in such a reconstruction is to find the origin of philosophy's search for certain knowledge. According to Dewey, philosophy's major shortcomings are a result of Plato's influence on Greek civilization.[11] *Reconstruction in Philosophy* begins with a description of traditions and beliefs in classical Greece. Dewey sees a tension, in this period, between a "socially generalized . . . texture of tradition" in which imagination, social heritage, and community are the mechanisms for knowing and acting in the world, on one hand, and experimentalism, positivism, and matter-of-fact knowledge on the other hand (*RP,* 10). In other words, he identifies an antagonism between a belief in cultural and communal traditions as a useful source of knowledge and the early scientific search for facts-in-themselves.

The communal way of conceiving life involves poetry, story, drama, and memory to "re-enact an emotionally important experience," to organize "larger ethical traditions," and to create a sense of social unity. Such traditional ways of life in classical Greece marked one particular instigation for the creation of philosophy. The organization, systematization, and generalization of "ideas and principles of belief" that grounded traditions and social heritage helped grant Greece stability, authority, and prestige (*RP,* 11). However, "the requirements of continued existence" made "attention to the actual facts of the world" indispensable. Therefore, a body of positive and tested knowledge grew alongside traditional beliefs.

Over time this growing body of facts "promoted the development of the experimental habit of mind." Dewey argues that "for a long time the imaginative body of beliefs closely connected with the moral habits of a community" persisted "side by side with the growing body of matter of fact knowledge." A time came, however, when "matter of fact knowledge increased to such bulk and scope that it came into conflict with not merely the detail but with the spirit and temper of traditional and imaginative beliefs." According to Dewey, "this is just what happened in what we term the sophistic movement in Greece, within which originated philosophy proper in the sense in which the western world understands that term" (*RP*, 12–13).

The conflict between Plato and the sophists marks a critical moment in the history of philosophy for Dewey because it points to the obsession with matter-of-fact knowledge at the expense of tradition, imagination, and social cooperation:

> The ill-fame of the sophists may be used to suggest some of the striking contrasts between traditional emotionalized belief on the one hand and prosaic matter of fact knowledge on the other:—the purpose of the comparison being to bring out the point that while the advantages of what we call science were on the side of the latter, the advantages of social esteem and authority, and of intimate contact with what gives life its deeper lying values were on the side of traditional belief. To all appearances, the specific and verified knowledge had only a limited and technical scope. . . . While the artisan is expert as long as purely limited technical questions arise, he is helpless when it comes to the only really important questions, the moral questions as to values. Consequently his type of knowledge is inherently inferior and needs to be controlled by a higher kind of knowledge which will reveal ultimate ends and purposes, and thus put and keep technical and mechanical knowledge in its proper place. (*RP*, 14–15)

Plato's dialogues provide a glimpse into the dramatic conflict between "tradition and the newer claims of purely intellectual knowledge" (*RP*, 15).[12] Dewey does not state rhetoric's role in these conflicts, but traditional belief systems, social unity, and the ultimate ends that a community was to pursue were constructed or reinforced through the practice of rhetoric. To be more specific, teachers of rhetoric, such as the sophists and Isocrates, taught their students how to use knowledge to "reveal ultimate ends and purposes" to their audience. According to the sophists and Isocrates, rhetoric has the "capacity to bring and hold people together" and "to invent and satisfy desires" (Poulakos and Poulakos 1999, 113). Dewey, however, does not develop the significance of rhetoric as a practical art in the conflict he describes.

Instead of accepting custom, political authority, or tradition, Plato argued that we "must search out the reason of things" with "definiteness," "accuracy," and "verifiability" (*RP*, 17). This is possible through the development of a "method of rational investigation and proof," in the "sense of pruning away excrescences and eliminating factors which to the average citizen were all one with the basic beliefs" (19). Ultimately, such a method would produce a metaphysics that could serve as a "substitute for custom as the source and guarantor of higher moral values—that is the leading theme of the classical philosophy of Europe as evolved by Plato and Aristotle" (17). However, at this point in the history of philosophy, Plato could not replace rhetoric; he could only subject it to critical investigation and try to show that rhetoric, tradition, and social unity should be based on certain knowledge. Although philosophy aims "at a rational justification of things," without any complementary rhetoric it fails to convince "men of the truth of doctrines"—"there is no recourse save to magnify the signs of rigorous thought and rigid demonstration" (20). The major implication of this claim is that philosophy must use rhetoric to have an effect on life—an implication latent in Dewey's work but not fully expressed.

Since Plato's split with the sophists, philosophy has constructed an "elaborate terminology, a hair-splitting logic, and a fictitious devotion to the mere external forms of comprehensive and minute demonstration. Even at the best it has tended to produce an overdeveloped attachment to system for its own sake, and an over-pretentious claim to certainty" (*RP*, 21). For Dewey, William James was one of only "a few dissenters who have ventured to assert" that philosophy need not pursue this path but instead can enlarge man's "perceptions of the world" (21). By arrogating itself to the "office of demonstrating the existence of a transcendent, absolute or inner reality and of revealing to man the nature and features of this ultimate and higher reality," philosophy "claimed that it was in possession of a higher organ of knowledge . . . and that it is marked by a superior dignity and importance" (23). This, according to Dewey, was a major mistake. Philosophy emerges "out of social and emotional material," out of a sophistic concern with tradition, poetry, and imagination (25). Ultimately this implies that philosophy emerges out of the need to ground rhetoric more solidly on knowledge: "Instead of impersonal and purely speculative endeavors to contemplate as remote beholders the nature of absolute things-in-themselves, we have a living picture of the choice of thoughtful men about what they would have life to be, and to what ends they would have men shape their intelligent activities" (26). Here Dewey offers us a potentially provocative definition of rhetoric alongside his description of where philosophy went wrong.

The analysis of classical Greek life that begins *Reconstruction in Philosophy* is carried further in *The Quest for Certainty.* In the latter work, Dewey adds to the conflict between tradition and matter-of-fact knowledge by showing how Greek culture divided the world into those aspects of life that could be controlled and those that could not. The "practical arts" gave citizens the ability to control their environment, while religious rites and ceremonies dealt with the uncontrollable. It seems obvious that rhetoric should be considered a "practical art" capable of accomplishing precisely what Dewey describes, but Dewey makes reference to the "practical arts" without explicitly discussing rhetoric.

Philosophy, in contrast to the "practical arts," introduced a more systematic approach to the uncontrollable world. Through its attention to the "Real in itself, or Being in and of itself," philosophy was concerned with a suprahuman realm and subsequently with the highest and purest kind of knowledge, thus creating a hierarchical distinction between kinds of knowledge (*QC*, 17). According to Robert Westbrook, "Practical matters—those infected with non-being—were left to lower forms of wisdom, judgment, and technical expertise. Such lower forms of knowledge were inferior because they were not knowledge of the fully and purely Real. Only by contemplative philosophical insight could man find the certainty he sought beyond the contingencies of ordinary experience" (1991, 349). Thus, Plato turned away from precarious and uncertain human experience that required practical and contingent knowledge and instead turned toward a perfect and certain world of rational and quasi-religious forms.

Subsequent philosophies followed Plato's lead by turning away from the contingent, ordinary, and uncertain, leaving those areas of inquiry to the likes of rhetoricians, politicians, or artists. However, "The notion that thought, apart from action, can warrant complete certitude as to the status of supreme good, makes no contribution to the central problem of development of intelligent methods of regulation. It rather depresses and deadens effort in that direction. That is the chief indictment to be brought against the classic philosophic tradition"(*QC*, 36).[13] Dewey pushes this line of thought even further by claiming that current "methods of knowing" and "arts of practical action" should force us to question our conceptions of knowledge and practice. To extend Dewey's position, the goal is to show that methods of knowing (philosophy and science) ought to be linked to the arts of practical action (rhetoric) and that this link is especially important given Dewey's historical position.[14]

Plato's legacy left a mark on philosophy that has proved impossible to erase. By removing philosophy from the practical arts, from tradition and the social fabric of a culture, and placing greater emphasis on a pure realm of contemplation, Plato permanently cast doubt on any attempt to craft a philosophy of action. Not even Francis Bacon could escape the metaphysical trap set by Plato. *Reconstruction in Philosophy* points to Bacon as both the "real founder of modern thought" and the most unfortunate victim of the obsession with certain knowledge (*RP*, 28). Bacon's major philosophical contribution, according to Dewey, was the argument that classic logic falsely assumed that truth was already known and required demonstration. To replace this faulty logic, Bacon claimed that a method of discovery was the aim and test of genuine knowledge. This means that "the great need is the organization of co-operative research, whereby men attack nature collectively and the work of inquiry is carried on continuously" (37).

For Bacon philosophy became a method of discovering certain knowledge, and this was a great advance, according to Dewey. However, this change from classical philosophy has been only technical "rather than human and moral," which renders the change problematic: "While we have been reasonably successful in obtaining command of nature by means of science, our science is not yet such that this command is systematically and pre-eminently applied to the relief of human estate. . . . And this limitation defines the specific problem of philosophical reconstruction at the present time. For it emphasizes the larger social deficiencies that require intelligent diagnosis, and projection of aims and methods" (*RP,* 43). Bacon gave the individual mind competence to discover knowledge, but he "did not achieve a free and unbiased formulation of the meaning of the power to direct nature's forces through knowledge—that is, purposeful, experimental action acting to reshape beliefs and institutions" (50). The ancient tradition's separation of the practical arts from pure knowledge still informed early modern philosophy, according to Dewey.

Bacon's inability to escape from Plato's metaphysics both influenced and foreshadowed the inability of science, as understood during Dewey's time, to escape from that predicament as well. Both *Reconstruction in Philosophy* and *The Quest for Certainty* try to make clear the philosophical underpinnings of "modern science." In so doing, these works illustrate the devastating effect that the separation of philosophy from rhetoric has had on the development of science. According to Dewey, modern philosophy contributed two main ideas to the scientific revolution that perpetuated Plato's metaphysical quest for certainty: "These two ideas . . . are that knowledge is concerned with disclosure of the characteristics of antecedent existences and essences, and that the properties of value found therein provide the authoritative standards for the conduct of life" (*QC,* 71). These traits exclude any consideration of practical activity, and they reinforce the separation between subject and object. Furthermore, science falsely equates the known with the real and transforms knowers into observers of the real equipped with mathematical instruments for precise observation. The great advance of science, according to Dewey, was to escape the transcendental contemplation of certainty and to replace the metaphysical aspirations associated with such a trend with a precise method able to produce concrete facts. However, the scientific method was still infused with metaphysical assumptions about certainty, reality, and experience. This prevented science from acknowledging the practical aspects of its methods and the importance of attention to ordinary problems.

Modern philosophy was then forced to address the success of science. According to Dewey, philosophy's major concern became the "need of reconciling, of somehow adjusting, the findings of scientific knowledge with the validity of ideas concerning value" (*QC,* 49). *The Quest for Certainty* demonstrates how

Descartes, Kant, Fichte, and Hegel all "sought by examination of the structure of the knowing function . . . to show that no matter what the detailed conclusions of the special sciences, the ideal authority of truth, goodness, and beauty are secure possessions of ultimate Being independently of experience and human action" (62–63). This merely shows, however, that philosophy's "continued adherence to certain conceptions framed centuries ago and then embodied in the entire western tradition" prevent it from "reflection upon actual conditions of science and life" (72).

In addition the subject matter of philosophy is "more and more derived from the problems and conclusions of its own past history," and therefore it remains "aloof from the problems of a culture in which philosophers live" (*QC*, 70). By continuing to assume that "the object of knowledge is some form of ultimate Being which is antecedent to reflective inquiry and independent of it," and that "this antecedent Being has among its defining characteristics those properties which alone have authority over the formation of our judgments of value," philosophy has systematically ignored the practical questions of the moment that it ought to be addressing (69).

Dewey's history ends with a call for a "Copernican Revolution" in philosophy, or as he put it more humbly at an earlier point, a "reconstruction in philosophy." The principal aspect of this revolution or reconstruction is the integration of the practical arts with the search for knowledge and the eradication of the search for "ultimate Being" that began with Plato. I argue that the suggestions that Dewey makes for a reconstruction in philosophy all point to the primary concerns of rhetorical theory and practice. Read from the perspective of the rhetorical tradition, Dewey's history of philosophy suggests that we need to understand and develop the significance of rhetoric for any future philosophy. There are four key features of a reconstruction in philosophy.

First, philosophers must rethink and reconfigure the relationship between experience and reason: "We *use* our past experiences to construct new and better ones in the future. The very fact of experience thus includes the process by which it directs itself in its own betterment. Science, 'reason' is not therefore something laid from above upon experience. Suggested and tested in experience, it is also employed through inventions in a thousand ways to expand and enrich experience" (*RP*, 95). This is exactly the kind of lesson that Isocrates taught his students. The best orator was able to use past experiences to advance the best possible course of action for the community—in essence this is Isocrates' definition of *phronesis*.[15] The *Panegyricus* embodies this attitude toward discourse by reworking a historical tradition to advance a particular political agenda: "For the deeds of the past are, indeed, an inheritance common to us all; but the ability to make proper use of them at the appropriate time, to conceive the right sentiments about them in each instance, and to set them forth in finished phrase, is the peculiar gift of the wise" (9). As an example of Isocrates' approach to "*philosophia,*" the *Panegyricus* underscores the importance of *phronesis* as a tool for bettering the community through the use of experience.[16]

Second, philosophy must change its conception of the real and the ideal, which is founded on the assumption that the concrete events of daily experience should play no part in determining the real or the ideal. Such an assumption suggests that "the structures and objects which science and philosophy set up" create "a realm apart in which rational contemplation may rest satisfied" (*RP*, 117). For philosophy to assume a practical nature, to become "operative and experimental," its prime function should be "rationalizing the *possibilities* of experience, especially collective human experience," and not the contemplation of some independent real (122). The sophists claimed that rhetoric had the capacity to articulate and realize the possibilities of collective human experience. The sophistic belief that ends can be reached through the practice of rhetoric rested on the assumption that "people are endowed with the capacity to see themselves and the world not only as they are but as they can become" (J. Poulakos 1995, 68).[17] By shifting attention from the problem of the real and the ideal to the possible, philosophy must direct its effort toward more grounded, practical, constructive, and ultimately rhetorical areas of inquiry. If this is so, however, pragmatism shares with rhetoric the assumption that the world can be remade in a new fashion.

Third, philosophy requires a new understanding of logic, a logic that emancipates it from the quest for certainty. Logic is not purely formal; rather it is a "means of intentional reconstruction of experience" (*RP*, 134). This implies that "the problem of logical theory is none other than the problem of the possibility of the development and employment of intelligent methods in inquiries concerned with deliberate reconstruction of experience" (138). In other words, logic should not be thinking in the abstract; it should be thinking in concrete ways how to guide intelligent responses to situations. Essentially, logic becomes a tool for rhetoric, a way of grounding decision making and judgment in uncertain situations on a method of intelligent deliberation. What Dewey recommends is an updated version of Aristotle's *Rhetoric* and *Topics,* which discuss the role of nonscientific, or informal, logic in developing persuasive arguments. For example, the general topics were designed to guide a rhetor's thinking in relation to specific situations so as to identify the best available means of persuasion. This is also a prescription for the development of contemporary argument theory, embodied in works such as Chaim Perelman and L. Olbrechts-Tyteca's *The New Rhetoric* and Stephen Toulmin's *The Uses of Argument,* which display the capacity of reason to ground persuasion on intelligent methods of deliberation.

Fourth, philosophy must change its approach to moral theory. When burdened with Plato's metaphysics, philosophers locate questions of good and evil within theology, metaphysics, and Being-in-itself. Moral problems, however, should be a question of "reducing, alleviating, as far as may be removing, the evils of life" (*RP,* 177). In addition, instead of abstract thoughts about timeless notions of the good, philosophy should contribute "in however humble a way to methods that will assist us in discovering the causes of humanity's ills." Ultimately all questions of morality should also be questions of meliorism, or the "belief that the specific conditions which exist at one moment, be they comparatively bad or comparatively good, in any event may be bettered" (178). This is the focus of both Isocrates and Cicero.[18] For Cicero, rhetoric was a question of the "good man speaking well." Embodied in the concept of the "ideal statesman," Cicero ties oratory to ethics by virtue of its concern for other citizens: "For just as the aim of the pilot is a successful voyage . . . so this director of the commonwealth has as his aim for his fellow-citizens a happy life, fortified by wealth, rich in material resources, great in glory and honored for virtue. I want him to bring to perfection this achievement, which is the greatest and best possible among men" (*De Republica* 5.6.8). In addition, the primary function of a rhetor, or political leader, according to Isocrates, is to contribute to the betterment of the community. "The highest kind of oratory," according to Isocrates, "brings most profit to those who hear" (*Panegyricus* 4–5). Both Isocrates and Cicero craft a notion of ethics that is tied to improving the quality of life in the community and having the best interests of others in mind. In so doing, they established the importance of ethics for rhetorical action, but it is an ethics embedded in pragmatic meliorism.[19]

Dewey tells this history of philosophy to highlight the problems associated with a search for certainty and the potential benefit of connecting philosophy to the practical arts as they once were in classical Greece. If rhetoric was acknowledged as an important practical art in classical Athens, then it is clear that Plato's rejection of the sophists damaged philosophy by eradicating its connections to rhetoric.[20] Dewey's call for a reconstruction in philosophy would turn our attention away from certainty and toward intelligence as the primary means of acting rhetorically. Robert Westbrook eloquently describes the implications of such a move: "For Dewey, substituting intelligence for transcendent reason or uninterrogated desire in the moral life of a culture required vesting authority not in the insights of philosophers (or scientists) but in the deliberations of ordinary men and women skilled in the art of practical judgment—the lowly artisans with their humble, contingent, probable knowledge would claim the temple denied them by Plato and nearly every philosopher since" (1991, 360).

To any student of the history of rhetoric, this statement is a clear indication of the central role that rhetoric should play in Dewey's pragmatism and the central role that Dewey should have hoped rhetoric would play in the intelligent construction of our world. Cornel West expands this theme to include communication explicitly: "The claim is that once one gives up on the search for foundations and the quest for certainty, human inquiry into truth and knowledge shifts to the social and communal circumstances under which persons can communicate and cooperate in the process of acquiring knowledge" (1989, 213). To West's description one might add that such a process of communication seeks to acquire the kind of knowledge that can be used to shape the character and destiny of a community. When communication seeks to coordinate social action, influence human choices, or achieve desired consequences, it engages questions of rhetoric. Dewey's history of philosophy shows that the scientific and philosophic search for certain knowledge should be used as a resource for rhetorical action, not as the collection of facts and immutable truths, and as grounds for theorizing rhetoric's role in human affairs.

Science, Communication, and the Rhetorical Situation

Dewey's history of philosophy is a response to a particular rhetorical situation. At the beginning of both *Reconstruction in Philosophy* and *The Quest for Certainty* he argues that his historical analyses are the results of the intellectual situation within which he was embedded. However, Dewey's stronger claim is that philosophy, in all of its endeavors, should *always* be concerned with the occasions and opportunities provided through experiences at particular moments. Social problems should call philosophers to action just as they have called rhetoricians to action.

By demonstrating the centrality of the "problems of men" for philosophy, Dewey establishes the grounds for a consideration of the rhetorical situation. Lloyd Bitzer's 1968 article, "The Rhetorical Situation," marks a key contribution to twentieth-century rhetorical theory.[21] The central argument Bitzer advances is that "rhetorical works . . . obtain their character from the circumstances of the historic context in which they occur" (Lucaites, Condit, and Caudill 1999, 219). To state the case more thoroughly: "A work of rhetoric is *pragmatic;* it comes into existence for the sake of something beyond itself; it functions ultimately to produce action or change in the world; it performs some task. In short, rhetoric is a mode of altering reality . . . by the creation of discourse which changes reality through the mediation of thought and action" (219, italics mine). Bitzer explicitly identifies rhetoric with pragmatism because both are concerned with situations and both perform tasks in response to some exigence. In *Reconstruction in Philosophy* and *The Quest for Certainty,* Dewey consistently argues that philosophy, whether it acknowledges it or not, is a method of acting in the world, altering reality, and responding to situations. Bitzer begins to explicitly demonstrate and develop the theoretical implications of Dewey's position for rhetoric.

James Mackin claims that Dewey was, in fact, "an important influence on Bitzer's thought" (Cherwitz 1990, 285). From Mackin's perspective, Bitzer offers a distinctly pragmatic rhetoric: "rhetoric as a discipline should seek to provide a better method for inquiry into rhetorical situations so that a more appropriate response can be discovered" (286). Both Bitzer and Dewey agree that without an exigence there would be no imperative to think about or change a situation. Mackin argues that rhetorical criticism, pluralism, relativism, and *phronesis* are all key aspects of a rhetorical theory that shares an intellectual orientation with Dewey's pragmatism. Mackin's essay illustrates some of the implications of combining pragmatism and rhetorical theory, and as such he focuses on the situational aspects of both of these. However, Dewey's contribution to the idea of the rhetorical situation extends much further than either Mackin or Bitzer acknowledge.

The very idea of thinking that Dewey crafts in *Reconstruction in Philosophy* and *The Quest for Certainty* is infused with situational or eventful aspects. Fundamentally he understands "thinking as a way of responding to difficulty" (*RP*, 140). This suggests that the very act of thinking is already a rhetorical activity: "Thinking which is a method of reconstructing experience treats observation of facts . . . as the indispensable step of defining the problem, of locating the trouble, of forcing home a definite, instead of a merely vague emotional, sense of what the difficulty is and where it lies. . . . The purpose is so to clarify the disturbed and confused situation that reasonable ways of dealing with it may be suggested" (141). In a chapter called "Rhetorical Thinking" in *Introduction to Rhetorical Theory,* Gerard Hauser links communication and rhetoric as "a discursive method for thinking" to Dewey's preoccupation with "the problems of society" (Hauser 2002, 16). Because rhetoric "provides reasons to believe, feel, and act in a particular way" in the light of a specific situation or event, "rhetorical discourse is a mode of thinking" (17). When Dewey describes the method of defining a problem, selecting and identifying a perspective on a problem, and suggesting possible solutions, he attributes a rhetorical dimension to thinking as a practical activity.

The claim that thinking is a kind of activity that responds to exigencies is grounded on the primacy that Dewey assigns to contingency and uncertainty—"the distinctive characteristic of practical activity, one which is so inherent that it cannot be eliminated, is the uncertainty which attends it." Practical activity, then, must deal "with individualized and unique situations which are never exactly duplicable and about which, accordingly, no complete assurance is possible" (*QC,* 6).[22] Every situation, replete with uncertainty, calls for practical action, the results of which are also uncertain. In fact, "judging, planning, choice, no matter how thoroughly conducted, and action no matter how prudently executed, never are the sole determinants of any outcome" (7).

Given such circumstances, philosophy, as a practical activity, must offer intelligent or prudent methods for deciding on the best course of action. This is another way of saying that the philosopher must cultivate *phronesis*—the ability to make wise decisions under difficult circumstances. Isocrates uses this concept, as well, to determine the nature of philosophy: "For since it is not in the nature of man to attain a science by the possession of which we can know positively what we should do or what we should say, in the next resort I hold that man to be wise who is able by his power of conjecture to arrive generally at the best course, and I hold that man to be a philosopher who occupies himself with the studies from which he will most quickly gain that kind of insight" (*Antidosis* 272). A wise, intelligent rhetorician or philosopher must be able to judge the best way to define a particular problem and thus the best way to solve that problem given uncertain circumstances. This is the primary function of philosophy for both Isocrates and Dewey.

If pragmatism can be said to have a central tenet, it is that the value of an action is judged by the consequences that result from that action. Dewey locates this tenet in the context of the rhetorical situation and *phronesis:* "If ideas, meanings, conceptions, notions, theories, systems are instrumental to an active reorganization of the given environment, to a removal of some specific trouble and perplexity, then the test of their validity and value lies in accomplishing this work. If they succeed in their office, they are reliable, sound, valid, good, true. If they fail to clear up confusion, uncertainty and evil when they are acted upon, then they are false . . . the satisfaction in question means a satisfaction of the needs and conditions of the problem out of which the idea, the purpose and method of action arises. It includes public and objective conditions" (*RP,* 156–57).[23] When Dewey asserts that practical activity must be made more intelligent, he implies that cultivating *phronesis* is the best means by which philosophers can act within a given rhetorical situation. The broader implication of this position is that what works to solve a problem is satisfying, effective, and reliable. By extension, what works acquires the character of that which is true, valid, or good.

Isocrates relies on *doxa* (or the common beliefs of an audience) and the reworking of past traditions to cultivate *phronesis*—a rhetor must rely on commonly held beliefs or past fact in new ways to judge the best course of action in the face of a unique and uncertain rhetorical situation. Dewey articulates a different but parallel view. In an attempt to escape the criticism that he is interested in "activity for its own sake," Dewey argues that the goal of philosophy is to secure action "directed by knowledge" and thus develop a "method and means, not an end." The aim of philosophy is "the securer, freer and more widely shared embodiment of values in experience by means of that active control of objects which knowledge alone makes possible." To cultivate *phronesis,* therefore, the philosopher must be concerned with the "*interaction* of our judgments about ends to be sought with knowledge of the means for achieving them" (*QC,* 37). The issue that faces the practical philosopher "is what do we need to *know,* how shall we obtain that knowledge and how shall we apply it?" For these reasons, empirical science is a key concern for the philosopher.

In the introduction to *The Problems of Men,* Dewey laments the inability of philosophers to agree on how their discipline is "related to those concerns and issues which today stand out as the problems of men" (1946, 4). As "deeply human" practical problems "have increased their range and their intensity" philosophy has "relegated them to a place that is subordinate" to abstract and technical problems. As these practical problems grow in number and intensity so too do "the applications of science in life by inventions and technological arts." Philosophy, however, remains mistakenly concerned with the "foundations" or "conditions" of scientific knowledge and not with the "actual and potential" consequences of scientific knowledge (7).

Pragmatism opposes this trend by affirming that the concern of "philosophy is wholly with *that part of the historic tradition called search for wisdom*—namely, search for the ends and values that give direction to our collective human activities." In addition, pragmatism suggests that the use of the methods of science "provides the means for conducting this search" (Dewey 1946, 11, italics mine). The *historic tradition* toward which Dewey gestures is, in fact, the rhetorical tradition. Although he remains seemingly unaware of that tradition, Dewey, by virtue of his intellectual commitments and his own discomfort with the tradition of philosophy, reworks key features of rhetorical theory such as *phronesis.* His intention is to bring science to bear on what we now call the "rhetorical situation" in order to better cultivate *phronesis.*

At the heart of Dewey's understanding of the relationship between science and philosophy lies "an alliance of ethics and science" (Westbrook 1991, 140). The emphasis that Dewey placed on the ethical implications of scientific work was a result of his attack on the epistemological assumptions fundamental to philosophy's quest for certainty. The major implication of this attack on epistemological certainty was a transformation in the roles that the philosopher and the scientist should play. Philosophy, if it is not concerned with a quest for certainty, ought to direct its attention to inventing intelligent methods to solve the problems of men. On a parallel view, scientists should not be considered the possessors of a body of knowledge but the practitioners of a method. By emphasizing the methodological aspect of science, Dewey illustrates the importance of practical activity in the pursuit of knowledge and repudiates the notion that scientists simply observe nature and add to the store of knowledge available to a culture. From Dewey's perspective, both scientists and philosophers are implicated in the problems of the moment and can offer intelligent direction for solving those problems.

According to Dewey, recent advances in science, at the time Heisenberg's Uncertainty Principle and Einstein's Theory of Relativity, demonstrate the impossibility of the quest for certainty and the role that practical activity plays in scientific understanding.[24] These advances indicated that knowledge no longer referred to the changeless attributes of natural substances. Instead, the focus of scientific inquiry was on "the deliberate institution of a definite and specified course of change" in an object. More specifically, "*the* method of physical inquiry is to introduce some change in order to see what other change ensues; the correlation between these changes, when measured by a series of operations, constitutes the definite and desired objects of knowledge" (*QC*, 84). The change in the method of scientific work implied a "complete reversal in the traditional relationship between knowledge and action." To cling to traditional assumptions about the mind and the organs of knowing is to ignore the fact that "science advances by adopting instruments and doings of directed practice, and the knowledge thus gained becomes a means of the development of arts which bring nature still further into actual and potential service of human purposes and valuations" (85). Science is a method of acting with and on objects, according to Dewey.

The major implication of Dewey's argument is that "knowing is itself a mode of practical action and is *the* way of interaction by which other natural interactions become subject to direction." In other words, "the experimental method" is a "way of operating upon and with the things of ordinary experience" so that we can "control" those "things" and "direct their changes as we desire" (*QC*, 106–7). In technical terms this means that data act as a substitute for objects because data are subject to use by and for people. In addition, data signify "subject-matter for further investigation" and ultimately the source of further problems for scientists to solve. In short, modern experimental science becomes "an art of control" (99–100).

If we follow Dewey's understanding of science as a method of practical action whose goal is to control our experience and direct changes in the natural world, then two critical aspects of rhetorical theory are at the center of the pragmatic understanding of science: invention and arrangement. Invention is the first of five canons of rhetoric developed in antiquity. It is that part of rhetoric concerned with discovering what might be communicated about a subject to persuade an audience. Hauser offers a clear definition of "invention" that parallels Dewey's discussion of science: "we may define invention as the method of finding 'sayables' (symbols) with the potential to transform some matter or question of an indeterminate nature into one that is determinate in the mind of the audience"; this implies that rhetorical inventions "provide frameworks that aid us in interpreting novel, conflicting, or ambiguous" events (Hauser 2002, 109). In this sense, science is a matter of inventing methods or symbolic acts that transform the subject matter of experience in order to cope with a particular exigence. The very idea of "data" is just this kind of symbolic invention because the "data" scientists invent provide a framework to think about particular problems, to create further uncertainty, and to use in acting upon the objects of science in new ways. No longer is science a matter of observing the natural properties of objects. It is now a question of inventing the best ways to act upon such objects so as to produce an effect that works to demonstrate control over the object acted upon and to solve the scientific problem at hand.

In antiquity invention referred to the process of finding arguments that had persuasive appeal given a particular audience, occasion, and context. For example, Aristotle explicitly identified "topics" in his *Rhetoric* to suggest methods for rhetorical invention. The goal of the "topics" was to help show all of the available means of persuasion. For an argument to have persuasive appeal the audience must agree to the truthfulness of the argument and its ability to solve the problem at hand; topics could aid in the invention of such arguments. When Dewey claims that science does not discover some antecedent reality and that scientists are not passive observers, he demonstrates the active role of invention in scientific practice. For example, the invention of a language, including words such as "electron," "quark," or "data," is a sign of the rhetoricity of science. In a way science acts in a similar fashion to Aristotle's topics, as a means of finding persuasive claims or effective results given a specific problem.

The results of the process of invention must then be organized or arranged. It is the need for social action that prompts the organization and arrangement of the knowledge acquired through invention—"the need for direction of action in large social fields is the source of a genuine demand for unification of scientific conclusions." According to Dewey, scientific conclusions are "organized when their bearing on life is disclosed" (*QC*, 312). Both invention and arrangement are useful because they act in response to rhetorical situations. In rhetorical discourse arrangement refers to the "planned ordering of a message to achieve the greatest persuasive effect" (Herrick 1998, 9). Arrangement points to the aesthetic and logical dimension of rhetoric and the necessity of shaping discourse into a form for maximum effect. In *Experience and Nature,* Dewey tries to demonstrate the artistic aspect of the scientific method: "Only action, interaction, can change or remake objects. The analogy of the skilled artist still holds. His intelligence is a factor in forming new objects which mark a fulfillment. But this is because intelligence is incarnate in overt action, using things as means to affect other things" (*EN,* 158). Scientific discovery and invention create a "transformation of both meanings and the existences of nature," and for this transformation to work it must be given an intelligent form by the scientist. Therefore, the results of experimentation are arranged in such a way that they can transform the object and our understanding of the natural world. Both kinds of arrangement require artistic skill just as arranging a speech to disclose a perspective on a specific situation requires artistic skill.

Viewed from the pragmatist perspective, scientific activity is a kind of rhetorical activity. By acting on, inventing, and arranging the objects of science, one engages in the constitutive task of developing and disclosing a particular perspective on the natural world. Such a view grounds Dewey's claim that the activity of science is best directed toward the "problems of men." This view also makes scientific activity a more useful resource for rhetoric instead of a special and superior method of producing abstract knowledge. If science is involved with the project of invention and arrangement while practically influencing natural phenomena, then rhetorical theory can help disclose the larger meaning of scientific activity.

When investigating physical phenomena, the scientific method can operate with great precision, carefulness, and thoroughness and thus produces knowledge that more accurately yields expected results. For this reason social problems should seek direction from the scientific method and from knowledge produced with the scientific method. However, "the application of physical knowledge has taken place in a technical way for the sake of limited consequences" (*QC*, 199). Dewey's goal is to bring science to bear on problems in the social world so that "the operations in which physical science is used" can transform "distinctively human values in behalf of a human interest." The greatest benefit of such a transformation is that "knowledge of the things of ordinary perception, use and enjoyment" can be understood in a "genuine and fuller and deeper" way compared to the way in which these things are understood by "the scientist in his laboratory." In other words, scientific knowledge is most beneficial when used in response to everyday, social, or rhetorical situations.[25] Viewed from the rhetorical tradition, this argument could be extended to claim that science, itself, can be used as a persuasive and powerful rhetoric capable of solving social problems.[26] We can better understand this claim in the light of Dewey's theory of communication.

In order to use scientific knowledge for social problems and to establish a reciprocal relationship between science and the social world, Dewey's pragmatism relies on a particular vision of communication. Invention and arrangement must be supplemented with a method of delivery. In *The Public and Its Problems,* Dewey points to the connections between knowledge and communication. However, Dewey's thoughts about communication are often couched in vague and overly general statements, and for that reason it is difficult to understand how and why he uses the term. At one point he claims that "knowledge is communication" and that "record and communication are indispensable to knowledge" (*PP,* 176). Dewey's perspective can be understood by seeing his notion of communication as similar to the practice of rhetoric. In essence Dewey's vision of communication has a fundamentally rhetorical dimension that is critical to pragmatism. Rhetorical communication, according to Hauser, "attempts to coordinate social action" and thus "always contains a pragmatic intent." In addition, the goal of rhetorical communication "is to influence human choices on specific matters that require attention"; hence it is "designed to achieve desired consequences" (Hauser 2002, 3). The vision of communication that Dewey articulated most clearly in the 1920s shares important features with Hauser's understanding of rhetoric.

The most important feature of Dewey's position is that communication is a fundamentally social activity. *Democracy and Education* begins by stating the connections between communication and social communities: "Men live in a community by virtue of the things which they have in common; and communication is the way in which they come to possess things in common" (1916, 4). Furthermore, "communication is a process of sharing experience till it becomes common possession. It modifies the disposition of both the parties that partake in it" (9). In *Art as Experience* this position is elaborated even further: "Communication is the process of creating participation, of making common what had been isolated and singular" (1934, 244). The coordination of social action, the sharing of experiences, and the importance of participation, therefore, are essential aspects of communication for Dewey. His understanding of knowledge also possesses a social dimension: "knowledge is a function of association and communication; it depends upon tradition, upon tools and methods socially transmitted, developed and sanctioned" (*PP*, 158). Both communication and knowledge, then, serve to bring people into association. When people are brought into association, the meaning of the world they share is produced and regulated through both knowledge as a practical activity and communication as a practical activity.[27]

More important, both knowledge and communication are ways of reorganizing the world. Just as the scientist, in pursuit of knowledge, acts on objects in the world, "when communication occurs, all natural events are subject to reconsideration and revision" (*EN*, 166). This implies that communication, as a practical activity, employs invention and arrangement toward the same ends that science does. Not only are all natural events subject to reconsideration, but they are also capable of "immediate enhancement": "Communication is an exchange which procures something wanted; it involves a claim, appeal, order, direction or request, which realizes want at less cost than personal labor exacts, since it procures the cooperative assistance of others. Communication is also immediate enhancement of life, enjoyed for its own sake" (*EN*, 183).

In classical Greece a major interest of the sophists was the use of rhetoric to induce the cooperation of others or to create pleasure or enjoyment in the audience. For example, speeches such as *The Choice of Heracles* by Prodicus were delivered at festivals and served to entertain. Epideictic rhetoric, in general, sought to please audiences and was practiced as a vital part of Athenian culture.

Whether communication is used to reinterpret or redirect natural events, to induce cooperation, or to create pleasure, in each case Dewey is describing communication as rhetoric. In addition, the use of communication to build communities is the primary task of Isocrates' rhetoric. Takis Poulakos describes Isocrates' "conception of rhetoric as a citizenly instrument meant to promote actions for the betterment of the *polis*" (1997, 24). By emphasizing social order, community, and common welfare, Isocrates articulates rhetoric's potential to bring people together. In Dewey we find this rhetoric in a new variation.

For social cooperation to happen, persuasion must play a key role, and Dewey acknowledges this. In fact, *The Public and Its Problems* ends with a call for better methods of persuasion: "The essential need . . . is the improvement of the methods and conditions of debate, discussion, and persuasion. That is *the* problem of the public. We have asserted that this improvement depends essentially upon freeing and perfecting the processes of inquiry and the dissemination of their conclusions" (*PP*, 208). Methods of persuasion allow for the participation of the public in the process of democratic decision making, also known as deliberation. Dewey wants such methods of persuasion to be based on the conclusions of the scientific method, and he believes that improving methods of persuasion and deliberation will help to improve the life of the community.

In *Human Nature and Conduct*, Dewey attends to the importance of deliberation in human affairs: "A world that is at points and times indeterminate enough to call out deliberation and to give play to choice to shape its future is a world in which will is free, not because it is inherently vacillating and unstable, but because deliberation and choice are determining and stabilizing factors" (1922, 310). By pointing to the need for methods of persuasion and deliberation, Dewey essentially identifies the importance of rhetoric for American democracy. A great deal of *Human Nature and Conduct* is devoted to explaining the role of deliberation in individual decision making. When Dewey makes claims about improving the methods of debate, discussion, and persuasion, he shows how difficult and important deliberation is on a public scale. In both private and public matters, rhetoric provides the means to use the results of scientific inquiry. Improving the practice of rhetoric, therefore, can help the individual make better decisions, and more important, it can help improve the life of the community. In his discussions of communication and its relationship to the public, Dewey comes close to articulating the necessity of rhetoric without making that position explicit.

Language as a form of symbolic action further links rhetoric to Dewey's notions of communication and persuasion. Meanings are made, enhanced, or repaired in a community by using "channels formed by instrumentalities of which, in the end, language, the vehicle of thought as well as of communication is the most important" (*PP*, 210). In *How We Think*, Dewey elaborates on the use of language for persuasion and shows how the persuasive function of language is an integral part of education: "The primary motive for language is to influence (through the expression of desire, emotion, and thought) the activity of others; its secondary use is to enter into more intimate social relations with them" (1911, 179). This makes the problem of education into a problem of directing "*pupils' oral and written speech, used primarily for practical and social ends, so that gradually it shall become a conscious tool of conveying knowledge and assisting thought.*" The project of "modifying speech habits so as to render them accurate and flexible intellectual instruments" is a precise description of an education in rhetoric. Given Dewey's perspective on the importance of understanding philosophy as a practical activity, the argument that rhetoric is an essential aspect of education is a necessary consequence. Although Dewey did not identify this form of education as a matter of rhetoric, as interpreted in the light of the rhetorical tradition the consequences of his argument are clear.

The persuasive function of language demonstrates that language is a method of action, not a reflection of the natural world: "Language is always a form of action and in its instrumental use is always a means of concerted action for an end, while at the same time it finds in itself all the goods of its possible consequences. For there is no mode of action as fulfilling and as rewarding as is concerted consensus of action. . . . Language is specifically a mode of interaction of at least two beings, a speaker and a hearer; it presupposes an organized group to which these creatures belong, and from whom they have acquired their habits of speech. It is therefore a relationship, not a particularity" (*EN*, 185). Dewey uses this description of language to show that identifying words or meanings as objective refers only to the regulation of linguistic interaction and not to the naming of some antecedent reality. The obvious implication of such a position is that objective meanings become tacit laws for communication only through prolonged and habitual interaction between speakers and hearers. Words can also be used in new, creative ways, to bring speaker and hearer into meaningful relationships. When we understand language as a kind of action, or as an interaction between two people, it becomes clear that the practice of rhetoric can and does regulate meanings and relationships. This is precisely why language and communication are critical concerns for politics, community, and democracy.

If there is a defining characteristic of Dewey's perspective on politics, it is that "every serious political dispute turns upon the question whether a given political act is socially beneficial or harmful" (*PP*, 15). This is a reiteration of the basic Isocratean position on politics, philosophy, and discourse—without Isocrates' additional focus on honor. Any political decision, act, or struggle, then, involves consideration of what is best for the community and how to determine what is best for the community. The questions that surround this struggle are the driving force behind *The Public and Its Problems*. For democracy to be a success, according to Dewey, ordinary men and women must put their intelligence in the service of directing the affairs of the state while realizing all the varied ways in which citizens of a democracy are bound to one another in a community.

Ultimately, Dewey's vision included the notion of a "great community," a community whose success would rely on "the perfecting of the means and ways of communication of meanings so that genuinely shared interest in the consequences of interdependent activities may inform desire and effort and thereby direct action" (*PP,* 174). Accordingly, the first task of reformers and philosophers was to find methods of communication that would allow individuals in a democracy to participate in decision making and realize the interconnectedness of the community to which they belong.[28] Like Isocrates, and unlike practitioners and theorists of an agonistic or argumentative rhetoric, Dewey suggests a theory of rhetoric as communion, oriented toward the common good. His own practices as a scholar try to employ a rhetoric of communion to bridge the distance between philosophy and the social world.

Politics, democracy, and community are all tied intimately together in Dewey's pragmatism. They are tied together by the belief that communication as rhetoric is the primary means by which the connections between politics, democracy, and community can be realized and the promise of each fulfilled: "The highest and most difficult kind of inquiry and a subtle, delicate, vivid, and responsive art of communication must take possession of the physical machinery of transmission and circulation and breathe life into it. . . . Democracy will come into its own, for democracy is a name for a life of free and enriching communion. . . . It [democracy] will have its consummation when free social inquiry is indissolubly wedded to the art of full and moving communication" (*PP,* 184). In other words, when the results of the scientific method meet the art of rhetoric, democracy and the "great community" become possible.

As science marches on to produce more knowledge, and as the mechanisms of mass communication (the newspaper, radio, and television, for example) take root in American democracy, the need for the art of rhetoric becomes more important. In fact, the "great community" must provide the structures and the means for the practice of rhetoric, for the persuasive use of language, and for methods of communication that bind people together. The newspapers and the radio may appear to provide new mechanisms for communication, but their use must meet the highest standards of the best rhetoric. "Presentation is fundamentally important, and presentation is a question of art," according to Dewey (*PP,* 183). To extend this statement, presentation as an art of rhetoric is fundamentally important to a community, a democracy, and to politics in general. This is a major implication of Dewey's pragmatism, latent in his work but undeveloped. To address rhetorical situations, to use science for the betterment of the social world, and for philosophy to become practical, communication as rhetoric must be a significant feature of American democracy. Dewey has outlined both the practical and the intellectual conditions for the practice of rhetoric in American democracy.

Dewey's Reconstruction of Philosophy and the Possibility of an American Rhetoric

In *Reconstruction in Philosophy* and *The Quest for Certainty,* Dewey tries to transform philosophy from intellectual and technical speculation about things-in-themselves to an active and practical method of addressing social problems. The promise of pragmatism lies in the reemergence of rhetoric for such a project, as both an object of intellectual inquiry and a useful, artful tool for American democracy. Pragmatism claims that philosophy must become more concerned with the art of *phronesis,* the ability to judge the best uses of knowledge, to predict the consequences of social action, and to act in the best interests of the community. It also emphasizes the role of communication as a method for sharing experience, a means of creating associations between people and influencing the course of social action.

The idea that communication as rhetoric involves the delivery and composition of a message as well as the ability to coordinate social action; to bind people to one another; to direct, redirect, or enhance experience; and to identify and articulate the best course of action for a community finds inspiration in Dewey's philosophy of pragmatism. To accomplish such tasks, however, the practice of the art of rhetoric must be crafted to fit the contemporary rhetorical situation—a lesson that Dewey tried to teach philosophy. Given Dewey's intellectual position, both philosophers and rhetoricians should be concerned with the ends toward which Dewey points and the benefits he promises. The development of pragmatism does not promise an increase in the store of knowledge or greater certitude about the natural world. Instead, it promises to develop the human capacity for making intelligent decisions in difficult circumstances, the enhancement of individual experience, advancement of the public good, and participation in democratic decision making.

Because of his interest in these issues, Dewey's pragmatism creates the conditions for the invention of contemporary American rhetorics. However, he did not provide specific suggestions, methods, or structures for the actual practice of rhetoric in American culture, nor did he draw explicitly on the tradition of rhetoric or its concepts.[29] I argue that he identified the need for rhetoric but did not translate that need into suggestions for specific rhetorical practices. This is due in part to the circumstances of Dewey's own historical moment. Classical Athens had the benefit of a clear and coherent sociopolitical structure for the practice of rhetoric, which ultimately led to a rich set of competing theoretical perspectives able to provide students with a diverse set of tools for practical application.

Given the situation in Athens, an education in public speaking would theoretically provide one with the opportunity to practice rhetoric competently.

Dewey's context provided a radically different set of challenges: "The physical and external means of collecting information in regard to what is happening in the world have far outrun the intellectual phase of inquiry and organization of its results. Telegraph, telephone, and now the radio, cheap and quick mail, the printing press, capable of swift reduplication of material at low cost—all have attained a remarkable development. But when we ask what sort of material is recorded and how it is organized, when we ask about the intellectual form in which the material is presented, the tale to be told is very different" (*PP,* 179). The massive increases in the quantity of knowledge and the technological ability to disseminate information have left rhetoric in difficult circumstances. The goal of the philosophy of pragmatism is to point to the need for developing the art of rhetoric to complement the advances in other areas of intellectual activity. Dewey provides the theoretical grounds for a reconstruction of rhetoric in greater variety than oratory. However, he did not complete the whole project himself. That task was left for other pragmatists, such as Jane Addams.

Three

Jane Addams and the Practice of Deliberation

Hull-House as a Site for Rhetorical Action and Social Democracy

In July 1881 Jane Addams delivered the valedictory address to the graduating class at Rockford Seminary. Addams spoke of Cassandra, the Trojan prophetess who, conscious of an important truth, tried in vain to convince the Trojans that the Greeks would destroy Troy. According to Addams, Cassandra failed to convince the Trojans because she lacked "*auetoritas* [*sic*], the right of the speaker to make themselves [*sic*] heard" (*JAR* 1881, 11).[1] By speaking of Cassandra on this occasion, Addams implied that American women, in a similar fashion, lacked a voice in the political affairs of the state. Also, by identifying *auctoritas* as the reason for Cassandra's inability to influence events in Troy, Addams implied that rhetorical authority was an important issue for effective participation in politics. Rhetorical authority grants the speaker not just the power to speak but also the added potential to persuade or to convince.[2] Addams's concern was that too many women possessed important truths but lacked the authority to be heard. Her life became a struggle to invent methods by which women and immigrants could obtain rhetorical authority within the machinery of American politics.

Eight years later Addams founded Hull-House, her first organized attempt to participate in public life in Chicago. From Hull-House she engaged in a wide array of activities as a sociologist, a progressive reformer, a social democrat, a political activist, and a humanitarian. These activities were carried out in search of a "voice" in political and social affairs—a "voice" of her own but, more important, a "voice" for women in general and immigrants.[3] By virtue of her desire to avoid Cassandra's fate and obtain rhetorical authority, Addams's primary concern at Hull-House was to find mechanisms for participation in public affairs, solving pressing problems, and making the community better—all of which link her to both the pragmatist and the rhetorical traditions.

By pursuing such goals through life at Hull-House, Addams engaged in the practice of deliberative rhetoric. By identifying the necessity of participation in political affairs, as early as her valedictory address, she shared the classical concern with having a voice in democratic decision making, a concern at the center of rhetorical theory in Athens. Students of the sophists and Isocrates sought training in the art of public speaking so that they could acquire rhetorical authority for guiding decision and judgment in the Ekklesia. Hull-House did not attempt to offer its neighbors instruction in the art of public speaking; even so, its central goal parallels the goal of a rhetorical education in classical Athens. Finding the mechanisms to participate in decision making and practical ways to guide decision and judgment were the impetus behind both Hull-House and education in classical rhetoric.

What makes Addams remarkable as a pragmatist and a rhetorician is her ability to develop a distinct perspective on the complexity of deliberation in a modern, large-scale democracy and her ability to practice pragmatism successfully given her own circumstances.[4] In Chicago around the turn of the twentieth century, a cacophony of languages and cultures coexisted and expanded in diversity and size, forming a new kind of urban experience in America. Participation in politics was difficult, as were more fundamental issues of understanding and communicating within such a complex environment. As a woman, Addams was not allowed to participate directly in political affairs (either through holding office or voting). To supplement traditional connections between rhetoric and politics, embodied in notions of deliberation as public address, Addams emphasized methods of bridging distances, identifying similarities, and demonstrating unity—all through the creation of Hull-House as an institution.

Instead of an agonistic rhetoric, which employs argument and debate with the intention of deciding on a specific course of action, Addams practiced a cooperative rhetoric that sought to bring individuals together. Her intention was to establish a "social democracy" through which many people could participate in the articulation of a collective voice. Insofar as the power of a collective voice is the result of the social unity that brings such a voice into being, Addams believed that it was necessary to think about participation in politics as an issue of communality, social ethics, and institutional cooperation. For those reasons, her rhetoric departs from traditional rhetorics that focus on debate as the essence of politics, but her position is uniquely pragmatist in that it suggests a community-centered rhetoric tested by its consequences. Addams's pragmatism is informed by her search for a deliberative rhetoric that would grant her "voice" authority. In pursuing such goals, her pragmatism prescribes a unique method of deliberation that extends the classical Athenian conception of citizen-participation in politics. A concern with social democracy, sociology, and social ethics contributes to a specific meaning of citizenship that grounds a new kind of rhetorical consciousness. It is precisely this new rhetorical consciousness that Addams breathed life into through all of her endeavors.

Addams's role as a pragmatist and as a deliberative rhetorician can be explored, first, by locating her work within the tradition begun by James and Dewey and within the tradition of rhetorical deliberation. She realized the intellectual commitments of James and Dewey and extended basic notions of rhetoric as deliberation. Her pragmatism and rhetoric operated then at Hull-House to craft a new kind of rhetorical action suitable for a "social democracy." Sociology as a social ethics must be part of both her rhetoric and her pragmatism, and both contribute to the health of a large-scale "social democracy." In important ways rhetoric and pragmatism intersect around notions of politics and democracy, and Addams helped bring that intersection into sharp relief.

Addams as Pragmatist and Deliberative Rhetorician

In Addams's own words, "every student of [her] time had become more or less a disciple of pragmatism and its great teachers in the United States" (*JAR* 1922, 322). This does not mean that Addams's lifework is a direct result of the influence of James and Dewey. Drawing direct lines of influence in this case is not easy. For example, Christopher Lasch claims that "it is difficult to say whether Dewey influenced Jane Addams or Jane Addams influenced Dewey. They influenced each other and generously acknowledged their mutual obligation" (*STJ*, 176). Dewey, in fact, lectured frequently at Hull-House and remained committed to many of Addams's social reform projects. In letters to his wife Alice, Dewey recounted several exchanges with Addams that left a permanent mark on his thinking.[5] Thus, the issue of shared intellectual commitments is more significant than the issue of influence. The responses to the problems of the day and the basic orientation to solving those problems connect Addams to the pragmatist tradition.

Gioia Diliberto's biography of Addams is entitled *A Useful Woman*, signifying that pragmatism is at the heart of Addams's endeavors. As someone who "worked tirelessly to abolish child labor, sweatshops, tenements, unsafe factories, filthy streets, and corrupt politicians," Addams embodied Dewey's intellectual commitment to the problems of the moment; and as a "gifted speaker and writer," she addressed those problems with an intelligence grounded in experience and knowledge (Diliberto 1999, 17). The belief that the consequences of an idea test an idea's validity found concrete expression in Addams's manner of addressing important political issues. Ever in search of methods for making the community better, she epitomized the spirit of pragmatic meliorism. The "useful" work that Diliberto recounts in her biography illustrates the concrete experiences within which Addams used knowledge, tested ideas, and ultimately found effective methods for making the community better.[6] In short, her ideas had consequences.

Despite her many achievements, however, Addams is often considered an ancillary figure in the history of pragmatism. In *The Metaphysical Club,* Louis Menand briefly recounts her part in the Pullman Strike as well as her influence on Dewey (2001, 306–12). In *The American Evasion of Philosophy,* Cornel West makes only a brief reference to her work at Hull-House and her relationship to Dewey (1989, 83–84). In *The Promise of Pragmatism,* John Patrick Diggins does not mention Addams at all.[7] In *Meaning and Action,* H. S. Thayer makes just one brief mention of Addams's work at Hull-House (1981, 75).[8] When Addams is mentioned as part of the pragmatist tradition, the common assumption is that her contributions were those of a reformer, not those of an exponent of the basic pragmatist intellectual orientation to the world. Because of her effective role in politics and social activism, her intellectual contributions are often overlooked, or at least considered far less significant than those of philosophers such as James, Dewey, C. S. Peirce, or Sidney Hook. Addams's pragmatism, however, is grounded on her success as a social reformer and as an engaged political activist. Accordingly, her own reflections on her achievements provide important intellectual insights into pragmatism as an orientation to the world.

Mary Jo Deegan's *Jane Addams and the Men of the Chicago School, 1892–1918* and Charlene Haddock Seigfried's *Pragmatism and Feminism* are two accounts that do claim for Addams an important and substantial place in the pragmatist tradition. Deegan argues for understanding Addams as a founding mother of the Chicago School of sociology. By piecing together a network of mutual influences, she also claims that Addams was one of the first-generation originators of philosophical pragmatism. Deegan makes the bold assertion that it is out of the "collegial contacts and intellectual exchanges" of Dewey and George Herbert Mead with Addams and other residents of Hull-House that "Chicago pragmatism was born"; Addams, Dewey, and Mead all "wanted to combine scientific and objective observation with ethical and moral values to generate a just and liberated society" (Deegan 1988, 5–6).

Seigfried extends Deegan's argument by claiming that "many aspects of Addams's thought develop and expand on pragmatist themes in original ways. Her perspectivism and her pluralism were more concretely grounded. She was more explicit than the male pragmatists about the value of the insights of women and of disadvantaged ethnic groups" (Seigfried 1996, 76). Addams also built on the "themes of experiment, experience, and democracy," which were important to "pragmatist theory," in order to "transform" life in Chicago (78). Deegan and Seigfried begin to correct the oversight made by other historians of pragmatism.

In an extension of Deegan and Seigfried's work, Addams's place in the pragmatist tradition can be developed by treating her work as a prescription for an effective deliberative rhetoric. According to Seigfried, Addams's focus on "social democracy, as extended from a theory of political governance to a practice of organized life, is . . . conceived as a means for guaranteeing the dignity and freedom of persons by its structural incorporation of the widest possible inclusiveness and participation in determining the conditions for our existence" (1996, 79). Such a project suggests that she can be understood as a rhetorician, and that the practice of rhetoric is an important part of her project. Treating her engagement in political and social affairs as a way of practicing rhetoric shows how pragmatism can work successfully in specific cases *and* how pragmatism can contribute key ideas to the rhetorical tradition.

In classical rhetoric, deliberation is a standard topos that consists of the careful consideration of possibilities or alternatives with the intention of deciding on a specific course of action. The uncertainty of the future persistently opens a variety of possibilities for individuals, communities, or nations, and the process of deliberation leads to decisions meant to affect the future. A deliberative rhetoric advises people or communities to decide or act in a certain manner. The rhetorician, then, offers reasoned arguments, emotional appeals, and evidence to persuade people or communities to make a specific decision or follow a specific course of action. Because deliberation must involve a choice within a context replete with uncertainty, competing perspectives are inevitable, and rhetors are charged with the responsibility of guiding their audience to what appears to be the best alternative.

Democratic politics, the practice of government and the management of public affairs, requires deliberative rhetoric. Political decisions attempt to influence, control, or motivate a public or community and often involve policies that prescribe specific courses of action. When the political process implicates more than one person in decision making, deliberative rhetoric becomes the primary practice through which decisions are reached. Through much of the fifth and fourth centuries B.C.E. Athens was ruled by a democratic political system that implicated all of the "citizens" of Athens in the political process of making decisions.[9] Although specific sociocultural factors allowed some "citizens" greater opportunity to control political affairs, deliberative rhetoric was nonetheless a key component of Athenian democracy.[10] In fact, the birth of rhetoric is tied closely to the function of democracy in Athens.

According to Josiah Ober's *Mass and Elite in Democratic Athens,* oratory, rhetoric, and deliberative speeches played a central part in defining Athenian politics and regulating relations between Athenians. Rhetorical ability and education helped distinguish orators as leaders and granted some citizens more political power than others. Although Ober identifies many other factors for effective participation in democratic decision making, he argues that "Athenians expected an individual politician to state his personal opinion on any given subject in open debate with individuals offering differing opinions" (1989, 123). That form of open debate was carried out in the Assembly. An issue was brought before an audience of citizens (whoever wanted to attend or participate), and after deliberation a decision would be made. Crowds at the Assembly averaged around six thousand citizens (132), and so deliberation could not proceed by means of discussion. To include all citizens equally, "the Athenians relied on mass communication by means of direct, spoken language" (Yunis 1996, 1).

The combination of the Assembly as the central decision-making institution, the number of citizens participating in the political process, and the need to arrive at a decision binding on the community and rendered by the citizens functioned so as to link democracy inextricably to the practice of rhetoric. This meant that democracy and deliberative rhetoric were inseparable, and the connection between the two helped create competing rhetorical theories that vied for adherents and political power. Such competing perspectives demonstrated that in the Athenian experience the practice of rhetoric was considered the most useful means by which a citizen could participate in, and affect the political affairs of, the state.

Participation in political affairs was a distinctly different matter in Jane Addams's experience of American democracy. However, the issues of participation and deliberation were just as important for Addams as for the Athenians. In *The Good Citizen,* Michael Schudson traces the history of citizen-participation in American politics by attending to the practice and the meaning of voting. According to Schudson's account, Addams lived through a key moment in the transformation of political participation. Between 1865 and 1920 voting changed "from a social to a civic act" (Schudson 1998, 147). At one end of this transformation, party politics made "spectacular political campaigning . . . carried on largely out of doors, in the streets, with elaborate rituals," a central act of public participation with parades and other forms of entertainment. The "social act" that Schudson points to as a key part of political participation brought citizens to vote through political parties that made civic life fun, emotional, enthusiastic, and at times spontaneous. However, reformers complained that such "social acts" did not make "the ordinary citizen an effective participant in the political process" (157). Although many citizens were voting and committing themselves to political parties, they played no major role in decision making and did not practice deliberative rhetoric in any way—voting only symbolized participation.

The civil service reform movement, the Mugwumps, and the Progressives helped transform political participation from a "social act" to a "civic act" by "rationalizing electoral behavior" (Schudson 1998, 147). As "spectacular campaigns" waned in popularity, "new educational campaigns" became a central force in voting. According to Schudson, "Progressive era politics instructed people in a citizenship of intelligence rather than passionate intensity. Political participation became less a relationship to party than a relationship to the state, less a connection to community than to principles and issues. The voter who kept up with the news read less to bask in the glow of his party's achievements than to pursue reports on the various issues, politicians, and parties of the day. . . . The new model of citizenship called for a voter more intelligent than loyal" (182). This new model of citizenship set the stage for debates over the "omnicompetent" citizen, crowd psychology, the role of the expert, propaganda, the influence of technology on democracy, and the future role of the political party (188–240). These issues were debated in the first half of the twentieth century to determine the best mechanisms for popular participation in politics. If citizens were to participate in political affairs and influence decision making, they must exercise an "intelligent" voice through voting—deliberative rhetoric must be grounded in knowledge. Was voting an adequate form of deliberative rhetoric, though? Did it actually signify participation in decision making?

As a member of the Progressive Party and an advocate of many social reforms, Addams played a part in the transformation in the meaning of participation, as well as other important progressive reforms.[11] Although she may have advocated a change in voting from a "social act" to a "civic act," Addams presents a distinct voice within debates surrounding notions of participation. As a woman, she did not have the right to vote, and so notions of participation based solely on the act of voting were not her only concern. Schudson admits that "women's groups as leading models of interest group organizing" were also important forms of participation (1998, 160). He also notes that "women pioneered interest groups because they were barred from direct participation in party politics." Although Addams worked for women's suffrage and campaigned for progressive reforms to make voting a "civic act," these issues were supplemented by her attention to participation in social organizations as a central part of deliberation and politics.

In essence, voting is a symbolic voice that operates as a mechanism for participation when a literal voice is not possible. In other words, direct participation by means of public address at a central decision making place such as the Athenian Assembly is unusual, if not impossible, in American democracy.[12] Voting is a definitively different form of rhetorical practice than public address (if it can be considered a kind of rhetorical practice at all). In fact, expressing a "symbolic voice" through casting a vote clearly demarcates, from other citizens, those citizens with a "literal voice" in creating persuasive messages. Addams was not content to see the project of deliberation as just a matter of voting or just a matter of public address. Politics, democracy, and the practice of deliberation required a much wider set of practices. Pragmatism points to those other practices as essential to the health of a democracy and suggests that political rhetoric is a complicated and varied art.

By attending to acts of participation in politics as both social and civic performances, Addams teaches us to think about participation outside of voting and public address. She argues that other methods of organization and participation are essential to American democracy so that everyone can have a voice in political affairs. Deliberative rhetoric in American democracy pursues the same goals as it did in Athenian democracy, but the methods for practicing deliberative rhetoric must change to include the majority of citizens in actual decision-making procedures. Addams's pragmatism is a search for a deliberative rhetoric in which all citizens can participate and which requires both a civic and a social dimension.

As Addams became a formidable voice in national and international affairs, she relied on organizations, groups, parties, and movements to help advocate specific courses of action. For example, she was a devoted member of the woman suffrage movement and the Women's International League for Peace and Freedom, and she was a key figure in organizing several labor unions. This was a sign that the American political process relied on the deliberative authority of organized movements, not the singular voice of any one citizen or the civic function of voting. At times this meant that one had to compromise one's own particular perspective because a chorus of many was far more persuasive than the voice of one.[13] This did not mean that public speaking was not a part of the deliberative process—Addams, in fact, was a prolific lecturer throughout her years at Hull-House. It did imply that deliberation in American politics relied on a vast array of organizations, unions, political parties, and social movements—all of which sought to guide the decision-making process through a variety of strategies and forms of mass communication that included but went beyond direct speech.

Comparing Athenian democracy with Addams's democratic experience is useful because it points to a general understanding of rhetoric as a mechanism for guiding decision and judgment. It also shows that American democracy lacked obvious or well-developed methods of rhetoric that could achieve those ends while allowing as many citizens as possible the opportunity to participate—Dewey pointed to this fact at the end of *The Public and Its Problems*. Voting was no substitute for the kind of rhetoric practiced in Athens, and Addams knew that. For those reasons her pragmatism seeks rhetorical strategies that use knowledge and experience to guide decision and judgment, that allows many people the opportunity to participate in politics, and that relies on communication as a means of bringing communities together. The success of Hull-House suggests that the promise of pragmatism can be fulfilled through varied ways of practicing deliberative rhetoric.

Citizenship in a "Social Democracy"—Hull-House and Rhetorical Action

In search of an effective deliberative rhetoric on which to ground her pragmatism, Addams turned to the social, cultural, and physical space of Chicago to create a "social democracy." When Addams claimed that it was time "to add a social ethic to democracy," she was identifying the social as a prerequisite for successful and effective democratic decision making (*DSE,* xii). In other words, a "social ethic" for American democracy was a necessity, a foundation, because it provided the structure or organization through which many people could participate in politics. However, the term "social democracy" lacked the institutional clarity of the Athenian Assembly. How could one "add the social function to democracy?" (*JAR* 1893, 14). What would such a process entail? Addams turned to the "settlement house" as a practical realization of the meaning of "social democracy." If the "settlement house" was to have the kind of success that Addams expected, though, she needed to demonstrate that such an institution was, in fact, necessary.

Addams's essay "The Subjective Necessity for Social Settlements" identifies the "motives which constitute the subjective pressure toward social settlements" and argues for the importance of a social dimension in democracy (*JAR* 1893, 15). According to Addams, the major function of Hull-House (and the other settlement houses) was "to make social intercourse express the growing sense of economic unity of society. . . . It [Hull-House] was opened on the theory that the dependence of classes on each other is reciprocal" (14). Challenging the notion that "political equality alone would secure all good to all men," Addams traces a litany of political abuses that separate and alienate citizens from one another and fail to demonstrate the economic unity of society. The political abuses she describes reflect the Progressive beliefs of her day and demonstrate her own political position (Schneider and Schneider 1993, 7–11). For example, she claims that African Americans were free and possessed the right to vote but remained "in a practical social ostracism" (*JAR* 1893, 15). Immigrants were given the right to vote, but Americans identified them "with epithets deriding [their] past life or present preoccupation, and [felt] no need to invite" them into their "houses" (15). In addition, the voting system was corrupt, with entire "city wards in which many of the votes [were] sold for drinks and dollars," and political "bossism," prone to scandal and corruption, ruled local politics. These abuses led Addams to claim that America was entering "the second phase of democracy" (16). The "French Philosophers" entered the first by identifying the need for political equality and for natural rights (equality, liberty, and fraternity).[14] However, the French philosophical program had clearly stalled in America, given the abuses in the American system. The second phase of democracy, then, must involve the social realization of the French philosophical goals and ideals.

Settlement houses were a viable alternative because the "social organism" had so severely and thoroughly "broken down through large districts" of many American cities (*JAR* 1893, 16). Extreme poverty and total lack of fellowship or local tradition marred cities such as Chicago. Social disintegration was coincidental with the political disintegration that Addams identified. Under such conditions, democratic ideals such as equality and the participation of all in the decision-making process were impossible. Addams did not believe that political parties alone could achieve such democratic ideals.

The first phase of democracy had established political institutions with a guiding constitution and the right to vote. Although Addams identified the first phase as a fundamental step in the construction of a democratic state, she insisted that a second phase was necessary. This second phase must create social organizations capable of: 1) demonstrating the interdependence of all classes and types of people; 2) disseminating and interpreting information openly and fairly to all citizens; 3) educating all citizens; and 4) fostering a higher civic life through common social intercourse.[15] Because Chicago and other cities were increasingly diverse and industrial, with ever-expanding populations, traditional assumptions about the effectiveness of democracy needed support from social organizations capable of those tasks. Without a "social" aspect of democracy there was no way that political institutions could live up to the ideal of collective decisions binding on all citizens. The settlement house was a rhetorical space comparable to the Athenian Assembly because it opened the possibility for participation in political life and tried to invent mechanisms for guiding decision and judgment.[16]

Generating the kinds of social conditions that Addams thought necessary for democracy required a radically different set of rhetorical practices. In what Addams identified as the "first phase of democracy," rhetorical practices had remained much closer to the practice of public address. Ideally, professional politicians persuaded citizens to vote for them, and then those professional politicians engaged in deliberation over specific courses of action as an embodied voice of their constituents. These politicians could be kept in check by the rules agreed on in a constitution. A constitution could secure the rights of citizens and provide equal protection to those without a literal voice in the decision-making process. Addams demonstrated that this system could not work in an efficient, open, or successful manner. Poverty, inequality, corruption, class, race, and sex discrimination all worked to prevent the mass of citizens from genuine participation in deliberation and politics. The Constitution and the right to vote were meant as theoretical protection from these problems, but such problems persisted.

Instead of relying on politicians to represent citizens and instead of relying on constitutional rights for protection, Addams advocated the development of social structures and organizations capable of supporting the economic and social unity of citizens. Citizens could then work within those social organizations to begin to exercise their voice in political deliberation—voting and constitutional protections were supplemented with more proactive methods. Traditional deliberative rhetoric, then, cannot aid in the operations of a democracy without first attending to a sense of social unity among citizens. The challenge of large-scale democracy, according to Addams, is to find mechanisms and organizations capable of bringing diverse people together. In addition, deliberative rhetoric was still needed in the "second phase of democracy" precisely because the French philosophical ideals of the first phase existed only in theory, not in practice.

Once the conditions for an effective democracy are altered, the notion of citizenship is also altered. Jean Bethke Elshtain, in her introduction to *The Jane Addams Reader* and in *Jane Addams and the Dream of American Democracy,* consistently claims that the major function of Hull-House was "to create citizens" (*JAR*, xxi).[17] In Athenian democracy the notion of citizenship meant full and equal legal and political privileges that included the ability to participate in the Assembly and in the legal proceedings held in the courts (Ober 1989, 5). Addams faced the challenge of reimagining the notion of citizenship given her own context. One could say that American citizenship, at the time, meant equal protection under the laws of the Constitution and the right to elect representatives to make political decisions. However, Addams had already demonstrated corruption in the voting system and social abuses of constitutional protections. In addition, Addams, as a woman, could not vote for representatives who would change undesirable situations. This meant that settlement houses, if they were to produce citizens, had to define citizenship in a much broader way—in a way that could bring about the broader notion of "social democracy."

The clearest example of a broader notion of citizenship and social democracy is Addams's belief that women needed to respond to both a "family claim" and a "social claim." The traditional "family claim" required women to maintain the home, care for and educate the children, and provide for the "head of the household." However, the "family claim" excluded women from participation in public life outside the home, even if activities outside the home affected the maintenance of the home. One way to remedy this problem was for women to acquire the right to vote. For Addams, however, citizenship could not be reduced only to voting:

> The family as well as the state we are all called upon to maintain as the highest institutions which the race has evolved for its safeguard and protection. But merely to preserve these institutions is not enough. There come periods of reconstruction, during which the task is laid upon a passing generation, to enlarge the function and carry forward the ideal

> of a long-established institution. There is no doubt that many women, consciously and unconsciously, are struggling with this task. The family, like every other element of human life, is susceptible to progress, and from epoch to epoch its tendencies and aspirations are enlarged, although its duties can never be abrogated and its obligations can never be cancelled. . . . The family in its entirety must be carried out into the larger life. Its various members together must recognize and acknowledge the validity of the social obligation. (*DSE* 1902, 79–80)

Clearly it was not a question of adding the right to vote to the "family claim" but rather a question of expanding the "family claim" so that women could respond to and participate in pressing "social claims."[18] Many women saw an "unnecessary conflict between the social and the family claims." However, the "social claim" was meant to call women to act as citizens by expanding their role beyond maintaining the home.[19] For Addams, the first aspect of citizenship, then, was the ability to respond to "social claims" through activities that expanded the notion of the "family claim." This is a concrete translation of Dewey's argument that philosophy should respond to the "problems of men."

With the recognition and response to the "social claim" in place, the second aspect of citizenship was the creation of a self or an "identity" through fellowship with other citizens. If Hull-House was to be a place of "civic education," then it must serve as a "vehicle for the creation of community and the sustaining of identities. Indeed, the central role Hull-House played in generating identity is the hallmark of its mission" (Elshtain 2002, 152–53). For Addams, identity replaces the notion of an individual, literal voice in affairs because it is an essential part of participation in the "social aspect of democracy." However, Addams's notion of identity and selfhood is quite different than the claims of postmodern identity politics.[20] Identity was not to be used as a rhetorical tool or topic for political debate; nor was identity to be contested, defended, or guarded. "For Addams, it is in giving the self that one truly discovers oneself. The self requires social and cultural forms and channels through which to flow" (153). Throughout *Twenty Years at Hull-House,* Addams consistently uses the pronoun "we" or simply "Hull-House" as a noun to describe various activities, signifying that her own identity was bound to that of others and to the social and cultural organizations to which she belonged.

For a more specific example of identity formation, Addams recounts a story about the Greek immigrant community in her neighborhood (*TYH,* 242–44). The Greek community performed plays for a variety of audiences at the Hull-House theater. These plays functioned as a celebration of Greek life, but more important, they were a way of bringing different parts of the community together to share in the celebration of a particular culture. In performing these plays, Greek immigrants were able to forge an identity in Chicago *through* enjoying the fellowship of other Chicago residents. The social space that Hull-House offered these residents made identity formation possible. The goal of such cultural activities was "to develop new ways of being that underwrote forms of autonomy *within* relationships, not in opposition to them" (Elshtain 2002, 174). This meant that notions of selfhood were possible only within social relationships, not outside of or against others. It also meant that the task of selfhood, and it is a task if it requires social participation, was a key component of citizenship and, by extension, democracy. Such a task introduced a citizen into the wider social claims of the community and made possible the orchestration of effective political bodies such as labor unions. The door to Hull-House was continuously open because the settlement house signified hospitality, fellowship, and solidarity—all of which were necessary to forming an identity.

The argument that citizenship required active responses to "social claims" and some notion of selfhood or identity would have seemed obvious to an Athenian democrat. The obligation to respond to "social claims" and partake in democratic deliberations was part of being an Athenian citizen.[21] However, according to Addams, American culture lacked these characteristics of Greek democracy. Without a sense of self or identity and without a felt need to respond to "social claims" it was difficult to see how voting, as a democratic function, could sustain a healthy, effective, and open democracy. Without the social dimension of democracy and without a broad notion of citizenship, it was difficult to put an effective deliberative rhetoric to work. If one eliminates the institutional clarity of voting and equal protection under the Constitution as the two primary characteristics of citizenship, then how exactly can one become or be a citizen? By what means or what processes can individuals actively respond to the social claims of their community or develop an identity through fellowship? If these issues lacked theoretical clarity, Addams made up for such ambiguities in the practical results that Hull-House was able to produce. As an institution, Hull-House had the goal of creating citizenship in a social democracy. In so doing, Hull-House adds to our notion of deliberative rhetoric by suggesting that rhetoric produces social cohesion as a prerequisite for effective deliberation. One way to understand this position is to consider it in the light of Plato's debate with the sophists.

In Plato's *Protagoras,* Socrates asks Protagoras to explain his claim that virtue can be taught. Protagoras's response involves the story of how Zeus imparted respect for others and justice to all men. For Protagoras, Zeus's goal was "to bring order into our cities and create a bond of friendship and union" (Plato *Protagoras* 322c). Respect and justice, then, were the foundations for the belief that any man could offer counsel in the affairs of the state: "[W]hen the subject of their counsel involves political wisdom, which must always follow the path of justice and moderation, they [Athenians] listen to every man's opinion, for they think that everyone must share in this kind of virtue; otherwise the state could not exist" (323a).

Hull-House, as an institution, continued Zeus's project of imparting respect and justice (in this instance to the citizens of Chicago) and thus attempted to bring order to the city and the bonds of friendship and union to its residents. Hull-House also laid the groundwork for the participation of all in political life. Order, friendship, and union, which are made possible through respect and justice, were to be fostered, upheld, and extended through the participation of all citizens in the life of the community. Protagoras claimed that, by partaking in deliberation, Athenian citizens spoke in accordance with the laws of Athens and the ethical standards of their community. Deliberation, then, involved individuals articulating their own interests as citizens, aware of the common good and of the virtues that held the community together. By encouraging residents of Chicago to respond to the "social claim" Addams hoped that political deliberation could serve the same function.

The myth that Protagoras recounts in Plato's dialogue serves to justify the role of the teacher of rhetoric (Protagoras, of course, was a prominent player of that role). A rhetorical education in Athens helped students practice, polish, and perfect methods of persuasive speech used in giving advice to the community. Such instruction, according to Protagoras, could assist in the development of virtuous citizens precisely because individual expression was tied to community standards of excellence (Plato *Protagoras* 327d–329). Every citizen, possessed of respect and justice, could become more virtuous through participation in deliberation because that process helps the community realize the ideals of justice and respect that create the bonds between and among all citizens. Protagoras's claim that "man is the measure of all things" underpins this perspective on deliberation. On the surface this is a relativist argument. However, Protagoras's claim is far more complex than the simple idea that "all truth is relative." To claim that "man is the measure of all things" is to claim that communities determine and understand what is good or bad, right or wrong through the articulation of ideas from within that community. The "human-measure" principle invites citizens to understand themselves as the guiding force behind *both* their own well-being and the well-being of the community, and to understand their beliefs, decisions, and values as the forces that lead to community action and community standards. This is why a rhetorical education was considered crucial for democratic deliberation.[22]

Recounting Protagoras's justification of his teaching in Plato's dialogue points out the similarity between Protagoras's conception of deliberation and the necessity for rhetorical education, on one hand, and Jane Addams's dreams for an effective democracy, on the other. The argument that citizens learn how to be virtuous through participation in the affairs of the state was an integral part of both Protagoras's and Addams's conceptions of democracy. In addition, the assumption that "man (and woman) is the measure of all things" works as an underlying theme in both Protagoras's rhetorical teachings and Addams's pragmatism. However, Addams could not teach those who came to Hull-House the principles of basic persuasive speech. If man and woman are the measure of all things, then they need a more complex set of practices to negotiate community values, beliefs, and standards. This is precisely why Addams insisted on social institutions as a prerequisite for effective democratic deliberation. Hull-House aimed to "develop whatever social life its neighborhood may afford, to focus and give form to that life, to bring to bear upon it the results of cultivation and training; but it [Hull-House] receives in exchange for the music of isolated voices the volume and strength of the chorus" (*TYH,* 83). The immediate training that Hull-House offered was in social organization so a collective voice could be created.

In Addams's conception of the democratic process, there are several kinds of communities and several layers of expression and identification within those communities. First is the relation between a person and the neighborhood: "the depth and strength of his [a resident's] relation to the neighborhood must depend very largely upon the genuine friendships he has been able to make" (*TYH,* 294). Interpersonal bonds, then, are important if the problems in the neighborhood are to be addressed. However, there is also the relation between a resident and the city: "his [a resident's] relation to the city as a whole comes largely through his identification with those groups who are carrying forward the reforms which a settlement neighborhood so badly needs and with which residence has made him familiar." One could also imagine third and fourth relations between state and nation. Both of these would necessarily involve participation in some social organization that responds to a bigger set of problems.

Through the process of participation in, and identification with, various communities, "life in the Settlement discovers above all what has been called 'the extraordinary pliability of human nature,' and it seems impossible to set any bounds to the moral capabilities which might unfold under ideal civic and educational conditions. But in order to obtain these conditions, the Settlement recognizes the need of cooperation, both with the radical and the conservative, and from the very nature of the case the Settlement cannot limit its friends to any one political party or economic school. . . . The educational activities of a Settlement, as well as its philanthropic, civic, and social undertakings, are but different manifestations of the attempt to socialize democracy, as is the very existence of the Settlement itself" (*TYH,* 295). The settlement, then, functioned for Addams as the Athenian Assembly did for Protagoras—it was an institution for the realization of community goals and standards, and a place for the expression of an individual's own voice. In addition, some form of rhetorical education is necessary for participation in the community, and the settlement house offered that kind of education. The settlement house was the first institution that a citizen could belong to, and through it a citizen could participate in other organizations that advocated specific causes. Through social clubs, labor union organizing, art studios, public lectures, and civic appeals to the Chicago Board of Education and Board of Health citizens learned about, participated in, and helped found community goals and standards.

Participation, then, required a rhetorical education that could produce the volume necessary to have a collective voice heard in deliberations on a local, national, or international scale. In order to develop this kind of rhetorical education, settlement houses offered "classes in citizenship in which the principles of American institutions are expounded" (*TYH,* 271). What Addams identified in her time at Hull-House was the need to explain American institutions to various immigrant populations and women so that they could then begin to participate in larger public institutions: "The early settlements practically staked their future upon an identification with the alien and considered his interpretation their main business. We stuck to this at some cost, for we believed that especially in times of crisis it was our mission to interpret American institutions to those who were bewildered concerning them" (*JAR* 1919, 244). However, it was not only a matter of interpreting American institutions to immigrant communities; it was also a matter of interpreting different people to one another: "We have no method by which to discover men, to spiritualize, to understand, to hold intercourse with aliens and to receive what they bring. A century old abstraction breaks down before this vigorous test of concrete cases and their demand for sympathetic interpretation" (*JAR* 1907, 149). Throughout many of her essays on education Addams insists that the most valuable function of the settlement lay in "interpretation and synthesis" (*JOE* 1899, 97).[23]

This kind of education was not being offered in universities. Addams, in fact, claimed that "it may be necessary that the University be supplemented by the settlement, or something answering thereto" (*JOE* 1899, 93). Universities, according to Addams, seemed interested only in laboratories whose goal was "research and the extension of the bounds of knowledge" (77). Although there were classes at the settlement, their main function was to bring students to participate in the life of the community. Universities sought knowledge, and were at times associated with the settlements, but the settlements sought action.[24] In addition, "a settlement constantly endeavors to make its neighborhood realize that it belongs to the city as a whole, and can only improve as the city improves" (93). In adopting this position Addams clearly aligned herself with the rhetorical task of education: "Let us assume that the dominating interest in knowledge has become its use, the conditions under which it may be most effectively employed in human conduct; and that at last certain people have consciously formed themselves into groups for the express purpose of effective application.

. . . The ideal and developed settlement would attempt to test the value of human knowledge by action, and realization, quite as the complete and ideal University would concern itself with the discovery of knowledge in all branches. The settlement stands for application as opposed to research" (*STJ* 1929, 186–87).

There are two primary functions of a rhetorical education, then, according to Addams. The first is to explain institutions to people, and to interpret one people to another. The second is to develop a collective voice so that action, the application of knowledge, can become possible. It was Addams's articulation of the task of education that drew her thinking in line with classical rhetorical theory. To accomplish this task, though, she needed more than persuasive speaking tactics. One central rhetorical task was the act of interpretation that could result in the construction of a collective voice, or a "chorus."

The use of Hull-House for founding and helping labor unions illustrates the power of the collective voice. The labor movement, in general, "may be called a concerted effort among the workers in all trades to obtain a more equitable distribution of the product, and to secure a more orderly existence for the laborer" (*JAR* 1895, 49). An attempt was made to aid in this endeavor through organizing various tradespeople at Hull-House. The simple act of providing a physical space for unions to meet and decide on actions and policies was a key part of organization. In addition, the act of bringing different tradespeople into contact with one another to share ideas and solutions was a simple but important task. Those in the sewing trades (shirt-makers and cloak-makers) had immediate success by using Hull-House to organize and strike, which resulted in fewer hours and higher wages (*TYH,* 151).

The settlement house also worked to infuse unions with higher ideals and a broader vision. Instead of insisting that a labor union work against the principal owners of capital, the settlement provided the labor movement with "a consciousness of its historical development" and accentuated "the ultimate ethical aims of the movement" (*JAR* 1895, 60). "The ultimate ethical aim," according to Addams, is the realization of the economic and social unity of society—it is an understanding that what is best for all is best for the individual.[25] Labor movements were in danger of forgetting this ethical appeal and instead focusing on tactics of class warfare. When this happened, the rhetorical effectiveness of the collective voice was compromised. This is exactly what occurred during the Pullman Strike.[26] The task of the settlement was not to side with labor but to interpret each side to the other so that each side could see the economic interconnections of all parties involved.

For Addams, labor unions and other organized political movements had to distinguish between rhetoric as self-expression and rhetoric as collective expression: "There is no doubt that the great difficulty we experience in reducing to action our imperfect code of social ethics arises from the fact that we have not yet learned to act together, and find it far from easy even to fuse our principles and aims into a satisfactory statement" (*DSE,* 137). This is not to say that self-expression plays no part in deliberation. "If, as is many times stated, we are passing from an age of individualism to one of association, there is no doubt that" the individual still remains an important rhetorical voice. It takes individual initiative to develop collective action, and Addams's Hull-House stands as an example of this. However, rhetorical self-expression must be combined with a "social ethic" for deliberation to be successful: "A man who takes the betterment of humanity for his aim and end must take the daily experiences of humanity for the constant correction of his process" (176–77). In other words, individual acts of self-expression must take the collective benefit of all into consideration to be most effective—any rhetorical act must be backed by a collective voice of many in order to have an effective impact.

Hull-House combined a new sense of rhetorical education with a new sense of rhetorical action to have a significant impact on life in Chicago. This was a crucial aspect of the "second phase of democracy": "It is on behalf of the average workingmen that our increasing democracy impels us to make a new demand upon the educator. As the political expression of democracy has claimed for the workingmen the free right of citizenship, so a code of social ethics is now insisting that he shall be a conscious member of society, having some notionof his social and industrial value" (*DSE,* 192). This combination of rhetorical education and rhetorical action was undoubtedly a success. Hull-House as a collective voice was able to repair public sanitation problems, health problems, child-care problems, and child-labor problems. For example, Hull-House demonstrated the close connection between typhoid cases in Chicago and bacteriological problems resulting from plumbing systems in the city. By extensive research and appeals to the city sanitation and health departments, Hull-House instigated legislation to improve the plumbing system in the city in order to solve the typhoid problem (*TYH,* 196). In addition, labor unions that actively met at Hull-House, and other international and national organizations that it supported, drew rhetorical effectiveness from Addams's project for a social democracy.

The impact that Hull-House had as an institution on deliberative debates in the city of Chicago cannot be questioned. From small reform projects such as prohibiting the sale of cocaine to minors (*TYH,* 197) to larger issues concerning the Illinois State Bureau of Labor (134), Hull-House actively guided decision and judgment on various issues. Addams was able to generate rhetorical authority for herself and for her neighbors. On what grounds, though, did this rhetorical authority rest? How can we explain the success of Hull-House as a site for rhetorical education and rhetorical action? Hull-House's rhetorical authority was supported by a "social ethic" in combination with sociological knowledge. Rhetorical education, the act of interpretation, and rhetorical action, the persuasive power of the collective voice, relied on sociology and ethics for success.

Sociology and Social Ethics

In the *Protagoras,* and in many of Plato's other dialogues, Socrates critiques the sophistic position on the practice of rhetoric. In response to Protagoras's claim that deliberation can improve an individual's moral character when grounded on justice and respect, Socrates argues that only knowledge of the good can insure that people make the right choice in any political debate. Again and again he insists that the project of rhetoric is dangerous if it is not based on knowledge. In the *Phaedrus,* Socrates advances this claim further by arguing that rhetorical discourse should be preceded by dialectic. Through the metaphor of the charioteer, the white horse and the black horse, he argues that true love is discovered by the soul that can tame the black horse (rhetoric) so that the white horse (philosophy/dialectic) can work as a team with the black horse to return the soul to true love.[27] In both the *Protagoras* and the *Phaedrus,* Socrates claims that rhetoric is empty, dangerous, and unsound without the kind of proper philosophical wisdom obtained through the method of dialectic. For rhetoric, the result is that political deliberation can be carried out only by those who possess knowledge of the good. For this reason Plato argues in *The Republic* that "philosopher-kings" should control the city-state.

Jane Addams answers Plato's general critique of deliberative rhetoric on many levels. She did not seek or possess knowledge of the forms; rather she insisted on grounding rhetorical action on sociological knowledge obtained through empirical investigation. Addams was a charter member of the American Sociological Society, founded in 1905, and was one of a few women to address the group on several occasions. In addition, she consistently referred to her work as sociology, not social work or philanthropy. Most telling, however, is the publication of several books containing careful collection of data, thick description, and sociological analyses of her empirical investigations—*Hull-House Maps and Papers, The Spirit of Youth and the City Streets, Democracy and Social Ethics,* and *Peace and Bread in Time of War.*

Mary Jo Deegan claims that Addams had considerable influence on the Chicago School of Sociology (which served through the 1920s as the paradigm for the discipline). In fact, Deegan argues that *Hull-House Maps and Papers* was one of the founding texts of the discipline of sociology.[28] She supports this argument by tracing the connections between Hull-House and the University of Chicago as well as the intellectual connections between Addams and notable sociologists such as Robert Park and George Herbert Mead. As a sociologist, Addams pursued empirical investigation of social problems in order to respond to "social claims" and solve neighborhood problems—she shared this perspective with the other members of the Chicago school.

Two examples clearly demonstrate Addams's combination of sociology and rhetorical action. First, *Hull-House Maps and Papers* established several key precedents for conducting sociological research: the use of mapping as a statistical technique to reveal patterns of social groups; emphasis on the city as a factor structuring daily lives; and the analysis of immigrant groups and their disorganization in the city as a function of debilitating economic conditions. In the final chapter of this collection of essays Addams uses sociological data to advocate labor union action. She did not offer unqualified support for labor unions, but she did argue that unions were an essential means for breaking the cycle of poverty in Chicago. The collection of information in *Hull-House Maps and Papers* was not meant to be absorbed passively but rather to be used to better the conditions of daily life in Chicago.

Addams recounts a second, more specific example in *Twenty Years at Hull-House.* During her first few years in Chicago's industrial district, one of the most striking features of the neighborhood "was the presence of huge wooden garbage boxes fastened to the street pavement in which the undistributed refuse accumulated daily" (*TYH,* 185). Beyond the foul smell, the overwhelming amount of garbage and the inefficient means of disposal caused serious health concerns for the children in the neighborhood. The Hull-House Woman's Club decided to collect evidence of health violations and inadequate garbage removal. Addams presented the findings to city officials, which resulted in her being appointed "garbage inspector." As garbage inspector Addams was able to establish a more efficient and effective means of garbage disposal and helped lower the incidence of childhood sickness and death in her ward. The sociological investigation performed by the Hull-House Woman's Club made subsequent rhetorical action effective.

The empirical investigations that Addams conducted were based on her belief that the residents of a city "should know their own neighborhoods more thoroughly than any other, and that their experiences there should affect their convictions" (*TYH,* 203). Rhetorical intervention in social problems should be firmly grounded on knowledge collected using the empirical method. Addams embodied the pragmatist belief that scientific knowledge was a key rhetorical resource for persuasion. However, knowledge was not the only resource for conviction and action. Just as Plato believed that the deliberative rhetorician should have knowledge of the good, Addams believed that rhetorical action should be tempered by a "social ethic." In fact her sociological writings are paralleled by her ethical writings.

Democracy and Social Ethics is Addams's clearest treatment of the meaning and significance of a "social ethic." Addams insisted that the word "social" be added to her analysis of ethics because the public life of a democratic state should be guided by a set of moral principles, not simply by ethical individuals within that democratic state. *Democracy and Social Ethics* advances the argument that "ethical maladjustment in social affairs arises from the fact that we are acting upon a code of ethics adapted to individual relationships, but not to the larger social relationships to which it is bunglingly applied" (221).

Ethics, then, is embodied in the solidarity of the group and not in individual citizens. This, however, creates a difficult tension between individual citizens and larger social organizations. In order to provide an individual citizen with "a sense of conviction that his individual needs must be merged into the needs of the many, and are only important as they are thus merged, the appeal cannot be made along the lines of self-interest. The demand should become universalized; in this process it would also become clarified, and the basis of our political organization become perforce social and ethical" (*DSE,* 269–70). In other words, it must be made clear to each citizen that "his individual needs are common needs" and that those needs "can be legitimately supplied for him when they are supplied for all" (269). The social activities fostered and developed at Hull-House were meant to produce a "social ethic" by demonstrating the ways in which the community is tied together: "In this effort toward a higher morality in our social relations, we must demand that the individual shall be willing to lose the sense of personal achievement, and shall be content to realize his activity only in connection with the activity of the many" (275). In effect, self-interest was to be replaced with solidarity.

The enactment of this kind of social ethic has important implications for rhetorical practice. The most frequent criticism of the art of rhetoric, made most vociferously by Plato, rests on the idea of a slick and elegant orator able to advance his or her own self-interest through the power of persuasive speaking that rests not on knowledge but on artifice. By insisting on the importance of a social ethic, Addams identified a nobler brand of rhetorical action resting on the best interest of the community as a whole. Such a sentiment directs rhetoric's power toward the bridging of distances between people (psychological or physical), the building of communities, and the development of social solidarity. Rhetoric's power is thus put into the service of social democracy.

Isocrates offered a similar argument in favor of just such a conception of rhetoric. In training students to enter political life in Athens, Isocrates taught that orators should be concerned with the outcomes of deliberation and the effects of decisions on the polis: "I have singled out the highest kind of oratory, that which deals with the greatest affairs and, while best displaying the ability of those who speak, brings most profit to those who hear" (*Panegyricus* 4–5). The full potential of rhetoric, then, is realized when the community benefits most from some action or decision. For a rhetor to be successful she must understand the good of the community and be able to make specific suggestions for the realization of the good of the community.

Norman Clark uses the notion of "the critical servant" to describe Isocrates' contribution to rhetoric.[29] According to Clark, critical servants propose a "practical, useful course of action to the community" that is judged by determining if the action and the rhetor advancing it are serving the good of the people. The concept of "the critical servant" combines an ethical orator who possesses appropriate intentions and relevant experience in the community with a purposive, pragmatic act that attempts to imagine how the community could be better. Servitude is "the giving over of one's will to fulfill the important function of addressing the needs of the community"; it is a willing choice to use rhetoric to remake the community so all are better off (Clark 1996, 117). The Isocratean notion of the "critical servant" is clearly comparable to the ethical mandate that Addams used to advocate specific rhetorical actions.

Isocrates trained political leaders, and so the ethical standards of the rhetor are judged on an individual basis—a leader must have virtuous intentions.[30] By contrast, Addams argued that labor unions, movements, and large social organizations should embody the ethical standards of "critical service." The best example of this is Addams's position on the physical violence associated with many labor strikes and the self-interest manifested in those strikes. Labor unions were founded on the idea that all of the different economic classes and interests were interrelated. This is why Addams continued to stress that the function of the settlement house was to interpret opposing forces to one another, display the interconnections between people, and to remain impartial in a dispute. This meant that physical violence during strikes threatened the social ethic of the community, and that labor unions needed to accept the brotherhood of the entire working class regardless of profession. This model of deliberative rhetoric is not agonistic or conflict-driven; rather it focuses on community. Ethically this means that the burden is shifted from the individual "critical servant" to the rhetorical actions of the whole group. If groups, unions, or any larger social structures degenerate into selfishness or the protection of self-interests, then the rhetorical practices of those groups are not ethical and will not lead to the betterment of the community. In this way Addams worked within and exceeded Isocrates' conception of deliberative rhetoric. When the single voice is replaced with the chorus, the standards of "critical service" still apply, but this time on a larger scale.

The combination of sociological knowledge and social ethics laid the foundation for much of Addams's rhetorical action. The constant search for knowledge about the pressing problems of the moment combined with the belief that deliberation should consider the best interests of the community generated a set of rhetorical practices that fit within the model of classical rhetoric while meeting the new challenges of a large-scale democracy. This combination of sociological knowledge and social ethics also marks another moment of historical tension between philosophy and rhetoric. Although Addams was not interested in the philosophical pursuit of the forms, the pragmatistic pursuit of scientific knowledge of society pressed the search for knowledge further. The scientific method replaced Plato's dialectic and became the pragmatist's preferred method for finding reliable truths as James and Dewey illustrated. However, Addams was careful to argue that such a search for truth should not end in passive or empty observation. She was able to combine Plato's claim that deliberative rhetoric should be based on knowledge with Isocrates' claim that the rhetor should be concerned with practical actions in the best interest of the community. Addams was able to draw the projects of philosophy and rhetoric together through her concern with political deliberation.

The Politics of Pragmatism—Rhetoric's Role in Democracy

In *The American Evasion of Philosophy,* Cornel West claims that "American pragmatism is a diverse and heterogeneous tradition. But its common denominator consists of a future-oriented instrumentalism that tries to deploy thought as a weapon to enable more effective action" (1989, 5). In comparison, Aristotle describes deliberation in the *Rhetoric* in the following way: "Political speaking urges us to do or not to do something. . . . The political orator is concerned with the future: it is about things to be done hereafter that he advises. . . . The political orator aims to establish the expediency or harmfulness of a proposed course of action" (1358b). In this juxtaposition of the general aims of pragmatism and deliberative rhetoric it is obvious that the two projects share a great deal. Perhaps substituting "language" for "knowledge" in West's explanation of pragmatism would make a more rigorous connection between the two, but the pragmatists lacked the social and political conditions that made oratory the key component of rhetoric. Pragmatists, instead, searched for ways to use knowledge to guide future decisions concerning social problems. Jane Addams, of course, fits easily into West's description of pragmatism. The contributions that Addams made to the larger intellectual tradition of pragmatism value and explore the meaning of deliberative rhetoric.

There are several important and specific contributions that Addams makes to pragmatism and deliberative rhetoric. First is her continued attention to what Aristotle called "practical wisdom." In the *Rhetoric,* Aristotle claims that "the function of rhetoric is to deal with things about which we deliberate, but for which we have no systematic rules" (1357a). The person of "practical wisdom" is able to negotiate the particularities of every new situation in such a way that general precedents or guidelines do not impede decision making. This means that good judgment is adaptable and flexible and must result from experience with particular cases. Addams was committed to just this kind of "wisdom." In *Twenty Years at Hull-House* she claims that "life cannot be administered by general rules and regulations; that [the] wisdom to deal with a man's difficulties comes only through some knowledge of his life and habits as a whole" (108).

Deliberation, in other words, must be based on knowledge gained from experiencing the particular lives of individual people. Hull-House was devoted to this endeavor. This is also a concern of pragmatism in general. It is precisely abstract philosophical knowledge that James and Dewey worked so diligently to reject in favor of "experience."

The result of the turn toward experience, the concrete, and the factual, which Aristotle advocates for the deliberative rhetorician and which James, Dewey, and Addams advocate for pragmatism, is the production of a method and a way of acting. When James argues that the pragmatist "turns toward concreteness," he also suggests that we turn "towards action and towards power" (*PR*, 20). Such a turn produces a "really vital question for us all": "What is the world going to be? What is life eventually to make of itself?" (47). The pragmatic method attempts to make the world better by investigating the concrete and from that imagining the possible. This, of course, is an exact description of Addams's entire lifework, but it is also a description of the role that rhetoric played in ancient Athens. Persuasive speech was a way of acting and making; rhetoric was a constructive art concerned with addressing the problems of the moment and imagining what the world could be. John Poulakos, in fact, defines rhetoric as "the art which seeks to capture in opportune moments that which is appropriate and attempts to suggest that which is possible" (Lucaites, Condit, and Caudill 1999, 26). The concepts of timeliness and appropriateness embedded in Poulakos's definition guide the rhetor to the pressing problems facing a particular audience at a particular time, but the rhetor tries to move the audience to new possibilities. If we are to take anything from Hull-House and Addams's work, it is the importance of investigating timely and appropriate problems combined with the effort to invent ways of making the community better.

Pragmatism's belief that the validity of an idea is tested by its consequences inspires the combination of concrete experiences with the search for methods of practical action. Addams lived this idea by making sure that all of Hull-House's many endeavors had some consequences on life in her neighborhood or in Chicago. This is also the test for an effective rhetoric. Rhetorical discourse is judged by its ability to influence or persuade an audience. Specifically, deliberative rhetoric is judged by its ability to guide the community in the most expedient fashion—this is part of Aristotle's definition of political oratory. Any knowledge, any idea, or any fact is only important if it can be used by the rhetor to induce some kind of effect. Addams, by seeking methods, practices, and ideas that could have important consequences for the quality of life in Chicago, performed the rhetorical and pragmatic task of pressing knowledge into action in search of truly beneficial consequences.

What separates rhetoric from pragmatism, however, is the role that language plays in affecting the life of the community. The classical rhetor could influence, control, or affect an audience through direct, spoken argument at the Ekklesia, in the courts, or at a festival. Pragmatism is less concerned with the power of language to shape the world because, as Addams hinted at in her valedictory address at Rockford Seminary, many people lacked occasions for public speaking or the rhetorical authority to be heard. Addams was acutely concerned with having a voice in political and social affairs. Her work is best seen as a search for practices or methods that allowed individual citizens to intervene or participate in public affairs through established institutions so that all citizens could influence or affect the future course of their community, city, and country. Linguistic techniques and persuasive public speaking tactics may be important, but they are not sufficient. This did not mean that rhetorical practice was easily translated from persuasive public speaking to some other art of expression or communication. In fact, one of the most basic struggles that pragmatists faced was the need to invent new modes of expression and communication. Addams tried to solve these problems through the creation of the settlement house as an important part of a community.

The most striking difference between rhetorical practice based on persuasive public speaking and the kinds of rhetorical practices the pragmatists were struggling to invent is the difference between self-expression and group-expression. In *Peace and Bread in Time of War,* Addams traces her experiences as a member of the Women's International League for Peace and Freedom. Throughout this work she continues to emphasize the importance of the uniformity of expression and the role of the larger organization or institution. If members of the Women's International League for Peace and Freedom were successfully to advocate a peaceful solution to World War I, then they needed to emphasize and use the collective voice they possessed.

After the war Addams argued that "there is little doubt that the more often representatives of various nations meet in conference the more they discover that many problems are world-wide in their implications and can only be solved if the nations come together to consider them. They also learn the technique of conferring together" (*STJ* 1932, 261). Here Addams expresses her faith in the possibility of finding and acting on a collective voice. Communicating as a group was the most effective method available to reach an ethical solution to the problems the world faced. This idea of group expression, however, opens an endless series of questions about rhetorical practice. What kinds of rhetorical methods can actually bring people together to produce a collective voice? What are the best means for expressing that collective voice? What are the ethical implications for the actions of the group? How do the actions of a group affect the identity of an individual member of that group? How does deliberation, or decision making, happen when larger groups are charged with the responsibility of guiding the affairs of the state? What role does language play in rhetorical practices based on the group instead of the individual? How does language influence an audience through methods other than basic public speaking? These are the theoretical questions that Addams struggled to answer. In attempting to answer them, she exceeded classical rhetorical theory and classical notions of deliberation; but she had to exceed them—the world she experienced demanded that she do so.

It would be easy to continue to cite examples of Addams's pragmatism. Her work at Hull-House actively developed many of the same ideas and themes that the more influential pragmatist philosophers only wrote about. She brings issues of politics and democracy into specific relief by suggesting that American democracy requires a unique deliberative rhetoric founded on social organization, sociological knowledge, and a social ethic. Her search for an appropriate and timely deliberative rhetoric was the defining characteristic of her pragmatism.

At this point it should be clear that Addams confronted many of the same questions that classical rhetorical theorists had confronted. Although she was challenged by a different set of circumstances and by a different context, her aims were in line with classical rhetorical theory—to have all citizens contribute to the decision-making process and participate in the affairs of the state. By working within the tradition of deliberative rhetoric, Addams pushed pragmatism into rhetorical action and thus demonstrated the connection between the two. The confluence of pragmatism and rhetorical theory in Addams's work should arouse wonder about what rhetoric can be outside of Athens and what pragmatism can contribute to the project of democracy in America. Jane Addams's work marks a beginning for such a project. If the universe is "unfinished, growing in all sorts of places, especially in the places where thinking beings are at work," as William James tells us, then not only is the art of rhetoric unfinished but it is also a vital part of constructing a new and better universe *(PR,* 100). Jane Addams's pragmatism is one iteration of many possible deliberative rhetorics available for our imagination and our use.

Four

Oliver Wendell Holmes Jr. and Legal Rhetoric

Judgment, Competition, and the Free Trade in Ideas

On Memorial Day, May 30, 1895, at a meeting called by the graduating class of Harvard University, Oliver Wendell Holmes Jr. delivered an address entitled "A Soldier's Faith."[1] As part of the Twentieth Massachusetts Regiment in the Union army, Holmes fought in some of the bloodiest battles of the Civil War.[2] "A Soldier's Faith" displays the residual impact of the war on his thinking: "I believe that the struggle for life is the order of the world, at which it is vain to repine" (*MFJH,* 19).[3] In that struggle, "man has in him that unspeakable somewhat which makes him capable of miracle, able to lift himself by the might of his own soul, unaided, able to face annihilation for a blind belief" (21). From this speech the general contours of his thinking are clear: life is a risk and a struggle, and we must act on faith without certain knowledge and often times under fire.[4] Through his work on the Supreme Judicial Court of Massachusetts and the United States Supreme Court, Holmes translated these general beliefs into specific judicial opinions and a unique legal pragmatism. Metaphors of war, struggle, and competition consistently appear in his court opinions and thus condition the judgments he made. Moreover, such metaphors strip his legal thought of claims to transcendent justice or objective logic. Instead, a judge, when deciding a case, picks a winner in a struggle and in so doing crafts a particular and contingent notion of justice and law.

Holmes's opinions were also his method of practicing philosophy.[5] Through careful attention to particular cases, he reflected on the role of experience, competition, knowledge, and general propositions in human decision making. The opinions he wrote are the grounds for a muscular and agonistic pragmatism built firmly on Darwin's theories and a celebration of military heroism. These philosophical reflections and judicial opinions are, in turn, expressed in a unique and aphoristic literary style. Richard Posner observes that Holmes is best understood as a "writer-philosopher" whose "distinction as a lawyer, judge, and legal theorist lies precisely in the infusion of literary skill and philosophical insight into his legal work" (*EH,* xvi). In other words, interpreting Holmes's judicial opinions requires attention to his method of articulating those opinions, the philosophy he develops through them, and the language he employs.

In order to understand the intersection between judicial decision making, legal philosophy, and literary style, I interpret Holmes's work in the light of the classical conception of forensic rhetoric. Such a comparison will demonstrate the central role of rhetorical processes in legal decision making and ground Holmes's philosophy and literary style in specific features of rhetorical theory. Holmes's pragmatism lays the foundation for a philosophy of legal rhetoric uniquely fit to American democracy. Through specific opinions that concern such issues as free speech, due process, and civil liability, he extends classical conceptions of forensic rhetoric by inventing pragmatic methods and standards for adjudication. Holmes's "soldier's faith" exemplifies a commitment to the inevitability of conflict. His legal pragmatism shapes the conflicts that arise in the course of human affairs and attempts to manage those conflicts so as to obviate the violence that he encountered during the Civil War. I interpret his perspective on conflict as a commitment to the need for rhetoric in negotiating disagreements without recourse to violence.

According to Holmes's pragmatism, legal rhetoric requires attention to experience and power as central forces in Darwinian struggle and competition. These two preoccupations, with experience and power, form the foundation for a sophistic legal philosophy and consistently function as references points for Holmes's judicial opinions. Understanding what Holmes means by experience and how he envisions the relationship between law and power is essential for understanding his legal philosophy. These concepts can be interpreted in the light of his most famous First Amendment decisions and his metaphor of the "free trade in ideas." As is evidenced by his "free trade" metaphor, Holmes's opinions display the capacity of language as an instrument that shapes the law. As an attempt to subvert formalist legal theory and any reverence for general rules, his opinions are interpretations of the particularity of the situation at hand. In addition, as a function of style his opinions display the capacity of eloquence for contributing to the ongoing construction of the common law. Explicating both the philosophical aspects of Holmes's legal thought and his method of adjudication will further demonstrate the necessity of rhetoric for legal pragmatism and democratic life.

Holmes's role as pragmatist and legal rhetorician can be seen, first, by evaluating his work within the tradition most clearly established by James and Dewey and within the classical tradition of forensic oratory. He realizes many of the intellectual commitments of pragmatist thought and extends basic notions of pragmatism and rhetoric in his judicial opinions. Second, his pragmatism can be defined by his attention to experience and power, and is embodied in his decisions concerning the First Amendment. Such a position provides theoretical insight into his legal philosophy and demonstrates the necessity of rhetoric for such a philosophy. Third, his pragmatism employs a specific method of legal decision making, a method that attends to the act of interpretation given the unique circumstances of a particular case and is embodied in the eloquence of his judicial opinions. Fourth, Holmes's specific contributions to rhetorical theory in the context of the American legal system can be demonstrated by examining the connection between law, pragmatism, and rhetoric.

Holmes's Pragmatism and Legal Rhetoric

While a student at Harvard Law School, Holmes knew William James well. The two shared an affectionate friendship for several years. Louis Menand claims that both were members of a group called "The Metaphysical Club," which met several times in Boston to discuss philosophy, literature, and science. As the two grew older, however, their friendship cooled. Although they continued to send their work to one another, personality differences led to a reciprocal annoyance. James thought that Holmes was "cold-blooded," egotistic, and conceited.[6] Holmes saw James as nervous, overly eager, and prone to long-winded explanations.[7] In addition, Holmes considered James's pragmatism "humbug" and had no patience for his spiritualism (*EH* 1908, 70). Nonetheless, the two shared specific intellectual commitments, especially regarding Darwinism.

Holmes's commitment to Darwin's ideas is evident in his lack of sympathy for the losers in life's competitions. In "A Soldier's Faith" he claims that he rejoiced "at every dangerous sport" that he saw "pursued." In dangerous sports he saw the Darwinian improvement of mankind: "If once in a while in our rough riding a neck is broken, I regard it, not as a waste, but as a price well paid for the breeding of a race fit for headship and command" (*MFJH,* 23). Moreover, he argued, our participation in these games is the only way we can determine those most fit for survival, and ultimately those most fit to decide questions of truth, justice, or morality.

According to Holmes, every participant in these games or struggles holds very personal beliefs, but no one player's beliefs have a greater a priori claim to truth than those of any of the other players. This skepticism leads to a dilemma because it makes any value judgment an entirely personal affair and leaves no basis for agreement between competing value judgments. Thus, Holmes constantly sought ways of judging values more objectively, and Darwinism provided the best solution. Having seen in the Civil War that only force ended debate,

Holmes believed that the only way to determine objectively the superiority of one claim over another is to bow to the winner. The only objective truth is "the majority vote of the nation that could lick all others" (*MFJH* 1918, 395). Of course, from this perspective, nothing can be absolutely true, certain, and fixed. In a world ruled only by power there can be no static and everlasting order, mundane or divine. There must be constant change, for today's winner may be tomorrow's loser, and with a new winner there will be a new truth. Constant change and pluralism were also the starting points for James's pragmatism.

Holmes often translated these beliefs into specific legal decisions, while James articulated the scientific and philosophical importance of pluralism and uncertainty. Thus, Holmes developed a form of social Darwinism that at times is harsher than what the other pragmatists may have accepted. For example, in *Buck v. Bell* (1927) he upheld a 1924 Virginia statute permitting sterilization of inmates in institutions for the "feeble-minded" (*MFJH*, 356). Carrie Buck was the daughter of a feeble-minded mother and had a feeble-minded child. Against the protection of individual liberties Holmes set the decisive social value of preventing the deterioration of the race. Recalling the Civil War, he argued, "We have seen more than once that the public welfare may call upon the best citizens for their lives. It would be strange if it could not call upon those who already sap the strength of the state for the lesser sacrifices, often not felt to be such by those concerned, in order to prevent our being swamped with incompetence. It is better for all the world, if instead of waiting to execute degenerate offspring for crime, or to let them starve for their imbecility, society can prevent those who are manifestly unfit from continuing their kind. The principle that sustains compulsory vaccination is broad enough to cover cutting the Fallopian tubes. . . . Three generations of imbeciles are enough" (358). In this opinion Holmes intends that the law should reflect Darwinian struggle and aid to victory those most fit to participate fully in society. In other words, given his skepticism of final truths and ultimate values, "the more powerful interests must be more or less reflected in legislation, which like every other device of man or beast, must tend in the long run to aid the survival of the fittest" (*MFJH* 1873, 50).

Holmes's Darwinism combines a rugged individualism with a constant attention to community. In his position as a judge he was forced to reconcile individual liberties with community welfare, and in the Buck case he demonstrates how his Darwinism is translated into a commitment to the collective welfare of the community. In other cases, most notably his First Amendment opinions, Holmes protected civil liberties using the same argument—that the free expression of ideas is necessary for the collective welfare of the community. Even in cases such as *Vegelahn v. Guntner* (1896) and *Plant v. Woods* (1900), the rights of labor unions to organize were defended with reference to the "free struggle of life" (*MFJH* 1896, 115).[8] In Menand's words, "Holmes did not defend the interests of labor because he wished to see those interests prevail. He defended them because he believed that every social interest should have its chance. He believed in experiment" (2001, 67). In the light of his Darwinism, therefore, Holmes understood the law as an instrument of external social forces, a struggle for resources and power among historic social blocs. Judges, according to such a perspective, were charged with the responsibility of keeping the struggle open to competing claims while keeping in mind the general will of the people.

Despite opinions such as *Buck v. Bell* and the glorification of war in "A Soldier's Faith," which many pragmatists would probably find abhorrent, Holmes's philosophy, which grew out of his Darwinism, is deeply pragmatist. In 1918 he claimed that "men to a great extent believe what they want to"—a position with which James would have sympathized (*EH,* 182). However, this did not translate into the claim that it was useless to talk about good or bad, or true or false beliefs. He argued, with the other pragmatists, that truth is a function of circumstances, and that in the long view of human affairs, custom and habit are contingent. In the short view, though, many people see their own customs and habits as necessary and irrevocable. Truth, he was fond of saying, is nothing other than what "I cannot help believing" (*MFJH* 1915, 392).[9] More important, we try to act on our truths—we do "what we can't help doing" and try "to make the world into the kind of world that we think we should like; but it hardly warrants our talking much about absolute truth."[10]

Holmes assumed that people are justified in defending what they have become accustomed to, and that there will be people who want to change the way things are. On this theory people are attempting to shift some part of the aggregate social burden from one set of shoulders to another. "Justice" and "fairness" are slogans propping up particular struggles, not eternal principles. What prevents the friction between competing conceptions of the right way of life from leading to violence is democracy.[11] In Holmes's time as a judge, the chief struggle in America was between labor and capital. Many of the opinions for which he became known constituted an intervention in that struggle, and his fundamental concern was to permit all parties the democratic means to attempt to make their interests prevail. "The life struggle is mitigated," he argued in one of his first law review articles, "by sympathy, prudence, and all the social and moral qualities. But in the last resort a man rightly prefers his own interests to that of his neighbors. And this is as true in legislation as in any other form of corporate action. All that can be expected from modern improvement is that legislation should easily and quickly, yet not too quickly, modify itself in accordance with the will of the de facto supreme power in the community, and that the spread of an educated sympathy should reduce the sacrifice of minorities to a minimum" (*MFJH* 1873, 50). Holmes, it should be clear, shares the pragmatist commitment to uncertainty, contingency, plurality, and democracy. However, his position is a muscular pragmatism that focuses much more explicitly on the role of power in negotiating those commitments.[12]

Perhaps the clearest indication of Holmes's pragmatism is his statement that "the prophecies of what the courts will do in fact, and nothing more pretentious, are what I mean by the law" (*MFJH* 1897, 75). In other words, it is not the law that determines the outcome of particular cases; it is what judges *say* is the law. Thus law is simply and empirically judicial behavior. A rule may be written down, it may express the will of the sovereign, or it may be justified by logic or approved by custom; but if the courts will not enforce it, it is not the law. Therefore, Holmes's legal philosophy focuses explicitly on the consequences of judicial action and is tested by the impact of a decision—perhaps the underlying premise connecting all of the different pragmatists discussed in this book.

In *Evolution and the Founders of Pragmatism,* Philip Wiener was the first to demonstrate the connections between Holmes and the other pragmatists by focusing explicitly on the influence of Darwinism on their thought. Around the same time Max Fisch described Holmes's theory of predicting what judges will do as a version of pragmatism, while Morton White demonstrated how this kind of legal theory was a rejection of formalist thought.[13] More recently Thomas Grey provided the most substantial and thorough account of the connections between Holmes and pragmatism.[14] Likewise, Richard Posner, as a judge and scholar, has consistently invoked Holmes as "the most illustrious figure in the history of American law" and the key inspiration for his version of legal pragmatism (*EH,* ix).[15] Furthermore, Louis Menand gives Holmes a central place in *The Metaphysical Club,* his intellectual history of the origins of pragmatism.[16] Menand argues that Holmes's belief that "certitude leads to violence" was the primary inspiration for the development of pragmatism as a philosophy that privileges the uncertain, contingent, and adaptable (2001, 61).[17] According to a pragmatist account of the world, beliefs are ever changing and we test our beliefs based on their adaptability. Holmes was committed to such an account of the world. That commitment remains the grounds for a great deal of scholarship that addresses the intersection of pragmatism and law.[18]

Although these interpretations of Holmes link his thought to pragmatism and clearly illustrate his enduring influence on the American legal system, they overlook the important function of rhetoric in law. Holmes's philosophy of law establishes the necessity of rhetoric for the process of adjudication. As the other pragmatists crafted a philosophy that continued to point to the significance and necessity of rhetoric, so too does Holmes. As a version of pragmatism that rejects claims to formal reasoning or an ideal form of justice in favor of commitments to competition, uncertainty, plurality, and power, Holmes's legal theory, if it seeks to reconcile disputes without recourse to violence, must place rhetorical processes at the center of jurisprudence. This claim becomes clear and convincing when the classical Greek connection between law and rhetoric is compared with Holmes's legal philosophy.

In the first book of Plato's *Republic,* Socrates discusses the meaning of "justice" with a sophist, Thrasymachus. Described by Plato as a "wild beast" who was prepared to "tear" the audience "to pieces," Thrasymachus first argues that the "just is nothing else than the advantage of the stronger" (Plato *Republic* 336c, 338c). The phrase "nothing else" in this definition points to the rejection of some notion of justice that extends beyond the human capacity to craft conceptions of good or bad. When pressed for further elucidation by Socrates, Thrasymachus argues that in each city it is the ruling body that is the stronger or superior. Whether this be a tyrant, a democracy, or an aristocracy, in each case it makes the laws in its own interest, so that in all cities one and the same thing is just: the interest of the ruling body (338d–339a).[19] This leads to the position that justice is obeying the laws. In the light of these arguments, Thrasymachus clearly anticipates Holmes's position.[20] To claim that justice rests with strength and the actions, rules, and regulations of the institutions that enforce the laws is precisely the argument that Holmes made as a judge.[21] The rest of *Republic* is devoted to dismissing Thrasymachus's claim and building a systematic and transcendent notion of justice founded on a belief in the balanced soul of the individual and the well-ordered state. The kind of definition of "justice" that Plato crafts is precisely the kind that Holmes despised. For someone who experienced the Civil War firsthand, a well-ordered soul and a well-ordered state were dangerous fictions that could only lead to violence.

More important, Thrasymachus's position is clearly connected to the actual function of the courts in Athens. The early development of legal rhetoric was tied to the structural changes of the Athenian courts that coincided with the shift from an aristocratic form of government to a democratic one.[22] During the fifth century B.C.E. legal proceedings were handed over to juries. Each year panels of 201 jurors were chosen from a designated pool and assigned to particular, private cases, while panels of 501 jurors were chosen for public trials. In such circumstances litigants, representing themselves, each had one chance to present a case in the form of a speech and one chance for rebuttal. Both sides were given equal time, and after both spoke, the jury would vote by secret ballot. A decision was reached by a simple majority, and the jury's verdict was final. These structural changes created the need for training in the composition and delivery of speeches to persuade a jury. This need was an extension of the need for a rhetorical education in political affairs.

From the sophists' perspective, "the court was an arena of symbolic competition" (Poulakos and Poulakos 1999, 9). This meant that the adjudication of legal disputes was a struggle between competing perspectives with victory determined by the person who presented the most compelling and well-reasoned arguments. Those capable of persuading the jury to see one point of view as opposed to another were also capable of crafting notions of guilt or innocence. Given such a perspective, the origins of Thrasymachus's position are clearer. Strength was a function of persuasive skill, and laws were crafted, enforced, and upheld through the power of persuasion located in the capacity of language to influence others. Victory in court, the outcome of a trial, determined the nature of justice. As such, verdicts of guilt or innocence were not predetermined truths but relative and situational determinations that depended on the speaker-jury interaction. This competitive dimension of the sophistic approach was supplemented by a belief in the ameliorative potential of competition. Protagoras's notion of *dissoi logoi* sets the stage for competition between opposing claims, but it also insures that good decision making happens through reasoned discourse when opposing sides are put into relationship with one another (see Schiappa 2003b, 89–116). Thrasymachus's position on justice is supported by this belief that competition makes law and politics better, and that improvements are achieved by virtue of conflicts between opposing sides. The commitment to competition and its ameliorative effects draws Holmes's work close to the sophistic conception of forensic rhetoric.

Unlike Holmes, however, the sophists conceived of the law from the perspective of those arguing the case. This led to a considerable attention to the creative use of language as the primary means of determining victory and producing reasoned discourse. Holmes, however, saw competition from the perspective of the judge or jury, those charged with deciding on the guilt or innocence of a particular person. In addition, the legal system in which Holmes was implicated was vastly different from the Athenian system. In both formal procedures and the existing body of texts that determined legal theory and practice, Holmes's experience was far removed from that of the sophists. However, the underlying assumptions behind the sophistic perspective on legal affairs and Holmes's are remarkably similar. Rhetorical practice, for the sophists, issued from the central place of competition and power in the courts, combined with the rejection of transcendent notions of justice and the belief that competition can improve the life of the polis. I argue that Holmes understands the work of the judge or jury as a rhetorical practice that issues from those same sophistic commitments, and that this is the defining characteristic of his legal pragmatism. In other words, his system of adjudication is premised on the assumption that the practice of rhetoric is a necessary component of managing competing claims in legal affairs and insuring that good decisions are made. Holmes crafts the means by which to judge rhetorical performance so as to predict the best outcome for the community and to keep the competition going.

Considering Holmes's focus on the judge's role in adjudication, his prescriptions for the practice of legal decision making are not aligned with the sophists' suggestions for improving one's public-speaking skills as a means to victory. Holmes observed the competition and tried to regulate the game so that all sides had a fair chance to win. This does not mean that Holmes's practices were not rhetorical practices. Instead, his contribution to the study of forensic rhetoric is unique because he examines the standards by which judges make decisions instead of the argumentative skills of those trying to persuade a judge or jury. For example, Holmes invented the "reasonable man" standard for use in liability cases: "The question of what a prudent man would do under given circumstances is . . . equivalent to the question of what are the teachings of experience as to the dangerous character of this or that conduct under these or those circumstances" (*MFJH* 1881, 70). Holmes wrote that the law does not hold a person liable unless "he might and ought to have foreseen the danger, or, in other words, unless a man of ordinary intelligence and forethought would have been to blame for acting as he did" (68). He repeatedly described his standard for foresight-based liability as identifying conduct that would be "blameworthy in the average man" or the "prudent man" (70).

The "average man," the "prudent man," and the "reasonable man" are all, of course, fictions. Holmes devised them as an external test for legal claims. As a test, these fictions are products of the historical moment, social circumstances, and cultural assumptions guiding the senses of average, reasonable, and prudent. In this way Holmes's standard is comparable to the concept of the "universal audience" articulated by Perelman and Olbrechts-Tyteca.[23] It is not an actual fact but an imagined and invented test for persuasive claims. Instead of predicting the persuasive capacity of arguments using the universal audience as a standard, however, Holmes attempts to predict the foresight of the average, prudent person. In the case of both, the universal audience and the reasonable man, one evaluates claims by comparing them to an artificially constructed standard. Theoretically, if one could convince a universal audience of a specific proposition, then one could convince any other particular, real audience. On a parallel view, if one could determine that a reasonable man could foresee the consequences of some action, then any person who acts in that way is liable for those consequences. Such concepts are aspects of rhetorical theory. No judge is in possession of a science by which to determine precisely what a reasonable man would do; nor can a philosopher determine the irrefutable features of the universal audience. These two concepts are simply theoretical means of prediction.

The "reasonable man" standard, therefore, can be understood as an aspect of Holmes's rhetorical theory. By clearly crafting a standard that is fictional and open to negotiation, he invented a flexible principle of adjudication subject to various interpretations. In Holmes's opinion, that is precisely how the law actually does operate. Without recourse to absolute logic or justice, Holmes had to invent rhetorical devices for judging cases—devices that could be used for a variety of purposes, as was the case with any proposed legal standards. Instead of focusing on the persuasive power of the litigants, however, Holmes focused on the community and the social standards of reasonableness. Community standards are implicated in the process of adjudication because they can predict the necessary conditions for keeping the competition alive and improving the overall welfare of the state. This is a rhetorical act founded on a sophistic view of legal affairs combined with a muscular version of pragmatism.

Experience, Power, and Free Speech

The "reasonable man" standard points to the importance of experience in crafting rhetorical devices for adjudication. Experience teaches the prudent person to foresee the impact of her actions and choices. According to *The Common Law,* experience was the central concern of Holmes's jurisprudence: "The life of the law has not been logic; it has been experience" (*MFJH,* 51). Such a statement was meant to reject any notion of a science of law founded on irrefutable general principles deduced logically. Experience, in Holmes's view, cannot be reduced to general propositions, even though those general propositions may be relevant: "All the pleasure in life is in general ideas. But all the use of life is in specific solutions—which cannot be reached through generalities any more than a picture can be painted by knowing some rules of method. They are reached by insight, tact, and specific knowledge."[24]

Holmes used this same idea in his dissent in *Lochner v. New York* (1905) by arguing that "general propositions do not decide concrete cases" (*MFJH,* 149). Logical reasoning from a priori truths is not the way people make practical choices. Accordingly, Holmes thought that learning the abstract legal doctrines on which judicial decisions are expressly based was poor training for a lawyer. Judges do account for these doctrines when they are explaining their decisions, but the doctrines are not sufficient to account for the decisions reached. Anything that might operate as a motive for a judge's decision—a moral conviction or a political preference—might be legally relevant if it helps the lawyers guess the correct result. Experience is the only way of managing in such circumstances.

Holmes's conception of experience is collective and social, not individual or psychological. The "reasonable man" standard is a clear indication of how experience can be thought of in terms of a collective or aggregate. This is a conventional approach to the law: "The substance of the law at any given time pretty nearly corresponds, so far as it goes, with what is then understood to be convenient."[25] In this case "convenient" is meant to highlight the social or conventional norms of a culture embodied in the collective experiences of the individuals who participate in that culture.

In the process of adjudication, how does one judge whether behavior counts as reckless or careless or accidental? One way to proceed would be to devise a series of general rules for conduct the violation of which would constitute negligence, but Holmes discounts this option because of his disdain for the utility of general rules. His alternative proposal was that judges should do what anyone does when presented with a difficult decision: evaluate the conduct at issue by the lessons of experience. "Experience," as he argues in *The Common Law,* "is the test by which it is decided whether the degree of danger attending given conduct under certain known circumstances is sufficient to throw risk upon the party pursuing it" (*MFJH,* 65).[26] To whose experience is he referring? Again, it is the experience of the fictional average person, or a jury. Reasonableness consists in the knowledge of the greater or lesser probability of an injury being caused by a specific action: "Even in the domain of knowledge, the law applies its principle of averages."[27]

This emphasis on common experience and reasonableness was tempered by Holmes's devotion to the passion and power of individual commitments derived from full participation in life. Again recalling his experience in the Civil War, he claimed that we "are born to act" and that the "stern experience of . . . youth" left the "feeling" that "through life" the "root of joy" is "to put all one's powers toward some great end" (*MFJH* 1913, 27). In pursuing such ends, however, one must realize that every person believes fervently in a variety of different ends as those most worth pursuing. It is not a question of pursuing the "right" end or of deducing the best possible end. Rejecting such certitudes, Holmes argued, "Life is painting a picture, not doing a sum," and that the results are that "twenty men of genius looking out of the same window" paint "twenty canvases, each unlike all the others" (26). We derive our own ends and paint our own pictures, but the one thing that ties us all together is our fervent pursuit of those ends: "Nothing could be more enchanting than to see a man nearly killing himself for an end which derives its worth simply from his having affirmed it."[28]

Holmes called this kind of commitment "nonsensical and sublime."[29] His frequent glorification of the death of soldiers committed to causes they did not understand bespoke the same perspective. He wrote of the "divine folly of honor which has no value but what [one's] own heart gives it" and of "man's most peculiar power—the power to deny the actual and to perish."[30] In an address in 1900 Holmes observed that "from the point of view of the world the end of life is life. Life is action, the use of one's powers. And to use them to their height is our joy and our duty, so it is the one end that justifies itself" (*MFJH,* 42). Such an attention to individual power was built on his Darwinian notion that life is a competition or a game. When Yale University awarded Holmes an honorary degree in 1886, he responded, "I never heard anyone profess indifference to a boat race. Why should you row a boat race? Why endure long months of pain in preparation for a fierce half-hour that will leave you all but dead? Does anyone ask the question? . . . Is life less than a boat race?" (*MFJH* 1913, 33).

Perhaps the greatest paradox of Holmes's thought was this: although he described judging in terms of "weighing considerations of social advantage," he valued personal action mostly for its expressive and blind commitment, not its instrumental or functional qualities (*MFJH* 1897, 81). For Holmes, blind commitment alone gave meaning to life, and it did not matter whether this commitment found expression in art, a legal career, a boat race, or death on a battlefield. Why, then, would Holmes be so concerned with what the "reasonable man" might think when blind faith and action gave life its meaning?

The ability to affirm a gamelike end and to make it one's own could make life worthwhile, but apart from the power to feel one's existence fully, life for Holmes was apparently a void: "my bet is that we have not the kind of cosmic importance that the parsons and philosophers teach. I doubt if a shudder would go through the spheres if the whole ant heap were kerosened" (*EH,* xxv–xxvi). As he once put it, "I wonder if cosmically an idea is any more important than the bowels."[31] Despite such a commitment to a deeply meaningless world, every person does have values. Even Holmes, despite these laments, had deep and passionate commitments. He called these values his "can't helps," and they were the grounds for his epistemology: "As I have probably said many times before, all I mean by truth is what I can't help believing—I don't know why I should assume except for practical purposes of conduct that [my] can't help has more cosmic worth than any other—I can't help preferring port to ditch-water, but I see no ground for supposing that the cosmos shares my weakness . . . [I] demand of my philosophy simply to show that I am not a fool for putting my heart into my job."[32] Knowledge, according to this perspective, is a matter of personal preferences or tastes—"our tastes are finalities."[33]

For an explanation of his commitment to both the power of the individual and the "reasonable man" standard of adjudication, it is instructive to consider Holmes's personal tastes in contrast to his judicial opinions. For example, his "can't helps" did not include a belief in natural justice or innate human rights. "I take no stock in abstract rights," he said, and "equally fail to respect the passion for equality."[34] Instead, "the passion for equality . . . seems to me merely idealizing envy." As he told Harold Laski, "You respect the rights of man—I don't, except those things a given crowd will fight for." On another occasion he observed, "All my life I have sneered at the natural rights of man." Not even the self-evident truths of the Declaration of Independence were among Holmes's "can't helps."

This fact, however, had little influence on his judicial opinions. In 1929 Holmes dissented from the Supreme Court's ruling that Rosika Schwimmer, a well-known pacifist, could not be a citizen of the United States. Schwimmer had refused to swear that she would bear arms in case of war. As Holmes put it, Schwimmer "wouldn't do what the law wouldn't let her do" (*EH,* 113).

A federal statute demanded a pledge to support and defend the Constitution against all enemies, foreign and domestic, and the Court's majority read this statute to preclude Schwimmer's naturalization. Holmes's dissent spoke eloquently of "freedom for the thought that we hate" (*MFJH,* 328). Then, commenting on Schwimmer's pacifism in a letter, Holmes revealed how much he did hate the thought: "What damned fools people are who believe things. . . . All 'isms seem to me silly—but this hyperaethereal respect for human life seems perhaps the silliest of all" (*EH,* 113).

The Schwimmer case reveals Holmes's commitment to allowing what he called in 1919 "free trade in ideas" (*MFJH,* 312). *Abrams v. U.S.* is perhaps the best-known case under the Espionage Act that attempted to outlaw speech against U.S. involvement in World War I. Jacob Abrams and several other Russian immigrants threw leaflets urging curtailment of war production from the roof of a loft in the garment district in New York City. Abrams was tried under the Espionage Act, convicted, and sentenced to twenty years in prison for the "intent" to "cripple or hinder the United States in the prosecution of war" (*MFJH* 1919, 305). In legal terms, the case turned on the meaning of "intent." By majority opinion the Court upheld the conviction, with Holmes and Louis Brandeis dissenting.

At the heart of his opinion, Holmes's commitment to power, experience, the "reasonable man," competition, and ultimately the significance and necessity of rhetoric are all immediately apparent:

> When men have realized that time has upset so many fighting faiths, they may come to believe even more than they believe the very foundations of their own conduct that the ultimate good desired is better reached by free trade in ideas—that the best test of truth is the power of the thought to get itself accepted in the competition of the market, and that truth is the only ground upon which their wishes safely can be carried out. That, at any rate, is the theory of our Constitution. It is an experiment, as all life is an experiment. Every year if not every day we have to wager our salvation upon some prophecy based upon imperfect knowledge. While that experiment is part of our system I think that we should be eternally vigilant against attempts to check the expression of opinions that we loathe and believe to be fraught with death, unless they so imminently threaten immediate interference with the lawful and pressing purposes of the law that an immediate check is required to save the country. (*MFJH* 1919, 312)

The most striking implication of this argument is that "the theory of our Constitution" is grounded in a specific epistemology. According to that epistemology, the test of truth is not whether a proposition reflects or mirrors reality, but whether a proposition is persuasive, whether the majority accepts it in the course of an open competition with other propositions. On another occasion Holmes argued that we "talk about truth and yet another man will say that he can see nothing in reasoning that seems to you conclusive. Truth is the unanimous consent of mankind to a system of propositions" (*EH* 1920, 115). In light of this fact one of Holmes's "can't helps," it seems, is that we cannot help but acknowledge that our system of government was established to allow for competing rhetorical acts. Moreover, he had a blind faith that open competition between rhetorical claims would generate the best possible outcome in the long run.

Also in the light of these "can't helps," the First Amendment becomes the most difficult and essential aspect of the Constitution. From Holmes's perspective, the First Amendment is not an inalienable human right but a command to protect the ongoing practice of rhetoric for the long-term benefit of the community. We must allow all speech to be heard because without such allowance we miss the possibility of testing our truth claims and being persuaded by new ones. Without such possibilities, the experiment of life cannot be run. The only danger lies in certain claims leading directly to violence or to the end of the experiment. That is why Holmes reserves the right for the government to "check" free speech if such speech presents a "clear and present danger" (*MFJH* 1919, 292–97).

The notion of "clear and present danger" is comparable to that of the "reasonable man" standard in that it is meant to craft an external test, open to negotiation and revision, subject to circumstance and context, by which to judge whether one's speech has jeopardized the experiment. In *Schenck v. U.S.* (1919) the defendants were Socialist Party officials who distributed leaflets to men who had been drafted to serve in World War I. These officials were also convicted under the Espionage Act for urging soldiers to refuse to serve. In this case Holmes wrote the opinion for the majority, upholding the conviction on the following grounds: "We admit that in many places and in ordinary times the defendants in saying all that was said in the circular would have been within their constitutional rights. But the character of every act depends on the circumstances in which it is done. . . . The most stringent protection of free speech would not protect a man in falsely shouting fire in a theater and causing panic. It does not even protect a man from an injunction against uttering words that may have all the effect of force. . . . The question in every case is whether the words used are used in such circumstances and are of such a nature as to create a clear and present danger that they will bring about the substantive evils that the Congress has a right to prevent" (*MFJH* 1919, 296–97). In the light of his experience in the Civil War, Holmes was committed equally to the competition between claims to truth as he was to the well-being of the larger community. It was the government that made possible the competition between ideas in the free market, and any idea that actually places that government in danger risks destroying the community that is open to testing a claim's validity. Therefore, if a speech incites violence and ultimately attempts to destroy the free trade in ideas, there is no way to test its truthfulness. Given specific circumstances, such speech should be outlawed.

The "clear and present danger" standard was further tested in *Gitlow v. N.Y.* (1925). Benjamin Gitlow was arrested and convicted under the Criminal Anarchy Act of 1902 for writing a Socialist pamphlet called "The Left Wing Manifesto." As a leader of the Socialist Party, Gitlow advanced a typical statement in favor of a proletarian revolution and the Communist reconstruction of society. However, in the light of a sweeping wave of antiradicalism, the state of New York tried to outlaw any provocation toward anarchy. The Supreme Court affirmed the conviction, with Holmes and Brandeis dissenting. The majority opinion used Holmes's "clear and present danger" test to convict Gitlow, but Holmes objected: "It is said that this manifesto is more than a theory, that it was an incitement. Every idea is an incitement. It offers itself for belief and if believed it is acted on unless some other belief outweighs it or some failure of energy stifles the movement at its birth. The only difference between the expression of an opinion and an incitement in the narrower sense is the speaker's enthusiasm for the result. Eloquence may set fire to reason. But whatever may be thought of the redundant discourse before us it had no chance of starting a present conflagration. If in the long run the beliefs expressed in proletarian dictatorship are destined to be accepted by the dominant forces of the community, the only meaning of free speech is that they should be given their chance and have their way" (*MFJH* 1925, 324–25). In this case Holmes did not think that Gitlow's ideas were particularly persuasive, and if they were they would have gained enough assent to establish the goals they sought. This is a striking endorsement of the power of eloquence. There could be no direct, harmful result of Gitlow's words other than their acceptance, for which they should have the chance to fight.

Freedom of speech and the power of the individual eventually conflict with the "reasonable man" standard and the "clear and present danger" test. Holmes reconciles such conflicts on a case-by-case basis and by using his experience to imagine the consequences of some act, not by reference to general propositions, logic, or case history. If the consequences of an act threaten "the experiment" that offers the only grounds to test truth, then that act must be restricted. Otherwise the courts are designed to make sure that every person has a chance to express her preferences and try to get them accepted by the majority. American democracy is built on the practice of rhetoric, the continued competition between different preferences, and a system that attempts to manage that competition without recourse to violence. The "reasonable man" and "clear and present danger" standards are rhetorical devices for predicting the consequences of specific actions, not scientific laws. They are designed to keep "the experiment" open to as many voices as possible.

The First Amendment is not only a question of individual freedom of speech; it also concerns the systems of communication for the dissemination of speech. In *Milwaukee Social Democratic Publishing Co. v. Burleson* (1921), Victor Berger, a militant Socialist and antiwar leader, was prohibited from using the mail to distribute his paper the "Milwaukee Leader." Invoking the Espionage Act, the postmaster banned the distribution of the paper because of its subversive content. The Supreme Court upheld the ban, with Holmes and Brandeis again dissenting. Holmes argued that the "United States may give up the Post Office when it sees fit," but while the U.S. Postal Service does operate, "the use of the mails is almost as much a part of free speech as the right to use our tongues." If that is the case, the postmaster has little say in deciding who gets to speak: "it would take very strong language to convince me that Congress ever intended to give such a practically despotic power to any one man" (*MFJH* 1921, 317). The mechanisms for the dissemination of speech are just as valuable and significant as is the act of speech. The larger implication of this opinion is that the free trade in ideas requires the use of a variety of forms of communication to ensure that each competitor is heard. Only under those conditions will the fittest ideas survive.

Holmes's decisions clearly demonstrate that rhetorical processes are necessary and essential aspects of American democracy, and that the courts are designed to insure the possibility of open debate and competition among competing claims. His legal philosophy is designed to keep rhetoric, as a form of public argument, open debate, and free expression alive without sacrificing the system that makes such things possible. In other words, Holmes's First Amendment decisions are a defense of rhetoric, equally cautious of both the danger and the promise of persuasion and eloquence.

What Holmes shares with the classical tradition is the sophistic belief in competition, power, and pluralism and the perspective that the courts are a mechanism for deciding on winners and losers and crafting notions of justice. What Holmes also shares with the classical tradition, perhaps more than any other pragmatist, is his own self-conscious practice of the art of rhetoric. In his case, his opinions are conditioned by the intellectual commitments of his pragmatism. Thus they are a rhetorical defense of the art of rhetoric. To take Thomas B. Farrell's definition, "rhetoric is the collaborative art of addressing and guiding decision and judgment—usually public judgment about matters that cannot be decided by force or expertise" (Farrell 1993, 1). This is an accurate description of Holmes's work on the bench. Through his opinions we see the residue of collaborative debate, the articulation of standards compatible with public judgment, and the eloquent defense of the "free trade in ideas." Through Holmes's legal rhetoric we have both an argument for the commitment to the necessity of rhetoric for human affairs and an example of how one can best practice legal rhetoric from which further theoretical reflection is possible.

Eloquence and Context in Judicial Opinions

Richard Posner argues that Holmes was "one of our greatest writers" and that "some of Holmes's best opinions, notably the *Lochner* dissent, possibly the most famous and influential of all his opinions, owe their distinction to their rhetorical skill"; in other words, "Holmes was a great judge *because* he was a great literary artist" (*EH,* xvii). Posner evaluates rhetorical skill from an "aesthetic perspective" and as "an instrument" with the capacity for the "persuasion, edification, mystification, entertainment, or whatnot, of its audience" (xviii). Assuming that Posner's description of Holmes as a literary artist is accurate, it is important to unpack the general features of his style of judicial decision making in the light of his theoretical commitment to the necessity of rhetoric.

Michael Oakeshott (1975) argues that conversation is the business of living, referring to the "conversation of mankind" (238). Conversation is not fated for any particular goal and is not guided by anything other than the impulses of those conversing. More to the point, he asserts the following: "A Morality, is neither a system of general principles nor a code of rules, but a vernacular language. General principles and even rules may be elicited from it, but (like other languages) it is not the creation of grammarians; it is made by speakers" (241). To be a judge is to be a converser, a participant in the vernaculars of both the larger community and the community of legal professionals. Just as in conversations among two people or a small group of people, these communal conversations meander, changing the conversers along the way. A person is, according to Oakeshott, a "character distinguished on account of limitless powers of self-transformation without self-destruction" (78–79). Holmes was committed to giving people the chance to remake themselves and to giving the larger community many chances to remake itself. We do not, however, remake ourselves through theories or general propositions but through conversations that require the creative use of language. It is the rhetorical give-and-take, the interaction between people of differing opinions, that shapes our vision of how we wish to be and in what sort of world we want to live. Holmes acted so as to make sure that the larger, public conversation was not closed off.

Oakeshott's account of conversation does not address the power of eloquence in the course of the "conversation of mankind." However, in Holmes's case his opinions are characterized by his eloquence.[35] Those opinions have contributed to larger conversations, and the fact that many of his dissents became the grounds for future decisions is evidence of their eloquence and persuasive power. Legal reasoning and judicial opinions are, in an obvious way, rhetorical acts that use various argumentative strategies. Holmes, however, consistently criticized "the fallacy . . . of logical form" and the view that law "can be worked out like mathematics from some general axioms of conduct" (*MFJH* 1897, 80). Thus, he states that "the logical method and form flatter that longing for certainty and for repose which is in every human mind. But certainty generally is illusion, and repose is not the destiny of man. Behind the logical form lies a judgment as to the relative worth and importance of competing legislative grounds, often an inarticulate and unconscious judgment, it is true, and yet the very root and nerve of the whole proceeding." Holmes's eloquence derived from his ability to get at this "inarticulate and unconscious judgment" so as to make the central questions of a case perspicuous. The kind of reasoning Holmes refers to could be described as what Aristotle called the "enthymeme" (*Rhetoric* 1355a–1356b).

The term "enthymeme" literally means "held in the mind," and enthymemes have at least one claim that the members of a community believe or hold in common. So clear is the agreement on a shared claim that it might not even be stated explicitly in an argument. In other words, the persuasive power of an enthymeme derives from its ability to play on the commonly held assumptions of an audience. In leaving those assumptions implicit, an enthymeme is a form of argument based on the "inarticulate and unconscious judgment" of an audience. In contrast, the syllogism, although it is similar in structure to the enthymeme, explicitly states its major premises and tries to derive truths about which we can be certain. The enthymeme, however, acknowledges that our "unconscious judgments" may change over time and are subject to circumstance, context, and the possibility of rearticulation. By associating logic with a "longing for certainty and for repose," Holmes rejected formal reasoning in favor of rhetorical reasoning. In both "The Path of the Law" and *The Common Law* he insists that "experience" is more important to jurisprudence than "logic" is. It is "experience" that points to the common assumptions of an audience and allows one to investigate the "unconscious judgments" on which legal reasoning rests.

This form of reasoning, and the style of writing that issues from it, is best illustrated by Holmes's dissent in *Lochner v. New York* (1905). A report by the New York Bureau of Statistics of Labor found that the baking industry exposed workers to health risks due to long hours and unsafe conditions.[36] In response to these findings, New York passed a statute designed to improve conditions and limit the number of hours bakers could work to ten a day or sixty a week. The owner of a bakery in Utica, New York, was convicted of a misdemeanor under the statute for allowing one of his employees to work more than sixty hours in one week. He claimed that the statute was unconstitutional because it interfered with the Fourteenth Amendment's "liberty of contract" clause. The court invalidated the statute, finding in favor of the owner of the bakery, with Holmes dissenting.

Holmes's dissent, which is merely two paragraphs long, does not waste any time with formal haggling over legal terms. The opening sentence states: "This case is decided upon an economic theory which a large part of the country does not entertain" (*MFJH* 1905, 148). In other words, the justices who struck down the law were arguing from an implied assumption that "the reasonable man" did not share. Even if Holmes "agreed with that theory" his agreement should "have nothing to do with the right of a majority to embody their opinions in the law." Moreover, "a constitution is not intended to embody a particular economic theory, whether of paternalism and the organic relation of the citizen to the state or of laissez faire. It is made for people of fundamentally differing views, and the accident of our finding certain opinions natural and familiar or novel and even shocking ought not to conclude our judgment upon the question whether statutes embodying them conflict with the Constitution of the United States" (149). Holmes was striking out at the idea that a judge's underlying assumptions often are the grounds for the decisions reached.[37] The test for these assumptions should be what a "reasonable man might think." A judge must be restrained from using those assumptions to argue particular cases.

In the opinion's most pithy statement, Holmes claimed that the "Fourteenth Amendment does not enact Mr. Herbert Spencer's *Social Statics*" (149). *Social Statics,* published in 1851, was Spencer's attempt to derive the classic doctrine of laissez-faire from the social laws that statistics was supposed to have revealed. Spencer's point was that there was something "natural" about laissez-faire economics. Holmes's point was that it was just an economic theory with no greater claim to authority than any other. Holmes's statement is also an example of a synecdoche—understanding a belief in the "natural" authority of laissez-faire in terms of one particular book. This synecdoche reveals the underlying assumption behind the opposing enthymeme, and by disputing that principal assumption Holmes is able to refute the entire argument with great clarity, precision, and force. Eventually the original decision was overruled and Holmes's dissent triumphed—changing economic theories made any assumption about laissez-faire economics suspect.

The *Lochner* opinion demonstrates three significant aspects of Holmes's style of argument and expression. First, his ability to display the underlying assumptions behind a case in a clear and concise manner is illustrated by his reference to Herbert Spencer. In many of his opinions he is able to show that legal reasoning is founded not on logic but on enthymematic arguments derived from experience, and that the persuasive effect of those enthymemes is grounded on the underlying assumptions they employ. Second, the general assumptions behind legal reasoning, whether implied or explicitly stated, do not decide specific cases. In *Lochner* he argued, "General propositions do not decide concrete cases. The decision will depend on a judgment or intuition more subtle than any articulate major premise" (*MFJH,* 149). The specific context and circumstances of a particular case are more relevant than any general rules, and his "clear and present danger" and "reasonable man" tests are both designed for interpretation within differing contexts. Third, Holmes believed in judicial tolerance or restraint. By tolerance, I mean his willingness to give the state legislatures the benefit of the doubt, and to assume the validity of their laws except when they were clearly (to the "reasonable man") in violation of the Constitution. By restraint, I mean his belief that judges should cultivate a form of detachment so that the judge's own opinions about social policy played no role in decision making.

Many of his opinions are written in an aphoristic style instead of in long, technical arguments that interpret the case at hand in the light of historical precedent and legal vocabulary. That is, his opinions tend to be short, instructive, and designed to have an impact on a wide range of audiences. Metaphors such as "the free trade in ideas" are meant to capture the underlying assumptions of a case by association with other concepts. Because law is nothing more than what judges are willing to do, the expression of law determines judicial action, and thus Holmes displays a sensitivity to language that reveals his awareness of the ongoing examination and interpretation of his words. James Boyd White sees a deep enough affinity between judicial opinion and poetry as to argue that our ways of reading both are similar. He claims that "law can best be understood as a set of literary practices that at once create new possibilities for meaning and action in life and constitute human communities in distinctive ways" (J. White 1985, 107). This implies that it is not the main idea expressed by a judicial opinion but "the reader's experience of the life of the text" that is more important (117). In other words, both poetry and judicial opinions are "open to the possibility of shifts in language and perception; more than that, each seeks to achieve such shifts" (119). Holmes's writings are a clear warrant for the comparison of poetry and law that White makes.

In their desire and ability to have an effect on future audiences, Holmes's opinions are also an example of rhetoric in action. As a part of larger debates and as a participant in questions of public judgment, Holmes was able to practice rhetoric in a way that many of the other pragmatists were not. His method of decision making was consciously bound by the context and circumstances presented by the case at hand, and his style of writing displayed an eloquence able to articulate with great clarity and simplicity the underlying assumptions of that case. Through his rejection of general principles and abstract thought, his pragmatic method of adjudication exemplifies and brings attention to the uses of rhetoric in the courts.

Pragmatism, Law, and the Practice of Rhetoric

Holmes's pragmatism places rhetoric at the center of legal affairs, as it once was in Athens, and he invents a specific philosophy and method of adjudication that highlights and channels rhetorical processes. James Boyd White, in *Heracles' Bow,* makes a more thorough connection between rhetoric and law, and in so doing develops much of what is implied in Holmes's thought. According to White, law "is most usefully seen as a branch of rhetoric," and by rhetoric he means "the central art by which culture and community are established, maintained, and transformed" (1985, 28). From this perspective, law is "something we do and something we teach," or "an activity" (33). In this way White reiterates Holmes's claim that law is nothing more than "what the courts will do" (*MFJH* 1897, 75). More specifically, law, like rhetoric, "always starts in a particular place among particular people" and "always takes place with given materials" (J. White 1985, 39). Thus general rules and propositions are relevant only if they can be brought to bear on the particularities of the situation at hand. When Holmes rejects the kind of general propositions offered by logic, he accepts the notion that law is a rhetorical activity about which certainty can never be achieved.

Developing this point further, White argues that both the rhetorician and the judge are "engaged in a process of meaning-making and community-building" under the "condition of radical uncertainty" (1985, 40). Accordingly, knowledge and the other resources for decision making "will thus not be scientific or theoretical but practical, experiential, the sense that one knows how to do things with language and with others. . . . This knowledge is itself not reducible to rules, nor subject to expression in rules, . . . rather it is the knowledge by which we learn to manage, evade, disappoint, surprise, and please each other." The major effect of thinking in this way is that law becomes something made, and that those in the legal professions are engaged in answering the question What kind of culture shall we have and what kind of community shall we be? As with the other pragmatists, Holmes understands his activities as part of a general, practical art of making, an art grounded in experience. I claim that this practical art of making is another name for rhetoric and that in Holmes's case he is founding and practicing a particular forensic rhetoric.

By virtue of his judicial opinions, Holmes offers a clear answer to the question concerning the kind of culture and community he believed we should have. His First Amendment decisions are a theoretical defense of rhetoric in the light of both community standards and personal convictions. In other words, he believed in experimenting, experience, individual power and action, competition, and the welfare of the community; and he thought that the best test of truth was a proposition's ability to get itself accepted by the majority. A culture and a community that favor such beliefs must see rhetorical processes as necessary components of human affairs and must secure the possibility and freedom for people to engage in such rhetorical processes unencumbered. Moreover, rhetorical processes have both winners and losers, but in the long run Holmes claimed that the entire community would benefit from the open competition between competing rhetorical acts. The best way to judge such competitions is by majority opinion, and the only time to curtail the freedom of speech is in the face of an imminent threat to the very community that makes free speech possible. The "reasonable man" and the "clear and present danger" standards are meant as rhetorical devices to test and predict community reaction. Holmes's legal philosophy offers these concepts as distinct contributions to rhetorical theory and belongs to the larger pragmatist tradition that defends and attempts to reinforce the necessity of rhetoric.

In the light of his legal theory, Holmes had a distinctive method for judicial decision making, which demonstrates the kind of legal culture and community to which he wanted to belong. By exposing the underlying assumptions behind legal arguments, by practicing judicial restraint in the face of ideas that he hated, and by making judgments based on circumstances and not logic, he practiced a pragmatist judicial rhetoric. This judicial rhetoric was the grounds for his eloquent, clear, and forceful decisions, the language of which still contributes to debates within and without the legal community. This judicial rhetoric also illustrates Holmes's preference for a language that reaches beyond the expertise and formal reasoning of much legal work to a language based firmly in experience and accessible to those outside the legal community.[38] Because Holmes's style of decision making requires a contextual test, he invited juries, "the reasonable man," or the larger community to read their own prejudices into his opinions and standards. Holmes thought that people would do that no matter what, and that the dominant opinion would have its way in the long run. It is not that Holmes had a deep faith in the judgment of the average person; rather he thought that the system did work that way and that his role as a judge was not to interfere with that process but to facilitate it. This made his rhetoric distinctly democratic.

According to Menand, the "Constitutional law of free speech is the most important benefit to come out of the way of thinking that emerged in Cambridge and elsewhere in the decades after the Civil War. It makes the value of an idea not its correspondence to a preexisting reality or a metaphysical truth, but simply the difference it makes in the life of the group" (2001, 431). This emphasis on free speech can be read as a defense of rhetoric. Holmes's preference for "free trade in ideas" risks the same defects that other market theories risk—no marketplace is ever truly competitive as there are barriers to entry. Even if some ideas never make it to the public arena and never have a chance at being persuasive, Holmes's defense of rhetoric is probabilistic. The more ideas that have their day, the more likely we are to come up with the best ideas. In terms of Darwinian science, the more individual variations, the greater the chance for the group to survive and prosper. We do not defend the right to free speech and to rhetoric because some individual may have Truth. We permit the free expression of ideas and open competition between claims because we need the resources of the whole group to generate the best ideas. Thinking is a social activity that requires tolerance of opposing ideas, that generates winners who can quickly turn to losers (or the reverse), and that is best expressed in the language of experience. These are pragmatist principles, and when translated into legal affairs they are the grounds for a defense of rhetoric.

Five

Alain Locke and Epideictic Rhetoric

The Promise of Cultural Pluralism and the Celebration of *The New Negro*

On March 21, 1924, Alain Locke presided over a party at New York City's Civic Club on East Thirty-fourth Street. As one of the few downtown establishments that admitted both blacks and whites to its dining room, the Civic Club was able to accommodate an eclectic gathering of prominent publishers, magazine editors, distinguished white writers, and many promising young black artists. On this occasion Locke served as master of ceremonies for the celebration of the publication of Jessie Fauset's first novel, *There Is Confusion.* The event was a key moment in launching the New Negro Movement, and Locke was literally and symbolically at the center of the celebration. As a result of this dinner, the literary magazine *Survey Graphic,* which had previously ignored black writers, devoted a full issue to "contemporary Negro life" with Locke as guest editor. In fulfilling both of these functions, Locke sought the means to celebrate the value and promise of New Negro art in a society decidedly hostile to such attempts. These acts of celebration were intended to announce the transformation of the role of African Americans in American culture.[1] Based on the success of the *Survey Graphic* issue, Locke edited *The New Negro,* published in December 1925, a central text in what became known as the Harlem Renaissance and the central statement of the transformation he had hinted at as master of ceremonies and in *Survey Graphic.*[2]

Locke was a philosopher, trained at Harvard in the shadow of William James, whose works outlined the intellectual conditions for the transformation he celebrated in the pages of *The New Negro.*[3] For Locke philosophy was a form of cultural criticism that focused on power, empowerment, and democracy.[4]

Accordingly he offered a pragmatic account of race, aesthetics, and value theory that situated philosophy in the social realities of the moment and that delivered a radical critique of those social realities. In this way his philosophy was tied to the exigencies of life as an African American, and it sought the mechanisms available for using philosophical insight to alter those exigencies. In his role as master of ceremonies and editor, Locke extended his philosophical insight so as to have a critical impact on the problems of the moment. He brought together different artists, presented artwork to the public, and articulated the larger meaning and significance of a variety of artworks.[5]

An understanding of Locke's philosophy and his role in the New Negro Movement can result from seeing his work as an argument for the importance of epideictic rhetoric. In the rhetorical tradition, "epideictic discourse exemplifies rhetoric as a language of transformation—of old to new."[6] Locke sought such a language of transformation in his art criticism and his editorial work. Moreover, his pragmatism laid the foundation for a philosophy of epideictic rhetoric that seeks a useful language of celebration, transformation, and solidarity for American social life and political affairs. By celebrating the value of African American art, Locke crafted a pragmatism attentive to issues of group identity, race, cultural pluralism, value relativism, and aesthetics. I argue that a concern with such issues uses and extends notions of classical epideictic rhetoric. Most important, Locke's pragmatism makes epideictic rhetoric (as a form of celebration, transformation, and aesthetic performance) an important part of a culturally plural democracy.

According to Locke's philosophy, practicing a pragmatic, epideictic rhetoric requires a theory of values that can account for, and sustain, a form of cultural pluralism.[7] These two preoccupations, value theory and cultural pluralism, ignited key questions about the uses of values and the potential, or the danger, of group identities. These questions were at the center of theories of epideictic rhetoric. A diversity of values inevitably causes conflict between larger communities that adhere to different value systems. In such cases people often make the mistake of believing that their value imperatives are timeless and universal. Locke sought mechanisms to teach people to hold their values less dogmatically, to bring different value systems into productive dialogue, and to advance an understanding of the historically located experiences and culturally specific values of various people. The practice of an epideictic rhetoric capable of displaying a diversity of values and bringing competing value systems into conversation could potentially produce and uphold a form of cultural pluralism. Much of Locke's philosophy is devoted to explaining the vital necessity and benefit of a cultural pluralism made possible by such practices.[8]

In addition to his claims about value, Locke engaged in acts of celebration using race to reconceptualize and transform notions of African American identity. In an attempt to subvert the biological racism inherent in stereotypical characterizations of Negro life, he sought ways to recalibrate race as a useful topos in politics and social life. The art produced in Harlem at that time was one mechanism for reconstructing race, and the attendant acts of celebration were meant to influence other competing value systems.[9] Locke's notion of reciprocity highlights ways of bringing different value systems into productive contact without resorting to violence. Epideictic rhetoric, I argue, is the principal means of conceptualizing and practicing such exchanges. Locke demonstrates this through his belief in the promise and necessity of celebrating New Negro art as a political mechanism for changing conditions of oppression, and as an intellectual mechanism for exploring value theory and cultural pluralism.

Locke realizes many of the intellectual commitments of pragmatist thought, and he extends basic notions of pragmatism by engaging in epideictic rhetoric. His pragmatism is defined by a philosophy of value and a belief in cultural pluralism. Such a position underpins his search for an epideictic rhetoric. *The New Negro* and Locke's conception of race can be seen as particular examples of epideictic practice. These practices are meant to highlight the possibility and potential of reciprocity between cultures. The connections between Locke's focus on aesthetics and the maintenance of a culturally plural democracy point to the ongoing significance of epideictic rhetoric for American culture and the promise of extending pragmatism to meet the pressing concerns of our contemporary moment.

The use of epideictic rhetoric to interpret Locke's work can offer a new critical perspective on one of the most vital, and often overlooked, social theorists and art critics of the last century. Locke still provides a useful resource for those studying and practicing epideictic rhetoric, and his work offers important insights into present issues concerning race, aesthetics, and cultural pluralism. The pragmatic account of epideictic rhetoric that Locke points to can help alter the way we understand communication in culturally plural democracies with competing value systems. This account also suggests the important role that epideictic rhetoric can play in democratic affairs, a role often overlooked for more obvious political and legal issues. Because of his specific and grounded attention to rhetorical processes involving race and aesthetics, Locke is a distinct and formidable voice of American pragmatism. By suggesting that epideictic rhetoric is necessary for a healthy American democracy, Locke's pragmatism is defined by its search for a specific set of ideas and practices meant to create a cosmopolitan American culture in which reciprocity and exchange trump domination and oppression.

Locke as Pragmatist and Epideictic Rhetorician

At the beginning of "Values and Imperatives," Locke contends that "[a]ll philosophies . . . are in ultimate derivation philosophies of life and not of abstract, disembodied 'objective' reality; products of time, place and situation, and thus systems of timed history rather than timeless eternity" (*PAL* 1935, 34). The attempt to connect philosophy to life, and the concomitant rejection of the abstract, is a common theme in pragmatist thought. In addition, the connection between philosophy and life demonstrates the pragmatic belief that philosophy should respond to the problems of the moment. Locke brought philosophy to bear on issues of race and culture—engaging in the kind of timely activity often prescribed by pragmatism. These concerns (connecting philosophy and life and attending to the problems of the moment) were also part of Locke's meliorism, or his belief that the world could be made better through critical investigation, another basic intellectual commitment of pragmatist thought.

In Locke's case, William James was the primary inspiration for such pragmatist impulses. Ross Posnock argues that "Locke continued to find James's work a fruitful way to rethink the relation between color and culture" (1998, 184). This was due to Locke's belief that James had hinted at a "vital connection between pluralism and democracy" and that it was important for others to elaborate on this connection. In 1942 he summarized his commitment to James's legacy: "When William James inaugurated his all-out campaign against intellectual absolutism, though radical empiricism and pragmatism were his shield and buckler, his trusty right-arm sword, we should remember, was pluralism. . . . Today, in our present culture crisis, it is both timely to recall this, and important . . . to ponder over it" (*PAL,* 53). Much of Locke's philosophy is devoted to working through the implications of a pluralistic value theory.

In 1908 in Oxford, Locke attended James's Hibbert Lectures, which were later published as *A Pluralistic Universe.*[10] He interpreted these lectures as "an indictment of philosophical thought that is grounded in the logic of difference/identity. Such thinking not only breeds separatism but is destructive of democratic equality" (Posnock 1998, 192). In other words, conceptual thought, as James had treated it in his lectures, was a mechanism for excluding and segregating. To conceptualize is to fix one thing and exclude other possibilities not of the same kind. Concepts thus become ways of denying contingency to create order and hierarchy. Although James's position is a critique of philosophy from within the philosophical tradition, his position animated Locke's introductory essay for *The New Negro.* In that essay Locke argues that the practices of separatism underlying the American conception of the Negro are untenable. In fact, he claims that it is a "delusion" to believe that the "trend of Negro advance is wholly separatist, and that the effect of its operation will be to encyst the Negro as a benign foreign body in the body politic. This cannot be—even if it were desirable" (*NN,* 12). It is impossible to separate the fate or well-being of one group from that of others in American culture.

John Dewey published *Experience and Nature* in 1925, the same year that Locke published *The New Negro.* In this work Dewey carries James's pluralism further by arguing that philosophy should be "a critique of prejudices." In fact,

Dewey claims that prejudices are embedded in the "classificatory device[s]" used by the "genteel tradition" to elevate "unity" at the cost of relegating "unreconciled diversity," "the recalcitrant particular . . . the ambiguousness and ambivalence of reality," to a "metaphysically inferior" order of existence (1925, 41–42). Critiquing prejudices, recovering mixture, dissolving segregation, redeeming what is classified as inferior, Dewey's stance in 1925 amounts to a theoretical perspective on Locke's critical practices. *Experience and Nature* evokes Dewey's activism on behalf of democratic equality in philosophical terms, while Locke's *New Negro* contextualizes the same lines of thought in issues of aesthetics and race relations. In 1934 Dewey published *Art as Experience*. Although he does not acknowledge Locke's influence, this work addresses the impact of social conditions on art, privileges diversifying and mixing over unity in making art, and demands that art be understood in terms of its social functions, its ability to improve life and change social conditions.[11] Locke, in the 1920s and 1930s, had already explored these themes. It is clear that Dewey and Locke shared similar perspectives on pluralism and aesthetics, despite the absence of direct connections.

Locke self-consciously extended James's work and explored similar lines of thought to those of John Dewey, but he rarely occupies a central place in the history of pragmatism. As with Addams, the major intellectual histories of pragmatism ignore Locke altogether or place him in an ancillary or anecdotal position. Diggins, Thayer, and even Cornel West fail to mention Locke. Instead, Horace Kallen is credited with developing the idea of "cultural pluralism" and is identified as a more important disciple of William James.[12] Louis Menand addresses Locke's place in debates about pluralism and his connection to James, but he gives Locke an ancillary place in the development of pragmatist thought. As with Addams, this is an unfortunate oversight. Locke's version of pragmatism concerns issues of race and aesthetics, highlights the potential of pragmatist criticism to change social realities, and extends beyond politics to consider the social function of art in creating community.

Ross Posnock's *Color & Culture* describes the connections between James, W. E. B. Du Bois, and Locke as three separate generations of Harvard pragmatists.[13] By exploring the relationship between these three figures and the different shades of pragmatism developed by each, Posnock begins to develop Locke's appropriate place in the pragmatist tradition: "Although the standard intellectual histories tell us that the prodigious career of John Dewey defines pragmatism after William James, this neglects the great flowering of pragmatism in the careers of prominent twentieth-century black intellectuals, specifically Du Bois and Alain Locke" (1998, 6). By virtue of a belief in the promise of aesthetic freedom and the practice of art that can resist racial stereotypes, the struggle to assert the "freedom of art" while "laboring for race uplift" inspired a useful revision of the more famous pragmatists. According to Posnock, this remains Locke's enduring contribution to the pragmatist tradition.

In addition to Posnock's account, Nancy Fraser's essay in *The Critical Pragmatism of Alain Locke* defines the theoretical ground on which to consider Locke's pragmatism as a unique and significant strand in the larger tradition inspired by James and Dewey. By virtue of her interpretation of *Race Contacts and Interracial Relations,* Fraser argues that "Locke understood difference in the light of power, domination, and political economy. Thus, unlike the pragmatist mainstream, he grasped that a dominated group might need to forge a cultural identity as a weapon of struggle against oppression" (*CP,* 17). From this perspective, Locke's version of pragmatism is useful because it "highlights some of the limits of the mainstream tradition of classical pragmatist social thought: its neglect of power, its emphasis on culture at the expense of political economy, and its tendency to posit imaginary holistic 'solutions' to difficult, sometimes irreconcilable, problems" (18). The contributions of James and Dewey are best supplemented by more grounded and concrete approaches to social realities. According to Fraser, Locke suggests that "systematically dominated social groups have pragmatic political needs for solidarity that differ from the needs of others," and "in the case of African Americans, such domination continues to encompass both cultural misrecognition and political-economic maldistribution." Therefore, Locke deploys pragmatist thought as a strategy for correcting the political and social inequalities in race relations and confronting issues of power and empowerment.

Fraser's article begins to redress the shortcomings of pragmatist anthologies that omit Locke. Leonard Harris, the editor of *The Critical Pragmatism of Alain Locke,* states clearly that "Alain Locke was a pragmatist" (*CP,* xi). However, he also claims that the implications of Locke's thought cannot be reduced to the intellectual preoccupations of pragmatism more generally construed. "The critical temper of his works, the central role of power and empowerment of the oppressed, and the concept of broad democracy" were the distinguishing characteristics of Locke's pragmatism. Thus the search for "socially warranted change" and the belief in the possibility of "tolerance, reciprocity, and diversity" to inform "democratic sensibilities and values" conditioned Locke's attention to specific methods for reshaping American culture.

One way to understand Locke's search for methods to alter the social realities of racism is in light of the practice of epideictic rhetoric. Such an interpretation highlights his attention to value theory, pluralism, and race while tying those issues to a specific form of rhetorical practice. This interpretation also extends the work begun by Posnock, Fraser, and Harris. Understanding Locke's engagement in issues of aesthetics and race as a way of practicing rhetoric shows that pragmatism can work successfully in specific cases *and* can contribute key intellectual ideas to the rhetorical tradition. Locke, then, can help us extend the potential of epideictic rhetoric for larger social issues and extend pragmatism through his grounded engagement in rhetorical processes.

In the rhetorical tradition, Aristotle identifies epideictic discourse as one of the three divisions of oratory (*Rhetoric* 1358b). Also known as ceremonial rhetoric, epideictic rhetoric praises or blames people, objects, deeds, or ideals. More specifically, epideictic rhetoric appeals to communal values that are important for the present and thus engages in acts of display that "uncover what [lies] hidden" through the use of "excess and exaggeration" (Poulakos and Poulakos 1999, 63). Updating Aristotle's original claims for the importance of epideictic rhetoric, Perelman and Olbrechts-Tyteca argue that epideictic discourse plays a "central part in the art of persuasion" (1969, 49). They suggest that it addresses the "unquestioned values" of an audience and thus is practiced as a method of education aimed at displaying, amplifying, and enhancing the values that bind an audience together in the present (51).

Perelman and Olbrechts-Tyteca contribute to a larger contemporary understanding of epideictic rhetoric that outlines and develops its civic function. For example, Brian Vickers (1988) claims that epideictic rhetoric's focus on values makes possible the development of civic cohesion. Donovan Ochs (1993), in a similar fashion, argues that epideictic rhetoric is a form of symbolic action whereby social cohesion is produced and audiences are bound together by common values. This civic conception of epideictic discourse demonstrates the lasting effects that this kind of rhetoric can have on its audience. From such a perspective epideictic rhetoric can be understood as constitutive of self, identity, and community.[14]

In classical Greece, "the epideictic genre developed through its connection to a number of civic occasions and societal functions" (Poulakos and Poulakos 1999, 62). Funeral orations, religious festivals, and athletic events "provided an institutionalized mechanism that fostered the development" of the epideictic genre as an "art of display."[15] Such occasions served at least three significant functions. First, speaking competitions held during athletic events and festivals required orators to display their skills at improvisation, composition, delivery, and dexterity with language. In other words, epideictic occasions highlighted an orator's ability to use language in an artful, entertaining, and pleasing manner. Second, epideictic rhetoric was designed to uncover "what lay hidden," or bring "into the open what remained covered" (63). When serving this function, speeches of display revealed "deep-seated meanings and concealed truths," and the orator made apparent what had been hidden. Third, funeral orations or religious ceremonies were moments for pointing out forms of excellence, self-evident truths, and commonly held values. In serving this function, epideictic rhetoric employed excess and exaggeration to display the dominant values of a culture and to perpetuate the prevalent system of beliefs. These three functions helped Athenians determine, uphold, and guide a system of values that gave the culture a larger sense of meaning.

Recent scholarship has articulated the significance of the epideictic genre for Greek culture and has suggested the potential it holds for contemporary rhetorical theory. Gerard Hauser, for example, argues that it is the basis for a "vibrant public sphere" (1999a, 14). Hauser's position rests on an interpretation of Aristotle, who "assigned epideictic the important duty of teaching public morality." Aristotle requires the epideictic orator to tell "the story of lived virtue" so as to practice a form of "community instruction" (17). The purpose of this interpretation is to show that "examining epideictic provides insight into how a public sphere may serve as the crucible in which a people constitute and validate their tradition" (18). By "inculcating a common vocabulary of excellence," epideictic rhetoric served, and can serve, a valuable function in creating community, making sound public judgments, and crafting a notion of virtue.

Takis Poulakos develops a similar line of thought by attending to Isocrates' notion of epideictic rhetoric. He argues that epideictic discourse can "shape the social sphere" and disclose "the capacity that participants of a society have to become social agents by articulating their own versions of the social order" (T. Poulakos 1988, 148). More important, Poulakos attends to the possibility of disagreement between or among competing values. "Conceived as a site of critique" or "conflicting values," epideictic rhetoric "provides an occasion for inquiry into conflicts and struggles over the contestation of specific values in specific societies." In other words, "the opposition between actual and possible valuations" can potentially frame "the question of epideictic rhetoric's relation to society" and did frame that relation in classical Athens (161).

Both Hauser and Poulakos link the practice of epideictic rhetoric to social, cultural, and public well-being, and they see the process of persuasion implicated in epideictic discourse to be an important practice in the maintenance of community life. This implies the need for "democratically secure space[s] for conflict and debate among participants regarding values, aims, and aspirations each proposes for our own society" (T. Poulakos 1988, 161). These spaces, and the debates that happen within them, would produce an intangible sense of public judgment about questions of virtue, not specific policies or laws. Christine Oravec argues that epideictic rhetoric "is itself a powerful and persuasive tool insofar as it 'proves' the significance of the praiseworthy object and insofar as it 'confirms' the judgments of the orator, thus lending insight and comprehension to the perception of the audience" (1976, 162). Given the institutionalized opportunities to practice this form of rhetoric in classical Greece, orators were able to develop, maintain, and reshape questions of values and virtue that brought the community together.

This brief account of epideictic rhetoric points to the role that persuasive acts of celebration can play in giving life to a social sphere in which audience and orator define the cardinal values of a community. Those values are unstable and uncertain, subject to the process of persuasion and an orator's ability to reshape the beliefs of an audience through speech. By fostering opportunities for this sort of rhetoric, Athenians acknowledged the importance of epideictic practices for democratic affairs. In other words, acts of celebration and display, occasions for the articulation of excellence and tradition, claims for common values and beliefs, and the use of a speaker's ethos, skill, and aesthetic sensibilities were all essential rhetorical processes for the maintenance of democracy in classical Athens. Hauser, Takis Poulakos, and others suggest that epideictic rhetoric could hold the potential to redeem our own public sphere and offer a space for debate over the values that bind our culture together. I argue that Locke attempts to practice such a rhetoric and to outline its importance for American democracy.

The New Negro celebrates the value and promise of African American art. In fact, Locke claims that hope for the present "rests in the revaluation by white and black alike of the Negro in terms of his artistic endowments and cultural contributions, past and prospective" (*NN*, 15). What Locke identifies is both a tradition of excellence in artistic ability and a transformation in the role of the Negro in larger social affairs brought about by new instances of artistic excellence in Harlem. By showcasing artworks, Locke finds a method of winning cultural recognition for African Americans. Much of his art criticism also deals with the tension between the larger tradition of excellence that gave the "Negro community" an identity and the idiosyncratic excellence of particular artists in Harlem during the 1920s.[16] Ultimately, Locke believed that "Harlem represents the latest thrust towards Democracy" because it created a social space for the reconciliation of the tension between great individual artists and a larger notion of community identity founded on values worth celebrating. In addition, the social space of Harlem enhanced the possibility of forming a positive group identity through art *and* developing singular artistic abilities in particular individuals.

In classical Athens epideictic rhetoric was closely tied to poetry, and the artistic skill of the orator was used in the service of beauty. Rhetoric was conceptualized as an art form, not lower than painting, poetry, sculpture, theater, or architecture but equally valid as a mechanism for expression and aesthetic contemplation. *The New Negro* does not include a single orator or public speaker. The purpose of the work, however, aligns it with rhetorical practice. In presenting art from Harlem to the larger American public, Locke sought to uncover what was hidden to many Americans—namely the artistic talent of Negro artists and the value of the Negro community for American society.

In pursuing these goals, *The New Negro* amplifies particular artworks and the role of art in general in developing and maintaining community life in

Harlem. In addition, such acts of celebration served a pedagogical function, educating those who did not know or did not have access to the vibrant and promising art produced in Harlem and attempting to teach others about the potential of African Americans to make valuable contributions to American culture: "He [the New Negro] now becomes a conscious contributor and lays aside the status of a beneficiary and ward for that of a collaborator and participant in American civilization. The great social gain in this is the releasing of our talented group from the arid fields of controversy and debate to the productive fields of creative expression. The especially cultural recognition they win should in turn prove the key to the revaluation of the Negro which must precede or accompany any considerable further betterment of race relationships. But whatever the general effect, the present generation will have added the motives of self-expression and spiritual development to the old and still unfinished task of making material headway and progress" (*NN*, 15–16). Here the combination of art and the act of celebration hold the potential of inciting material changes. In other words, practicing an epideictic rhetoric, a rhetoric capable of reshaping a social sphere in which African Americans are not valued, is a necessary prerequisite for larger political and economic changes.

Locke's attention to the promise and potential of art indicates a commitment to an epideictic conception of aesthetics. Through the practice of art Locke saw the process of displaying visions of a social order, the constitution and validation of tradition, an engagement in community-centered education, the development of a useful group identity based on common values, and the creation of a more vibrant public sphere that accepted the contributions of competing value systems as necessary rhetorical processes. In Harlem, Locke saw a democratic space for conflict and debate among eclectic and competing value systems and a diverse set of participants able to generate a well-informed and valuable identity that was subject to revision, persuasion, and further elaboration. Harlem was not a place where voices or artists were silenced but where the conversation among a variety of artists could produce community standards of excellence without political oppression based on biological racism. In *The New Negro,* Locke attempts to make race an object of celebration capable of validating a tradition, contributing to public notions of virtue, and acting as a tool in securing material progress. Given such a position, the community can be seen aesthetically, as an artwork still in progress. By this interpretation, Locke's goal was to use race in epideictic rhetorical processes to help alter community standards and beliefs before altering policies.

In Harlem during the 1920s Locke saw the opportunity and the need to revise American value systems that segregated and oppressed African Americans. He could not step to the podium at athletic events, religious ceremonies, or funerals to begin such a task. However, he could host parties, such as the one at the Civic Club in 1924, and edit books, such as *The New Negro*. In addition, Locke had to develop a theory of values that could account for revision, persuasion, and competition between diverse value systems. Such a theory would demonstrate an intellectual commitment to epideictic rhetoric because it would show the importance of displaying competing value systems and bringing those value systems into conversation. Understanding Locke's theory of values as a philosophy of epideictic rhetoric, then, can illustrate an important aspect of Locke's pragmatism and open the possibility for the practice of an epideictic rhetoric suitable to American democracy.

Cultural Pluralism and Locke's Philosophy of Value

Throughout many of his essays Locke argues that interethnic violence stems from the fact that people are motivated by conflicting, universalized value imperatives. In response to this situation, Locke challenges notions of value absolutism by focusing on the philosophical mistake of categorizing values as products of universal reason (the Kantian position) instead of as group-influenced personal feelings. His challenge is supported by the belief that cultural uniformity about values is undesirable and impossible. Leonard Harris claims that in Locke's view, "cultural diversity was inherently desirable" and a "multitude of ways of valuing is characteristic of our being and not a temporary phase of human history" (*PAL,* 17). Like James, then, Locke points to change and plurality as defining characteristics of human experience, and he does not seek ways of arresting or unifying that change or plurality but instead insists that we look for ways of managing and coping with uncertainty.

In "Values and Imperatives," Locke contends that our ways of valuing are "feeling-modes" that reflect both personal disposition and the influence of group norms that operate in the cultural context within which a person lives. These value feelings act as interpretive guides and imperatives to action in shaping our responses to situations. People can revise these value feelings on the basis of reasoned judgments or available experience, but often people regard their values as universal categorical imperatives, which is the grounds for inevitable conflict. This, though, does not entail declaring "for value-anarchism as a wishful way out" of the situation (*PAL* 1935, 36). Instead, this presents the "gravest problem of contemporary philosophy." How is it possible "to ground some normative principle or criterion of objective validity for values without resort to dogmatism and absolutism on the intellectual plane, and without falling into their corollaries, on the plane of social behavior and action, of intolerance and mass coercion"? In answering this question, Locke "calls for a functional analysis of value norms and a search for normative principles in the immediate context of valuation." This means that for "a practical understanding of the operative mechanisms of valuation and of the grounds for our agreements and conflicts over values" we must attend to values as "feeling-attitudes and dispositional imperatives of action-choices" and not as products of universal reason or judgment.[17] This is one of the tasks of epideictic rhetoric—to understand which values are important to the larger community at a particular moment and to provide a description of the reasons for holding those values.

This position extends James's pragmatism. Locke emphasizes feeling, experience, and action as potent factors in determining both the attitudes that define values and the "pragmatic consequences" that determine our actions. Like the other pragmatists, Locke seeks a "middle ground between" the "extremes of subjectivism and objectivism" because "human behavior is experimental" and "selectively preferential" (*PAL* 1935, 38). Classifying values "in terms of the mechanics of value-feelings" is a more useful method of understanding both how values work and why they arise, and such a position avoids "leaning too heavily upon logical definition" (41). This position also points to the claim that "our varied absolutes are . . . largely the rationalization of our preferred values and their imperatives. Their tap-root, it seems, stems more from the will to power than from the will to know" (46). In other words, objective, logical reasons for holding values come only after we act on our feelings: "The effective antidote to value absolutism lies in a systematic and realistic demonstration that values are rooted in attitudes, not in reality, and pertain to ourselves, not to the world." This "systematic realization" requires that we learn, in the words of Judith Green, "to understand the historically located experiences and culturally specific values of various, differing peoples through new culture-specific scholarship and, on that basis, to discover the commonalities within human experience that make certain basic values broadly humane" (*CP,* 87). Locke calls the philosophical framework for guiding such scholarship "cultural pluralism" or "value relativism."

In "A Functional View of Value Ultimates," Locke supports his form of pluralism and relativism by accounting for changes in normative values over time. A functional analysis of values demonstrates "that what is revealed or developed in experience as *better* becomes *the new good*" (*PAL* 1945, 84). In addition, a functional analysis investigates the process of change guiding the assertion of value ultimates: "The process continuity of the normative character of values is demonstrated not merely by the substitution of new value content for the old, but even more clearly by the displacement and retroactive de-valuing of the old, a procedure which transforms yesterday's good into a relatively bad. That which is felt or judged as relatively better . . . is preferred and so becomes normatively imperative." Analyzing the process of changing values shows that "in actual practice" value norms "have a progressively corrective character" and not the "stability of specific value content which endows our abstract values with normative ultimacy." Locke proceeds to describe the shifting conception of beauty over time. Thus he offers a case study in "value transposition" to argue for the potential of a functional analysis to support a form of pluralism. In addition, he cites Nietzsche's notion of "transvaluation" as a name for the process he describes.

In another essay Locke summarizes his position on values as attitudes toward facts that manifest a person's "feelings, desires, interests, purposes, needs, and acts" by outlining five main commitments that follow from his perspective (*PAL,* 111).[18] First, inherent in all values is a relation to personality not to universality or reason. Second, values arise "out of the mind's practical attitude, when it reacts upon stimulation." Third, values are qualities that are added to objects by people in order to express personal relations. Fourth, transvaluations should be regarded as normal and entirely legitimate. Fifth, we are blind to transvaluations "by the stability of words; for these change their form much less rapidly than their meaning" (125). The final commitment points to the rhetorical process at the center of a functional analysis of values. From Locke's perspective, language shapes and solidifies our value attitudes and thus obscures the process of change. However, as Nietzsche points out, transvaluation requires a poet who is able to use language in a new manner.[19] According to Locke, "every society, and nearly every soul, is full of conflicts between opposing valuations, and any variation in their relative strengths may entail a change in values." Language may be the source of stability in such cases, but it is also a resource for change. Locke goes so far as to claim that stable, eternal values are fictions, potentially "dangerous fictions."[20] Rendering such stability fictional opens the possibility for linguistic invention that creates new fictions.

Returning to the notion of "culture-specific scholarship," Locke believes that a cross-disciplinary "anthropology in the broadest sense" would demonstrate the specific functional value adaptations that diverse people have made to their own environmental, historical, and political context (*PAL* 1944, 72). This form of scholarship must account for the role that language plays in shaping stable value systems and in contributing to transvaluations. In addition, Locke argues that the functional character of values makes it possible to evaluate, pragmatically, the relative insightfulness and usefulness of specific cultural values and to make progress in our understanding of broadly humane values such as human dignity, democracy, freedom, equality, group loyalty, and self-respect. The keys to overcoming the interethnic violence rooted in disagreements between value systems are the cross-cultural norms of tolerance and reciprocity based on a pluralistic understanding of the historical and functional character of varying group values.

This position implies that on pragmatic grounds scholarship that displays different value systems is useful in establishing the existence of pluralism. In addition, the norms of tolerance and reciprocity are equally useful in connecting competing value systems around concepts that lack rigid dogmatism and instead point to the fluid process of transvaluation: "What is achieved through relativistic rapprochement is, of course, somewhat different than the goal of the absolutists. It is fluid and functional unity rather than a fixed and irrevocable one, and its vital norms are equivalence and reciprocity rather than identity or complete agreement. But when we consider the odds against a complete community of culture for mankind, and the unlikelihood of any all-inclusive orthodoxy of human values, one is prepared to accept or even prefer an attainable concord of understanding and cooperation over against an unattainable unanimity of institutional beliefs" (*PAL* 1944, 71). Thus, a realistic understanding of values offers clues for "a more practical and consistent way" of holding them in a fluid and functional manner. More important, "it is here that the connection between pluralism and intellectual democracy becomes evident" (*PAL* 1942, 57). In attending to the fluid process described by Locke, value dogmatism is disregarded: "Value assertion would thus be a tolerant assertion of preference, not an intolerant insistence on agreement or finality. Value disciplines would take on [a] tentative and revisionist procedure."

Based on his theory of values and his cultural pluralism, Locke believes that his perspective gives rise to "three working principles" that underscore the flexible norms of tolerance and reciprocity. First, the principle of "cultural equivalence" demands that we search for "functional similarities in our analysis and comparisons of human cultures" and not differences (*PAL* 1944, 73). Second, the principle of "cultural reciprocity" demands that we recognize the "reciprocal character of all contacts between cultures." In other words, exchanges between value systems are an integral part of a plural democracy such as the one in the United States, and those acts of exchange shape value systems. Third, the principle of "limited cultural convertability" suggests that there are limits to the scope of cross-cultural exchange that we must respect so as to avoid domination. These three "working principles" point to the process of negotiation implicated in cross-cultural exchanges and the recognition of both functional value commonalities and valued diversity as twin aspects of democratic decision making and collaborative action. Locke suggests that we best develop our practical capacity to engage in cross-cultural conversation, collaboration, and negotiation so as to make a pluralist democracy possible.

"Intellectuals" play a significant role in this process, according to Locke, by engaging in scholarship and teaching that displays the diversity of values, the functional adaptation of values to specific conditions, and the commonalities that unite different value systems: "What intellectuals can do for the extension of the democratic way of life is to discipline our thinking critically into some sort of realistic worldmindedness. Broadening our cultural value and tempering our orthodoxies is of infinitely more service to enlarged democracy than direct praise or advocacy of democracy itself. For until broadened by relativism and reconstructed accordingly, our current democratic traditions and practice are not ready for world-wide application. Considerable political and cultural dogmatism, in the form of culture bias, nation worship, and racism, still stands in the way and must be invalidated and abandoned" (*PAL* 1942, 63). Here, Locke points to a concept that he variously calls "cosmopolitanism," "civilization-type," or "culture-citizenship." These concepts all imply the need for assimilation and adaptation regarding questions of value. Being able to acknowledge and understand diverse cultural value systems requires a form of cosmopolitanism derived from scholarship that demonstrates a functional understanding of values. In addition, participation in "culture-citizenship" subjects one's own value imperatives to reconsideration and revision based on interactions with other cultures. The "civilization-type" is not ruled by the desire for domination but instead respects diversity, seeks collaborative conversation regarding values, and is open to the prospect of adapting or changing value imperatives.

Locke understands values as feelings, as imperatives to action, and as demonstrative of a deep-seated cultural pluralism. He also considers the process of transvaluation as critical to his pluralism and as the grounds for his notion of cosmopolitanism. These concepts are useful on their own, but they become especially provocative in the light of the earlier discussion of epideictic rhetoric. As a pragmatist, Locke is concerned with the process of determining our values, and he rejects the assumption that we rely on antecedent first principles in engaging in that process. As is the case with the other pragmatists discussed, this perspective leads to an interest in rhetorical processes. By testing, upholding, and revising our values, we are constantly engaged in the process of negotiating our place in a community or a culture. Such a process involves practical and productive tools that use language and the art of persuasion. Locke's value theory, therefore, can be interpreted as an attempt to place rhetorical processes at the center of decision making regarding the construction of both individual and group identities and the development of value systems for American culture.

Drawing on some general themes from classical rhetoric can help explain this interpretation. Some scholars believe that the sophists engaged in the practice of epideictic rhetoric to demonstrate their expertise as orators and to recruit students. In delivering epideictic speeches the sophists also revealed a perspective on the function of rhetoric in Athens. For example, Prodicus's speech *The Choice of Heracles* recounts a standard Greek myth and in so doing demonstrates the importance of rhetoric. Prodicus recounts the story of Heracles coming of age and trying to choose between the path of virtue and the path of vice for his life. While Heracles stands at the crossroads deliberating on which path to choose, two women appear, each urging Heracles to follow her particular path to happiness. The two women are Virtue and Vice. Vice directs Heracles to the path promising pleasure, ease, leisure, and enjoyment. In contrast, Virtue directs him to the path whose rewards include love, honor, and admiration but that requires service to community, country, and friends as well as hard work and dedication. In Prodicus's version of the story, Virtue and Vice debate the relative merits of each path, and the story ends with no clear decision by Heracles.

This example of classical epideictic rhetoric highlights several useful themes that parallel Locke's value theory. First, the competition between Virtue and Vice points to a diversity of values in a plural society. No obvious, singular path presents itself to Heracles or any member of the audience. A plurality of paths is asking that we choose, just as for Locke a plurality of values is causing conflict and seeking to guide our imperatives to action in different ways. Second, such competition is worked out through the persuasive claims of each woman in Prodicus's story. This illustrates the importance of debate, argument, and rhetoric in reaching decisions. The dialogue between Virtue and Vice is designed to place the audience members in a better position regarding their own choices. In Locke's case, conflict and debate between competing value claims is a significant part of the process of determining value systems. Although Locke does not explicitly attend to the persuasive use of language in such conflicts, the processes he does point to obviously highlight the role of persuasion when competing value systems come into conflict. Third, because Prodicus's story ends with no clear decision, he is able to mark the uncertainty that attends our value choices and suggests that such choices are subject to revision. Both Locke and Prodicus demonstrate that valuations are not the result of fixed standards already in place but the outcome of democratic practices of deliberation and debate (practices constantly revising traditional notions of the good). Both Prodicus's speech and Locke's philosophy can actually be read as instances of a celebration of the commitment to deliberation regarding questions of value. In Prodicus's case, rhetoric has the capacity to influence people's choices and ultimately shape community values. Locke is less clear as to the mechanism that negotiates value conflicts or the process of transvaluation. He does not consider speech acts or language in general as the primary mechanism for negotiating those projects. However, reading Locke from the perspective of figures such as Prodicus demonstrates the possibility and necessity of rhetoric in negotiating such situations.

Developing this line of thinking further, Aristotle argues that epideictic rhetoric urges a specific course of action (*Rhetoric* 1368a). Embedded in the praise of an individual and the expression of a person's good qualities is the suggestion that the speaker would urge the audience to do as the person being praised has done. In fact, one motivation for epideictic speech is to suggest ways for the audience to act in the future. Such an argument aligns values with imperatives to action just as Locke did. In Aristotle's case, however, the act of linguistic display must employ the exaggeration of past excellence so as to inspire future action of the same kind. The social function of *The New Negro* is designed with exactly the same intention—to inspire future excellence based on past performance. More generally, however, Aristotle's position highlights the necessity of testing rhetoric by its consequences. Just as political rhetoric urges a course of action, so too does epideictic rhetoric if it expects the audience to perpetuate the value being praised. In other words, value feelings are stirred by the epideictic orator and thus inspire future action in accordance with particular commitments. Locke does not look to rhetoric or oratory for this function. Instead he looks for the mechanisms that transmit value systems from one person to another without relying on dogmatic claims and while staying open to the possibility of revising value feelings. I argue that Locke's theory of values, by attending to feelings, attitudes, and actions, points to a similar way of understanding acts of praise.

A summary of Locke's value theory as a philosophy for epideictic rhetoric can be useful at this point. First, by arguing that we must find ways to understand and negotiate conflicts between values without descending to violence, Locke attends to communicative processes that can bring competing value systems into productive dialogue. This is precisely what Prodicus demonstrates in *The Choice of Heracles*. Carrying on the sophistic tradition, I argue that one way to extend Locke's analysis is to claim that epideictic rhetoric is a necessary mechanism for negotiating cultural pluralism. The sophists use epideictic rhetoric to display a plurality of values and to aid audiences in decision making regarding those values, just as Locke attempts to do in his work on race and aesthetics.

Second, Locke describes the process of transvaluation, or change, regarding value systems over time. The sophists believed that language was the primary instrument in directing such changes. Like most forms of pragmatism, Locke's position seeks practical methods to direct those changes for the better, and he highlights tolerance and reciprocity as conditions for productive, nonviolent change. However, Locke misses the potential role that language plays in directing the process of transvaluation. Nonetheless, he does call for "exchanges" between competing value systems, and the results of such exchanges would be tolerance or adaptation, not domination or oppression. Prodicus's speech is about an exchange between competing value systems. Significantly, it does not end in domination but is open to the possibility of interpretation. Locke's theory of values, therefore, can be seen as a kind of neosophistic philosophy of epideictic rhetoric.

By virtue of his attention to pluralism, conflict, transvaluation, and exchange, Locke outlines the intellectual conditions for seeing epideictic rhetoric as a necessary instrument in maintaining a culturally plural democracy. His suggestion that cosmopolitanism should be a broad-based cultural goal given such diversity indicates the role that epideictic rhetorics can play in presenting and understanding competing value systems and in helping people to adapt and change in the light of new value imperatives. By celebrating the value of African American art in *The New Negro* and by attempting to display the value of race, Locke proceeded to engage in the practice of epideictic rhetoric outlined by his value theory. His cultural pluralism had, in fact, established the need for finding practical mechanisms for guiding the construction of value systems in a culture shot through with contingency, plurality, change, and competition.

The New Negro, Race, and Reciprocity

Both *Race Contacts and Interracial Relations* and *The New Negro* attempt a transvaluation of race, the first grounded on a rejection of biological and political racism and the second on a celebration of art. In effect, these works are Locke's method of outlining the intellectual conditions for, and the practical realization of, reciprocity and exchange. *Race Contacts and Interracial Relations* was first delivered as a series of lectures at Howard University in March and April 1916. The purpose of the lectures was to analyze and evaluate the different meanings of the term "race" and "to discriminate among them and to perpetuate [only] those meanings—those concepts—which are promising and really sound" (*RCIR,* 1). The result of this task is an analysis of race as a concept with three distinct meanings. The first, "theoretical" meaning, refers to biological and physical interpretations of race. The second, "practical" meaning, refers to a political-economic interpretation of race as a construct of imperialist domination. The third, "social" meaning, points to modern forms of solidarity. Locke evaluates each meaning for its promise, distinguishing between those meanings that can and should be "redeemed" and those that should be eliminated. Locke's arguments concerning each meaning of race illustrate how these early lectures laid the groundwork for his position in *The New Negro* and for the development of a rhetoric of reciprocity.

Locke's first lecture, "The Theoretical and Scientific Conception of Race," critically interrogates and demystifies the physical and biological racial theories of scientists. By exposing the epistemological deficiencies of such theories, he reduces racist biology to a pseudoscience. Specifically, biological racism conflates the descriptive project of classifying human groups with the normative project of distinguishing "superior" and "inferior" groups. Such "biological" theories neglect the extensive variations within human groups while exaggerating variations between groups, and they therefore maintain a false fetish of group purity. By contrast, Locke argues that racial groups "have neither purity of blood nor purity of type. They are the products of countless interminglings and infinite crossings of types" (*RCIR,* 10). Moreover, biological theories neglect history. By appealing to static, fixed racial types, these theories miss the dynamic development of human culture and biology—overlooking the process that Darwin described in *The Origin of the Species.* Locke concludes that "there are no static factors of race at all. . . . Race inequalities must have an historical explanation." This criticism operates from a distinctively pragmatic perspective. Although biological race is "an ethnic fiction," Locke argues that such fictions have harmful practical consequences. Thus he distinguishes between the plausible pragmatist claim that a group may need, in some circumstances, to consider itself an "ethnic unit" and the untenable, pseudoscientific view that a group is in fact such a unit.

In his second lecture Locke turns to the "political and practical conception of race" (*RCIR,* 22). In doing so he shifts his analysis from "the modern race creed" to the "modern race practice"—which he calls "imperialism." The central idea in this lecture is that race is a result of the practices of power. Refuting the prevailing view that white superiority is the basis for white supremacy, Locke argues that political supremacy spawns the idea of superiority: "The conception of 'inferior' races or 'backward' races and of 'advanced' races or 'superior' races largely comes from the political fortunes and political capacities of peoples . . . the people who have not been successful in acquiring dominance will be called the inferior people. . . . The ruling people not only dominate the group practically but control the . . . class distinctions . . . justifying their success in terms of . . . innate forms" (*RCIR,* 22–23). Locke proceeds to describe an international economic system of competitive commerce that helped establish the imperialist practices of the dominant groups. In this system European nation-states competed for domination over non-Western peoples by seeking markets for their goods. These commercial imperatives were rationalized by reference to Christianity, "civilization," and the deprecation of the cultural capacity of colonized peoples. Thus commercial imperialism led to racist theories and a "practical culture" of alleged Anglo-Saxon superiority.[21]

Locke continues this line of thought in his third and fourth lectures, but there he focuses explicitly on U.S. "race relations" as an extension of international imperialist politics. He argues that the belief in Anglo-Saxon superiority was institutionalized in Jim Crow laws and imperiled the social standing of colonial subjects living as minorities. The goal of this critical genealogy of imperialist practices is to put an end to race in the political sense of domination.

In his final lecture, "Racial Progress and Race Adjustment," Locke argues that something potentially useful and pragmatically defensible remains about the idea of race, and thus race should be "revised" and "redeemed." According to Nancy Fraser, "a properly reformulated social conception of race could serve a salutary function, helping to resolve racial antagonism and to advance the progress of civilization" (*CP,* 12). Any social conception of race would require a new sense of group belonging and solidarity appropriate for the exigencies of the moment and unimpeded by the desire for imperial domination or segregation based on biological theory or political practice. From Locke's perspective, formulating such a notion of solidarity requires two distinct concepts. The first, which refers to the general development of contemporary society, is called the "civilization type," while the second, which refers to the specific situation of subordinated groups within contemporary society, is called "secondary race consciousness" (*RCIR,* 97).

Locke claims that "the only kind of race that is left to believe in and to be applied to modern problems is what we call the idea of the social race [defined] as a conception of civilization type. . . . This is to be the race concept of the future" (*RCIR,* 88). This does not mean that the civilization type requires homogeneity of customs, beliefs, or even religion. Instead the civilization type is the product of assimilation made possible by interactions between ethnic groups. The emerging American civilization type would not be based on biology and cannot be identified by traits specific to any single constituent subgroup. Instead, it is a composite that incorporates traits previously associated with various groups. As the civilization type emerges, all of the parties involved in its formation are transformed. Thus, the American Negro would continue to contribute to the development of the American civilization type and assimilate to the other subgroups involved in its formation—dominant groups do not, and cannot, control assimilation. Locke's vision, however, does not end with an endorsement of the "melting pot" perspective on American culture.[22] The next turn in the argument leads to the development of a secondary race consciousness in tension with the civilization type.

Locke recommends secondary race consciousness to American Negroes on pragmatic grounds: "While social assimilation is in progress there seems to be necessary some . . . counter-doctrine [of] racial solidarity and culture. The stimulation of a secondary race-consciousness within a [dominated] group . . . is necessary for . . . practical reasons. The group needs . . . to get a right conception of itself, and it can only do that through stimulation of pride in itself. . . . Race pride or secondary race consciousness [is] the social equivalent to self-respect in the individual moral life" (*RCIR,* 96–97). In addition, this kind of self-respect will serve to stimulate the sort of "collective activity" that will accelerate Negro assimilation to the emerging civilization type. Therefore, secondary race pride and "loyalty to the joint or common civilization type" are not antithetical. Instead, the first serves as a necessary means of realizing the second. Locke proposes Negro "race pride" as a pragmatic strategy for realizing the long-term goal of assimilation guided by equal exchanges.

Locke argues that to create secondary race consciousness, cultural production is necessary. Cultural production requires the recovery of valuable African traditions, from which Negroes have been cut off by slavery, as well as the task of expressing African American traditions in public cultural forms such as literature, music, and painting. These public cultural forms will make recognition of the value of African Americans by the larger society possible. In the light of these lectures on race, then, *The New Negro* appears to be a bid for "culture-citizenship" as a step on the way to reversing political and economic inequalities.

In Harlem in the 1920s Locke saw a physical space for the creation of a secondary race consciousness. *The New Negro* and the Harlem Renaissance both highlight the complicated and dangerous attempt to forge a new sense of group identity while refuting and destroying old stereotypes.[23] Locke understood such a task as necessary for the full and equal participation of Negroes in American society. Race pride would replace exclusive and oppressive racist policies by offering alternative grounds on which to conduct cultural exchanges between various subgroups. Without race pride and the subsequent exchanges between different groups within American culture, political and economic equality cannot be achieved. However, *The New Negro* and the idea of race pride strike at a profound problem for a pragmatist such as Locke: how does one reconcile a philosophy that refuses the primacy of identity with the politics of racial group advocacy? In other words, how does one avoid the dangers that attend the original stereotypical characterizations of Negro life while inventing counterstereotypes?

Locke answers this dilemma in two ways. First, he turns all questions of race into questions of culture and not blood or biology: "if you have the same manners and customs and have allegiance to the same social system you belong to the same race . . . even though ethnically you may not" (*RCIR*, 79). Even when he references links to African culture by virtue of "forefathers" and "blood descendants," this blood link functions not on the biological level but instead as a social symbol of connection that provides special "cultural inspiration" through a "sense of direct cultural kinship" (*NN*, 256). Second, continuing to render questions of race into questions of culture points to the process of negotiating group identity, not the stereotypes that result from the process. Locke's larger point is that "if a 'New Negro' is not born and reborn every half generation or so, something is radically wrong" (*PAL* 1950, 231–32). Any stagnation of the continual process of developing new and better group identities would mean that the Negro has been arrested again in stereotype and remains "more formula than human being" (*NN*, 3). These two arguments provide the warrant for Locke's strategic essentialism. He believes that if some forms of essentialism are the products of cultural production (and not biological or political racism), then they can serve a useful function in animating and correcting the process of achieving the civilization type through reciprocity and exchange.

In the light of these two strategies, *The New Negro* formulates a striking and useful answer to a difficult question: How can the individual and collective identity of the New Negro be prevented from being as limiting as the old stereotypes were? By seeing the New Negro as an artist, Locke is able to postulate a particular aesthetic identity tied to cultural forms of expression and open to constant revision by other artists.[24] This implies the need for intense self-expression and speaking from experience rather than "moralism and guarded idealizations" (*NN,* 50). The aesthetic identity formulated is individually variable and open to change, and yet it can be representative because the self-expression of the Negro artist and the quality of Negro art arises out of Negro life. Locke contends that the misery and hardship that have been indelibly part of the Negro experience in America have given Negro life an aesthetic quality of its own: "With them, even ordinary living has epic depth and lyric intensity, and this, their material handicap, is their spiritual advantage. So in a day when art has run to classes, cliques, and coteries, and life lacks more and more a vital common background, the Negro artist, out of the depths of his group and personal experience, has to his hand almost the conditions of a classical art" (47). Since black individual self-expression is already aesthetic, it is also by implication a group expression, so that "race expression need not be deliberate to be vital."[25] Artists need no longer be self-conscious of representing and interpreting "the Negro" to a white world; they can simply "speak as Negroes" (48). In other words, by "speaking" through their art, Negro artists possess the ability to give voice to both their own identity and the identity of the community to which they belong.

In Locke's assumption concerning individual expression as group expression, the distinctions between artist, subject, and audience are overcome. Therefore, Harlem not only assumes mythical qualities for the New Negro as a place for emancipation and self-determination but also constitutes a place where the artist is embedded in and embraced by a community and yet not restrained by it. Harlem, in other words, is a place where the artist's work not only expresses a communal experience but also helps to shape that experience. It is on these grounds that Locke is able to project a new secondary race consciousness rooted in art. According to his position, such artistic representations can have enormous power in conditioning changes in political and economic realities.

In addition to his focus on self-expression and its connection to group expression, Locke consistently uses verb tenses hovering between the present and the future (between "it is" and "it promises to be") that emphasize Negro life in transition. For example, Locke claims that "in the very process of being transplanted, the Negro is becoming transformed" (*NN,* 6). Because of such formulations it is difficult to decide whether the New Negro, as a form of group identity, already exists or is being created. This is not a logical weakness, however; Locke's emphasis is on the transformation, not the foundation of a concept. Accordingly, the New Negro is a project and a projection, not a new fixed image. The "new aesthetic" and "philosophy of life" constructed by Negro artists and underlying new representations of Negroes in literature and art cannot proclaim fixed principles (49). Instead, such a "new aesthetic" can serve primarily to "break through the stereotypes to a new style, a distinctive fresh technique, and some sort of characteristic idiom" (267).[26]

As an act of celebration, *The New Negro* attempts to display and interpret the prominent features of this new style. Such an act of celebration highlights the contributions that Negroes can make to both art and culture. According to Locke, it is important "[t]o evolve from the racial substance something technically distinctive, something that as an idiom of style may become a contribution to the general resources of art. In flavor of language, flow of phrase, accent of rhythm in prose, verse and music, color and tone of imagery, idiom and timbre of emotion and symbolism, it is the ambition and promise of Negro artists to make a distinctive contribution" (*NN*, 51). This is a description of Langston Hughes, Claude McKay, Jean Toomer, Zora Neale Hurston, Jessie Fauset, and the other artists collected in the pages of *The New Negro*. Such a position warrants Locke's act of celebration. On another level, however, Locke's own interpretive and critical essays offer a new idiom of pragmatism and a new perspective on aesthetics that also issue from his cultural position as an African American. In other words, the act of celebration, and the philosophical justification of that act of celebration, grounds a larger perspective on the meaning, significance, and social function of the art being celebrated.

Locke's pragmatist aesthetics ties art closely to epideictic rhetoric. His essays in *The New Negro* respect art's formal values, as is made clear by his attention to idiom and technique. Those essays also understand art as a purposive activity with a social function. By focusing on art's use for "self-expression" and "self-determination," Locke argues that "the social promise of our recent art is as great as the artistic" (*NN*, 52). In other words, along with the "old and still unfinished task of making material headway," he advocates the contributions of Negro artists as the privileged means for the Negro's full social acceptance in American society: "The especially cultural recognition they win should in turn prove the key to the revaluation of the Negro which must precede or accompany any further betterment of race relationships" (15). The communicative process of revaluing the role of the Negro in American culture, conducted through both the artwork of the Harlem Renaissance and the celebration of that work, is a rhetorical process.

Considering Locke's aesthetics, his acts of celebration, and his conception of race in the light of epideictic rhetoric helps articulate the implications of his position for American democracy. The artwork celebrated in *The New Negro* is designed to promote the cultural recognition of African Americans *and* to advance "a new democracy in American culture" since democracy cannot tolerate cultural disrespect toward ethnic groups (*NN*, 9). Locke's pragmatist aesthetics recognizes that democracy, like art and culture, is best served by open exchange between different ways of thought and diverse ethnic voices.[27] Negro expression, therefore, must be treated as a well-respected, interactive part of American culture: "Democracy itself is obstructed and stagnated to the extent that any of its channels are closed. Indeed they cannot be selectively closed. So the choice is not between one way for the Negro and another for the rest, but between American institutions frustrated on the one hand and American ideals progressively fulfilled and realized on the other" (12). In short, Locke's focus on race pride and its expression through art and culture issues from a belief that if American democracy is to fulfill its promise, all voices must find mechanisms for participation and for outlining the collective identity and values by which an American civilization might live. By focusing on art, value theory, and group identity Locke has suggested that the practice of epideictic rhetoric is a necessary means for the creation of such a democracy, for the ongoing process of negotiating group identity, and for the construction of a better American community.

The key features of his epideictic rhetoric, however, are not the funeral oration, the speaking competition, or the practice of public speaking in general. Instead Locke's position emphasizes the importance of reciprocity and the general relevance of art and cultural expression broadly construed. Because life in Athens was marked by a relatively homogeneous culture, competition between ethnic subgroups did not obscure the process of finding a communal identity. This, however, is precisely the problem that Locke faced. Not only was American culture marked by an obvious pluralism, but it was also encumbered by a history of racism designed to segregate and oppress specific ethnic groups. In light of this fact, practicing epideictic rhetoric takes on a new significance. The necessity of expressing group identity issues from the need to conduct meaningful cultural exchanges between different ethnic groups. Epideictic rhetoric, therefore, is a way for a community to come to know itself and to come to know the other communities living in the same society. In addition, such exchanges lead to inevitable assimilation, transformation, and change, demonstrating the ongoing process of defining race, generating group identity, and determining values. This process, according to Locke, implicates a vast array of cultural practices, including but extending far beyond public speaking. The art produced in the Harlem Renaissance is an example of epideictic rhetoric because it was engaged in the process of determining group identity and could serve the function of displaying a group's values so that others might learn and understand. Locke's acts of celebration were meant to make that fact clear.

Locke suggests the New Negro as a conception of what African Americans might stand for and leaves this representation open to modifications. In other words, by voicing dissent from current forms of representation, he instigates the quest for new representations as a continuous search for a new consensus. I would add that Locke's position makes the production of a group identity such as the New Negro a rhetorical process. It is a process guided by what classical scholars would have called epideictic rhetoric because it praises or blames and in so doing highlights the use of values in the construction of community standards of excellence. Thus, Locke points to the connections between art and epideictic rhetoric, and the significance of those connections for creating a vibrant social space that conditions the possibility of democratic politics.

Locke departs from classical lines of thought, however, by emphasizing the culturally plural realities of American society, and thus he extends the significance of epideictic rhetoric by focusing on the importance of exchanges between different subgroups. Epideictic rhetoric, therefore, becomes a mechanism for exchange, assimilation, and transformation. Group expression and self-expression are both meant to foster exchanges that aid in the continued process of negotiation implicating the groups belonging to a democracy. Locke suggests reciprocity and exchange as a mechanism for overcoming violence, oppression, and segregation. I suggest that such exchanges are fundamentally rhetorical processes, processes in which persuasive voices have the capacity to regulate and influence the changes taking place. Eloquence in the form of a speech, story, painting, or play shapes the perceptions of the artist and audience and results in the articulation of new forms of identity, better value systems, and new forms of pragmatically grounded, epideictic rhetoric—a lesson that Locke makes clear.

Democracy and the Celebration of Aesthetics

The Harlem Renaissance program of using art to advance freedom and equality for African Americans derived from a belief in the central role of aesthetic experience in the achievement of new forms of solidarity and understanding. In this way the Harlem Renaissance was a striking experiment in cultural pluralism. Locke's role in this experiment was that of a mediator or cross-cultural interpreter. He sought to further human solidarity through specific acts of recognition, identification, and exchange with diverse groups.

Many writers associated with the Harlem Renaissance believed that realistic fiction, poetry, and drama would bring greater interracial understanding by exploring the psychology of racism as well as opening a space for the re-creation and expression of diversely "American" selves. However, by pragmatist standards the Harlem Renaissance did not succeed. Compared with the overt political activism of the civil rights movement in the 1960s, the kind of equality and reciprocity that Locke and others sought through aesthetics remained largely out of reach. Pragmatism seeks to test ideas in experience, revise or drop those ideas that fail, and pursue instead those that make life better. In Locke's case, how can we revise his ideas so that, in the crucible of experience, they are better able to produce the results sought?

Locke faced a double challenge: first, he needed to articulate the intellectual conditions for understanding the role of art in generating useful notions of group identity; and second, he needed to open spaces for the possibility of displaying that art and engaging in cross-cultural exchanges.[28] The celebration at the Civic Club in New York City highlights the difficulty of finding a space for pointing out the virtue of African American art, and Locke's philosophical writings demonstrate his search for a language with the capacity to express and articulate the important links between culture, race, and art. Two problems arise from this position. Locke is missing a robust account of exactly how to manage the interactions between subgroups as well as a clear indication of where those interactions are supposed to take place. By virtue of the recent interest in his scholarship, Locke's ideas are clearly still a vital and useful resource for our own moment. However, if we expect those ideas to have a larger impact on American life, we must extend them to offer a clear account of the mechanisms for negotiating cross-cultural exchanges and an argument for the creation of physical spaces to make such exchanges possible. The tradition of epideictic rhetoric offers an important resource for addressing these problems.

Locke's pragmatism, therefore, points to the need for finding an appropriate rhetoric for the health and maintenance of American democracy. Such a rhetoric, if it is to be appropriate, must find spaces for the articulation of community standards of excellence. The classical emphasis on the funeral oration, speaking competition, or festival must be extended or revised to account for contemporary cultural spaces in which art is used for the display of values, the development of community identity, and education. Connecting Locke to the rhetorical tradition warrants the further development of specific, institutional spaces for the practice of epideictic rhetoric. Such spaces would help us understand one another by demonstrating the values of various communities, suggesting ways to revise and reshape our own values, and pointing out ways to interact with different ethnic subgroups without resorting to violence. Most important, such spaces would establish the possibility for participation in epideictic rhetorics that celebrate a variety of traditions.

In addition, an appropriate, American epideictic rhetoric would demonstrate how art and language can display competing values, forge identities for larger communities, and regulate the interactions between different communities and different value systems. Locke's position suggests that rhetorics of celebration, transformation, and aesthetic performance are critical to the health and maintenance of culturally plural democracies because they can regulate and manage interactions between subgroups. If multiple value systems are inevitable, then such rhetorics are necessary means of creating productive dialogues between different value systems. More important, Locke offers an open-ended notion of community that is subject to revision and acts of persuasion, and that is highlighted by his notion of cosmopolitanism. The results of this kind of epideictic rhetoric would create a notion of world citizenship, which stresses reciprocity in an attempt to combat the idea of race as a political instrument for oppression.

Locke can be understood as part of the epideictic tradition for several reasons. First, he celebrates the value and promise of African American art. Second, such celebrations are meant to help forge and display a notion of community or group identity, which he sees as necessary means of combating racism. Third, he engages in acts of display that point out specific instances of artistic excellence to encourage the continued development of a tradition of excellence. Fourth, he tries to uncover what remains hidden to other communities in American society and in so doing tries to teach people about the virtue of African American art and culture. Fifth, he describes the role of values in determining human actions and seeks ways of revising those values in the face of competition and disagreement.

Locke also extends the tradition of classical rhetoric. From his perspective epideictic discourse plays a necessary role in regulating relationships and exchanges between competing value systems and subgroups. In other words, epideictic rhetoric is a necessary art to master if we are to live in a plural democracy and tolerate other values and reshape our own values through reciprocal exchanges. Mastering epideictic rhetoric requires one to become a cosmopolitan willing to be transformed through interactions with others. In addition, race is a necessary topos for epideictic rhetoric to negotiate because it is an integral part of group identity and value systems. Also, from this perspective many different kinds of art are implicated in epideictic rhetorical processes and seek to have an impact on social relations by offering representations of a group's identity.

Accordingly beauty, artistic expression, and aesthetics are useful for the maintenance of community life in democratic societies. In the words of John Dewey: "The level and style of the arts of literature, poetry, ceremony, amusement, and recreation which obtain in a community, furnishing the staple objects of enjoyment in that community, do more than all else to determine the current direction of ideas and endeavors in the community. They supply the meanings in terms of which life is judged, esteemed, and criticized" (*EN*, 159). Along with Dewey, Locke suggests that we critically interpret such arts to better understand their role in constructing the values by which we live. In such cases epideictic rhetoric offers grounds to conduct a form of critical interpretation of various artworks that can reveal the manner in which acts of cultural production guide our imperatives to action.

We need epideictic rhetoric in American democracy because it helps us understand one another while maintaining an open-ended tolerance for change, plurality, and revision. However, Locke does not mention rhetoric in his writings. Instead he focuses on methods for creating community and solidarity in plural democracies. From his perspective solidarity is tied closely to art and to reciprocity. Artistic expression can represent and define a community, and cross-cultural exchanges can bring diverse communities closer together. Locke's deepest concern is with creating a vibrant polis that can accommodate competing value systems and, in turn, condition the possibility for the practice of politics without racism. He is interested in using the arts as a method for grounding democracy on legitimate claims to equality. For Locke, culture and community exist in tension with plurality and change. Reconciling that tension without violence requires attention to epideictic rhetoric. In such a case epideictic rhetoric becomes a necessary mechanism for using aesthetics to regulate plurality in a democracy. Unfortunately American society lacks the institutional opportunities for, the intellectual commitment to, and a theoretical understanding of the practice of epideictic rhetoric. Locke offers us the possibility to rethink such issues.

Conclusion

The Many Varieties of Pragmatism and American Rhetoric

A central claim of this book is that both pragmatism and rhetoric are committed to pluralism. As such, an attempt was made to set the scene for, and contribute to, the development of other pragmatisms and other rhetorics. Implied through the structure of the book is that, on the one hand, William James and John Dewey constitute a mainstream with which any critic of pragmatism must contend. On the other hand, classical figures such as the sophists, Aristotle, and Isocrates also constitute a mainstream with which any rhetorical theorist must contend. This is not meant to imply that the conversation ends with these central figures. Instead, the message is that the variety of first-generation pragmatisms and the variety of classical rhetorics facilitated the development of both. In light of this claim, it is important to move from notions of pragmatism and rhetoric in the singular to pragmatisms and rhetorics in the plural.

Developments in neopragmatism and contemporary rhetorical theory point to this growing pluralism. The many voices associated with both pragmatism and rhetoric illustrate the contingency, uncertainty, and adaptability that attend the intellectual work done in the name of both. Limiting the central argument of the text to the first-generation American pragmatists and classical rhetoric facilitated the explanation of the relationship between the two. However, such an argument demands that a clearer resolution of this relationship be made given the growing pluralism in both traditions.

The claim has been made that pragmatism, as an orientation to the world, was characterized by five central commitments: a belief in uncertainty, an epistemological anthropocentrism, pluralism, an attention to the relationship between the individual and the community, and a search for useful methods and tools. It is not my intention to view these characteristics as foundational, philosophical concepts. Instead, I view these five characteristics as conditions for the development of multiple rhetorics. In other words, pragmatism provides theoretical grounds that require the invention and use of a variety of rhetorics. Jane Addams, Oliver Wendell Holmes, and Alain Locke are just three possible figures inventing and using such rhetorics. William James valued variety, richness, and multiplicity as central features of his philosophy, and he taught that their presence was a sign of vitality and life. To end the conversation with Addams, Holmes, and Locke would be to ignore James's commitments. Thus, if pragmatism is to continue to flourish as an intellectual tradition, multiple rhetorics must flourish as well. The development of a variety of American rhetorics is necessary if the promise of pragmatism is to be fulfilled.

Read as intellectual history, this book demonstrates that American pragmatism is an important resource for thinking about the scope, function, and value of rhetoric for American society. The pragmatists developed a distinctively American philosophy that can best be understood as an attempt to find and practice appropriate rhetorics that are essential for a vibrant democracy. Read as rhetorical theory, this book demonstrates how specific philosophical arguments create the grounds for the development of various rhetorics. Pragmatism helps us to theorize the significance, centrality, and use of rhetorics for democratic affairs.

Two pressing questions remain: Have we witnessed this kind of flourishing of American rhetoric in the twentieth century? Has pragmatism fulfilled some of its potential with advances in rhetorical theory? Answering these questions does not involve arguing that contemporary rhetorical theorists are pragmatists and just do not know it. Instead, it involves arguing that contemporary rhetorical theorists use some of the characteristics of pragmatism. From a pragmatic perspective, questions of definition are not important or valuable. Such questions are replaced by questions concerning consequences, use, and effectiveness. By turning toward *some* of the varieties of contemporary rhetorical theory, one can see how the characteristics of pragmatism inspire and grow into a rich variety of rhetorics and how the promise of the philosophy of pragmatism is being fulfilled by the return of rhetoric.

Contemporary Rhetorical Theories as Neopragmatism

Kenneth Burke was not a pragmatist in any overt or obvious sense. He developed a sophisticated and influential rhetorical theory based on his focus on the function of language. Burke defines rhetoric as "the use of words by human agents to form attitudes or induce actions in other human agents" (1945, 41). This "symbolic means of inducing cooperation" is an essential function of language (43). Burke grounds rhetoric on the notion of identification. Rhetoric makes order possible and "designates the very process by which human societies are created, maintained, transformed, destroyed, and recreated" (Crusius 1999, 121). To persuade someone is to "talk his language by speech, gesture, tonality, order, image, attitude, idea, identifying your ways with his" (Burke 1969, 55)—one changes attitudes or actions by virtue of one's ability to identify with others. The notion of identification nicely supplements traditional views of persuasion.[1]

In the light of a pragmatist orientation to the world, what Burke provides is a sophisticated analysis of the manner in which language can create and sustain communities. His notion of identification rests on the belief that people communicate in order to eliminate division and illustrates the manner in which communication establishes what is common. This was precisely Dewey's interest in *The Public and Its Problems*. Burke goes further to develop a philosophy of language called "dramatism." This philosophy of language was designed to discover human motivation in various situations. Most important, it was a "technique of analysis of language and thought as basic modes of action rather than as means of conveying information" (Burke 1945, 74). Burke uses the "pentad" as a critical instrument in discovering motivation and showing how language is a form of action. Ultimately, he demonstrates how specific vocabularies can help one identify the motivations of individuals or groups. Furthermore, some of those vocabularies form "terministic screens" that direct one's attention and legitimate certain ideas and delegitimate others. The concept of the "terministic screen" illustrates how language actively works to regulate and organize one's reality. It also attests to the possibility for the multiplication of perspectives.

Although this is only a brief and simple overview of *some* of the aspects of Burke's rhetorical theory, there are important affinities between it and pragmatism. Clearly, Burke was a pluralist who sought methods of analysis to help show how various communities or groups cohered by virtue of their linguistic choices. At certain points in his work he even takes up the task of refuting the metaphysical dogmas that plagued philosophy according to James and Dewey. The purpose of providing this brief look at Burke's work is not to define him as a pragmatist and force him to occupy a place in that tradition. Instead, what is important here is the manner in which the basic characteristics of pragmatism are used toward ends that the first-generation pragmatists could never have predicted. This is precisely the purpose of pragmatism—it was designed as a philosophy that would ultimately extend beyond itself to invent tools, techniques, ideas, and instruments of change that it alone could not imagine. It is my contention that rhetorics and rhetorical theories are just those tools, techniques, ideas, and instruments. The spirit of pragmatism lives in work such as Burke's because of his interest in discovering tools to use in coping with a plural and ultimately ambiguous world.

There is ample evidence to suggest that Burke could not have written what he did without the pragmatists, especially James and Dewey. What this entails, therefore, is the argument that neopragmatism ought to turn toward rhetorical theory as an essential resource. The consequences of pragmatism, so James and Dewey hoped, would be the discovery of methods for acting and reflecting on the problems of the moment. The philosophical arguments they made were designed to make those consequences possible. This is to say that figures such as Burke, who develop sophisticated and valuable rhetorical theories, cross the disciplinary boundaries of higher academics to demand attention from both the larger university community *and* the publics involved in settling controversies and making difficult decisions. To name Burke for this end is to begin a conversation that includes countless other participants—a conversation that reflects on the potential of rhetoric to carry the project of pragmatism forward.

One can see the pragmatist impulse in Wayne Booth's work as well. In *Modern Dogma and the Rhetoric of Assent,* Booth searches for "good reasons" and "warrants of assent" in an age of doubt and skepticism. Toward the end of this work, Booth sounds a particularly pragmatist note:

> We have found, I think, without falling back on any traditional dogma or depending on any private revelations, a firm public value. And in a world where many claim that there are no shared values, it is no mean practical result to be able to point to one clear value you and I share, in full cognitive respectability: It is always good to maintain and improve the quality of our symbolic exchange with our fellow "selves"—to sharpen our symbolic powers so that we can understand and be understood, "taking in" other selves and thus expanding our own. What we say matters, and it matters how we say it. But the rules for good discourse or clear thinking can no longer be confined to logical prose—we must take in the proofs of personal appeal and commitment, of art and myth and ritual. . . . Perhaps even more important, in a world that talks of the threat of alienation and the loss of community, we have found a community that everyman can assent to: as old as Adam and as new as the morning's newscast, it is the community of those who want to discover good reasons together. (203)

This community, of course, is not stable or static; it changes by virtue of the participants in it. This sentiment is precisely the one that Dewey articulates at the end of *The Public and Its Problems,* arguing that the great community will be possible when methods of communication and debate are perfected. Pluralism, provisionality, community, the search for tools for use in argumentation and debate—all the central pragmatist characteristics are there. What Booth provides is a search for good reasons, a search that explicitly understands itself as rhetorical theory and criticism. However, again, the spirit of pragmatism lies at the heart of such a search.

In *Critical Understanding: The Powers and Limits of Pluralism,* Booth takes up the Jamesian task of analyzing pluralism as a philosophical and literary concept. According to Booth, literary criticism multiplies perspectives, and the resulting pluralism creates a problem for understanding and judgment. Fittingly, Booth argues that an appropriate response to this pluralism is a pragmatist one. Again, the point here is not that Booth is a pragmatist but that his work is a sign of pragmatism's capacity to extend beyond itself, to grow and flourish and be revitalized beyond the walls of philosophy departments. More important, Booth and Burke provide decidedly different variations and voices for contemporary rhetorical theory and criticism. They work from different perspectives, develop different concepts, and employ different critical tools. This variety is precisely the kind of end that pragmatism seeks.

Even philosophers of argumentation such as Stephen Toulmin have made a pragmatic/rhetorical turn in their work. Beginning in *The Uses of Argument,* Toulmin distinguishes between what he terms "substantial" and "analytic" arguments—the former are evaluated according to content and the latter according to form. Individuals who use analytic arguments base their claims on universal principles, while those who use substantial arguments ground their claims in the context of a particular situation rather than some abstract principle. Elsewhere, Toulmin calls these two types theoretical and practical arguments. The distinction between the two is grounded in "two very different accounts of ethics and morality: one that seeks eternal, invariant principles, the practical implications of which can be free of exceptions or qualifications, and another that pays closest attention to the specific details of particular moral cases and circumstances" (Toulmin and Jonsen 1988, 2). Toulmin's claim is that we have relied too much on theoretical arguments, and this has limited the range of methods of appropriate decision making useful in commonplace situations. His work seeks to emancipate people from the domination of theoretical argumentation. Like Booth, Toulmin is in search of good reasons and methods for analyzing the use of reasons in everyday contexts. Just as James and Dewey distanced themselves from the philosophical tradition in order to focus on the problems of the moment, so too does Toulmin.[2]

Toulmin's work has had a considerable impact on rhetorical theory as it provides a concrete analysis of argumentation by showing how warrants are used to move from available data to claims in specific situations. This perspective on argumentation is distinctly different from Booth's and develops out of a different tradition. Even so, the pragmatist impulse to "intellectualize practice," as Dewey once put it, remains. Disparate figures such as Booth and Toulmin are brought together by questions of rhetorical theory. Theories of argumentation, such as the one that Toulmin provides, are critical for pragmatism if it is to hold to claims about pluralism and provisionality. Toulmin's model of argument provides a mechanism for grounding decisions not on absolute, universal principles but on contextual claims made on the basis of probability and the uniqueness of a situation. This is precisely the kind of grounds that pragmatism has sought and continues to seek.

In a similar fashion, the rhetoric-of-inquiry project at the University of Iowa investigated the role of argument in the human sciences by turning away from "foundationalism" and rejecting the notion that there are rules for inquiry in scholarship that stand apart from actual practices. In *The Rhetoric of the Human Sciences* (an anthology of essays that resulted from the rhetoric-of-inquiry project), John Nelson, Allan Megill, and Deirdre McCloskey claim that John Dewey "philosophically and politically . . . provided a rhetorical way of relating scholarship to politics" (1987, 8). According to Nelson, Megill, and McCloskey, Dewey is one of the philosophers who helped weaken the Cartesian base of contemporary philosophy. This change has led to an emphasis on the uses of argument in the conduct of inquiry, along with a concern for the quality of speaking and writing in scholarship and an emphasis on the interaction between style and substance. This anthology ends on a pluralist note with an outline of a variety of rhetorics of inquiry. On the whole, the rhetoric-of-inquiry project and *The Rhetoric of the Human Sciences* show how rhetorics cross disciplines and engage basic and pressing questions concerning the use and communication of knowledge. Again, the spirit of pragmatism lies close to this project (most clearly in Richard Rorty's essay for that volume, "Science as Solidarity"). In each of the various essays one sees different takes on the meaning, significance, and scope of rhetoric, but each acknowledges that rhetoric functions in some undeniably important ways and that reflecting on rhetoric's role can help work through the relationship between scholarship and public affairs.

Contemporary rhetorical theory is a various and multisplendored endeavor. It has many voices, not all of which agree. It has many ends and tries to produce many different consequences. However, underlying these rhetorical theories are the same intellectual commitments that gave birth to classical rhetoric and American pragmatism. The erosion of the Cartesian spirit referred to in *The Rhetoric of the Human Sciences* turns us toward the battles waged by James and Dewey to direct philosophy toward "the problems of men." This turn is first and foremost one toward rhetoric, broadly construed as an intellectual endeavor, and rhetorics, narrowly construed as sets of strategies for coping with uncertainty and plurality. Neopragmatism can help facilitate rhetoric's full move to the center of intellectual affairs; the fate of pragmatism depends on this move. Moreover, in contemporary rhetorical theory one sees that pragmatism is related to rhetoric in many different ways. That is, the relationship between an orientation to the world based on uncertainty, plurality, epistemological anthropocentrism, and rhetoric can be theorized from a variety of perspectives and toward a variety of ends. This variety is just what a pragmatist seeks. Attending to the relationship between the two can enhance both rhetorical theory and neopragmatism. One contemporary pragmatist/rhetorician does attend explicitly to this relationship: Stanley Fish. In Fish's work we see one possible variation on the relationship between pragmatism and rhetoric.[3]

Stanley Fish as Neopragmatist Rhetorician

This book has argued that antifoundationalist lines of thought require the practice of rhetoric to guide decision making and ground knowledge claims. This is also Stanley Fish's argument: "another word for anti-foundationalism *is* rhetoric" (1989, 347). Pragmatism is an antifoundationalist line of thought. It does not seek a set of first principles or independent and general criteria by which beliefs can be justified. Rather it posits that truth and human practices are grounded on tradition, history, experience, and language. Pragmatism critiques the pursuit of first principles by arguing that foundationalists cannot deliver what they promise and that it is impossible to tie our beliefs to something independent of everyday, local meanings and values.

Given such a position, critics are likely to charge pragmatism with justifying the position that "anything goes."[4] According to Fish, however, this is hardly so: "When the formalist dream of finding invariant meanings underwritten by God or the structure of rationality is exploded, what remains is not dust and ashes but the solidity *and* plasticity of the world human beings continually make and remake" (Dickstein 1998, 419). In the world that we are in the process of making and remaking, only the things that succeed, that prove useful, actually "go." The relativist charge that "anything goes" is a straw-man argument that ignores the actual operations of rhetoric that ground our beliefs on local and provisionary truths. The last part of a famous sentence written by James demonstrates the centrality of rhetoric in human affairs: "The true is the name of whatever proves itself useful in the way of belief, and good, too, for definite, assignable reasons" (*PR*, 30).

According to Fish, "we come to beliefs by virtue of our situations and our histories in relation to which certain routes of evidence and persuasion are already part of the structure of our understandings"; moreover, we connect our beliefs "with the routes of evidence and persuasion constitutive of the understanding of others" (Dickstein 1998, 432). In such circumstances success is no guarantee, but we are ever engaged in the process of trying to get our beliefs accepted as pieces of the larger, public truth. Pragmatism describes a world of rhetorical processes, and that is crucial for its antifoundationalist attitude. This leads Fish to claim that if "pragmatism is true it has nothing to say to us; no politics follow from it or is blocked by it; no morality attaches to it or is enjoined by it" (419). Instead of prescribing beliefs or attempting to justify truth, pragmatism commits us to the practice of rhetoric. According to Fish, in the absence of foundations, we "fall back on and deploy rhetorics . . . and what we will do with these rhetorics is use them as clubs against our opponents all the while daring them to deny the force of a way of talking that has captured the heart and mind of America. The advantage of vocabularies or rhetorics over foundations is that they are already available in a storehouse of stock arguments, a storehouse Aristotle first furnished in his *Rhetoric,* and one we have been adding to ever since. Foundations have to be sought, and as pragmatism tells us, they are never found. Rhetorics in long short and middle versions are already there for the quarrying and, what is even better, using them in a moment of need commits you to nothing, necessarily in the next moment" (421). Pragmatism recommends that we use rhetoric to advance our own beliefs and persuade others, and so it recommends self-conscious reflection on our rhetorical practices.

A pragmatist, therefore, holds the position that beliefs cannot be justified by independent and abstract criteria. However, such a belief "will not lead me to lose confidence in my other beliefs or inhabit them more loosely than would be the case if I had another account of them" (Dickstein 1998, 420). The "contingent and revisable traditions of inquiry" that anchor our beliefs direct our attention to the competition between opposing claims. Such a competition is rhetorical in that it relies on the persuasiveness of one claim over all others. It is at this point that the relationship between pragmatism, rhetoric, and democracy becomes clear—all three begin from "a recognition of the intractability of difference" (431). Given such a perspective, democracy "is a device for managing the narrow partialities that . . . will always inform the activities of human actors. And by the same reasoning, communication is not a vehicle for harmonizing those particularities; not . . . a cooperative venture, rather it is a competitive one, and the prize in the competition is the (temporary) right to label your way of talking 'undistorting,' a label you can claim only until some other way of talking, some other vocabulary elaborated with a superior force, takes it away from you." Pragmatism, rhetoric, and democracy advocate a pluralism that can be reconciled only through the communicative interactions of different people. More important, such communicative interactions give shape to the world that we inhabit and are open to revision by future persuasive claims.

Perhaps the best explanation of why both pragmatism and rhetoric emerged under democratic conditions is that they emphasized the untenability of foundations on which to anchor our truths *and* the need for communicative practices to decide which claims would emerge victorious from human competition. More important, however, both pragmatism and rhetoric attempt to pit provisionality, openness, and tolerance against inclinations toward closed-minded and bigoted dogmas. Thus they both suggest that democracies will not make people "less aggressive in holding their beliefs" but that democracies must develop mechanisms to ensure provisionality, openness, and tolerance so that beliefs do not become occasions for oppression (Dickstein 1998, 426). Pragmatism teaches that democracies require the open practice of rhetoric and that "all modes of discourse are rhetoric, where 'rhetorical' means proceeding on the basis of assumptions and distinctions that are open to challenge" (Fish 1989, 298). On a parallel view, classical rhetoric teaches that democracies require the practical application of nonscientific knowledge to difficult and uncertain situations and open participation and competition between different interpretations.

The result of Fish's line of thinking, and my reading of pragmatism, is "to move rhetoric from the disreputable periphery to the necessary center . . . the skill which produces belief and therefore establishes what, in a particular time and particular place, is true, is the skill essential in the building and maintaining of a civilized society. In the absence of a revealed truth, rhetoric is that skill" (Fish 1989, 480). For Fish, antifoundationalist thought and the developments of neopragmatism place rhetoric at the center of intellectual and human affairs. One consequence of this line of thinking is that the differences between, for example, science, on the one hand, and poetry, on the other, is not the difference between a foundational and accurate depiction of reality and an artistic production. Instead it is the difference between rhetorics that are more or less powerful in different, situated contexts. Different rhetorics acquire persuasive power through "historical achievements—achievements fashioned on the anvil of argument and debate" (298).

Fish's essay "Truth and Toilets," from which this line of argument was drawn, is the conclusion to *The Revival of Pragmatism,* an anthology of the latest generation of academics working within the tradition of James and Dewey. The final two paragraphs of his essay point to the similarity between pragmatism and rhetoric developed throughout this book. Fish argues that "if pragmatism is anything . . . it is an up-to-date version of rhetoric, that account of thought and action anchored in two famous pronouncements of Protagoras': 'About the gods I cannot say either that they are or that they are not' and 'Man is the measure of all things.' It's all there—the bracketing of ontological questions, and the location of knowledge, certainty and objectivity (of a revisable kind) in the ways of knowing that emerge in history. That is the lesson pragmatism teaches, that we live in a rhetorical world where arguments and evidence are always available, but always challengeable, and that the resources of that world are sufficient unto most days . . . everyone is already doing what Aristotle advises in the *Rhetoric,* looking around for the available means of persuasion" (Dickstein 1998, 432). If the revival of pragmatism is to continue and extend the work done by James and Dewey, then the next turn in its rebirth must be a turn toward rhetoric. Fish gestures in that direction. Pragmatism commits us to updating and expanding Aristotle's *Rhetoric,* and the best place to begin such a project is by reading pragmatism in the light of ancient Greek rhetorical theory. The more radical claim is that the fate of pragmatism runs parallel to the fate of rhetoric. One could argue that the revival of pragmatism is a parallel development of the rebirth of rhetoric in the last fifty years, and that combining the insights from both can explain that parallel development and help push both projects forward.

What Fish describes in "Truth and Toilets" and elsewhere are *some* of the ways that language, symbol systems, and modes of argument influence our thoughts, beliefs, and decisions. It would not be pragmatic to think that Fish serves all of the purposes that any rhetorician might have with these issues; Burke, Booth, Toulmin and others all point to other ways to think through such issues. The spirit of pluralism that attends both pragmatism and rhetoric indicates that Fish alone cannot nourish all of our rhetorical and pragmatic needs. He does mark a beginning in the project of developing the relationship between pragmatism and rhetoric, but it is only a beginning. Perhaps Fish's move to call pragmatism an "updated version of rhetoric" oversimplifies this relationship. To state the case in such a way is to sublimate pragmatism to the rhetorical tradition rather than to have a multiplicity of rhetorics as possible tools for the multiple purposes of pragmatism. In that case the relationship between rhetoric and pragmatism becomes more complicated and subject to the shifting demands of each of the varieties of pragmatism and rhetoric.

What Fish's work clearly demonstrates is that the five central commitments of pragmatism outlined in the introduction to this book require that we explain and account for the function of rhetoric in contemporary sociopolitical affairs. More important, Fish demonstrates that these five commitments encourage and facilitate the development of many rhetorics used for an ever-expanding variety of purposes. It is not just Fish's rhetoric that waits at the end of pragmatist thought but many possible rhetorics—those already included within the rhetorical tradition and those yet to be expressed and developed by the demands of the moment.

Another Turn—From the Classical to the American Context

Pragmatism appreciates the centrality of rhetoric in democratic affairs. Such a reading is warranted by the model of ancient Greek rhetorical theory and the significant similarities between pragmatism and Greek rhetoric. Pragmatism is appreciative of the centrality of rhetoric not by self-consciously reflecting on aspects of the rhetorical tradition but by following two distinct paths. First, James, Dewey, and others outline intellectual conditions that, if granted, necessitate the practice of rhetoric. In other words, their theoretical commitments imply the need for rhetoric in negotiating uncertainty, plurality, and ambiguity. Second, Addams, Locke, Holmes, and others highlight the practical conditions that call for the uses of rhetoric in politics, culture, and law. In other words, their recommendations for pragmatic action suggest ways to cultivate rhetorical practices in an American democracy. Comparing these two lines of thought with the development of Greek rhetorical theory demonstrates what pragmatism might learn from rhetoric and what rhetoric might learn from pragmatism.

The similarities between pragmatism and Greek rhetorical theory issue from the claim that philosophy is incomplete or inadequate if it focuses exclusively on the foundations of knowledge. The traditional assumptions of philosophy—its focus on abstract thought, its quest for certainty, and its belief in the possibility of a true account of reality—are built on its dismissal of rhetoric in Greek thought. However, pragmatism rejects those traditional assumptions, choosing instead to describe the world as uncertain, plural, and ambiguous. By offering both a description of the world and a critique of philosophy, pragmatism shows that we are always already engaged in rhetorical processes. Implied in this position is the claim that philosophies are improved by exploring their relationship to rhetoric and self-consciously reflecting on the role that rhetoric plays in shaping philosophical inquiry. More important, however, this position also implies that contemporary culture can be renewed and improved through self-conscious reflection on rhetoric's role in sociopolitical affairs. Seeking foundations for our knowledge, according to the pragmatists, does not aid us in making a better democratic culture. Only the development of the means of applying knowledge to difficult and uncertain circumstances can aid such a project, and that requires attention to rhetoric. Although none of the pragmatists understand themselves explicitly as rhetoricians, they all suggest the possibility and necessity of developing rhetorics based on pragmatist principles. Carrying the pragmatist project forward requires turning to such issues.

This book is only a beginning. It is open to and accepts revision, extension, and interpretation because it acknowledges its place in a larger conversation of competing claims. It seeks to outline a theoretical commitment to rhetoric implied by pragmatism and to show what can happen when that commitment is explored. Mining classical Greek sources for recommendations is one important way of engaging in that project, and one final lesson from Aristotle can be a suggestion for the future development of pragmatism. Aristotle divides all uses of language into three categories: theoretical, practical, and productive.[5] He uses this same system of classification when discussing types of knowledge. Within this scheme he identifies areas of study that correspond to each category: the theoretical is concerned with philosophy and science; the practical is concerned with politics and ethics; and the productive is concerned with rhetoric and poetics. This scheme allows Aristotle to investigate the varying uses and purposes of language and knowledge. Studying James, Dewey, Addams, Locke, and Holmes points to the ways in which language and knowledge are understood and used from a pragmatist perspective. The general features of these earlier claims can be summarized by reading them in the light of Aristotle's three categories.

Prior Analytics, Posterior Analytics, and *Topics* are all devoted to the art of logic and examine the theoretical and scientific use of language. In these works Aristotle claims that language functions as an instrument of knowledge, attempting to record and communicate facts with accuracy and precision. The goal of theoretical language is to make certain that words mirror the way things are. Knowledge derived from this kind of language is certain, general, and unambiguous. The pragmatists attempted to debunk the pursuit of theoretical knowledge, and the influence of Darwinian science demonstrated the limits of scientific thought that sought universality and certainty. More important, the pragmatists dismissed the kind of philosophy that issued from theoretical language as overly abstract and detached from the actual activities of people. Neopragmatism carries the project of debunking theoretical language even further by rejecting the very possibility of words as a mirror of reality.[6] Dewey's history of philosophy is an account of the dominance of overly theoretical language at the expense of the practical, and thus he recommends that philosophical inquiry turn to practical knowledge as its proper area of investigation.

In the *Politics* and the *Nicomachean Ethics,* Aristotle demonstrates how language functions as a mechanism for influencing individual behavior and collective action. The purpose of practical language is persuasion, and the goal is prudential action that aids the welfare of the community. The art of the practical use of language is rhetoric, according to Aristotle, and the rhetor must use knowledge gained from experience in difficult situations and apply that knowledge to new circumstances. This is the primary concern of each of the pragmatists described. In the case of James and Dewey, pragmatism was a question of applying philosophy to "the problems of men." In the case of Addams, Locke, and Holmes, pragmatism was a question of applying all forms of knowledge to the immediate and pressing concerns of the moment. The pragmatist concern with applying scientific knowledge to practical problems works precisely at the intersection of Aristotle's theoretical and practical categories, and it demonstrates the problems of thinking of one without the other. Dewey, in fact, believed that the theoretical and the practical are a false binary that must be overcome.

In the *Poetics* and the *Rhetoric,* Aristotle shows how language can be used in the formation of artistic discourse. The purpose of the rhetor or poet is to use the aesthetic resources of language for the cultivation and expression of a delightful work of art. The production of a work of art requires experience with materials as well as rules for making something out of those materials. In their reflections on aesthetics both Dewey and Locke begin to recommend what a pragmatist account of the productive use of language and knowledge might look like; and James's lectures and Holmes's judicial opinions are clear examples of the aesthetic capacity of language. However, the pragmatists do not pay sufficient attention to the production of persuasive discourse. Their explanation of the limits of the theoretical and their emphasis on the importance of the practical were not complemented with the development of a productive guide for engagement in rhetoric.

Aristotle's classification of knowledge and language highlights the great advance of pragmatism *and* its limits. In advocating the importance of the practical and illustrating the limits of the theoretical, the pragmatists correct what they perceive as an old and enduring imbalance. The next step in correcting the overemphasis on the theoretical is to fully account for the role of the productive and the aesthetic capacity of rhetoric. If, as Fish claims, pragmatism can be understood as an updated version of rhetoric, then it must be concerned with the production of persuasive discourse so that we are better able to compete and apply our knowledge to the uncertain circumstances of our moment.

Emphasizing the productive capacity of rhetoric in the light of pragmatist thought allows us to begin to use all the available means of persuasion to contribute to the ongoing construction of a better world. It also allows us to engage in the practical art of politics and the application of knowledge to democratic decision making. What pragmatism needs now is a renewed attention to the productive capacity of language within contemporary sociopolitical circumstances. Such a move would more fully account for the connection between philosophy and rhetoric and would provide better grounds on which to engage in practical action.

Such a move is not necessarily a turn toward oratory, as it was in the classical period. In our own moment, face-to-face spoken language has been supplemented by a variety of other technologically mediated forms of communication. Given this situation, Aristotle's *Rhetoric* may be a place to begin, but it cannot describe all the available means of persuasion. Jane Addams, Alain Locke, and Oliver Wendell Holmes all point to possible areas for the multiplication of rhetorics. The promise of pragmatism lies in extending its attention to the practical by reflecting more deeply on how rhetorical claims are produced and how they can shape American democracy. Perhaps this will involve thinking about rhetoric from outside the speaker-speech-audience perspective.

In any case, pragmatism can be made more useful by teaching two specific skills. First, the critical reception of messages must become part of the pragmatist project if we are to evaluate which claims will prove most prudent. This is a prescription for the practice of rhetorical criticism and the judgment of messages based on their use. More important, it is a prescription for a kind of postmodern rhetorical criticism, one that understands the complicated and sophisticated relationship between language, discourse, and persuasion. Second, we must continue to refine our capacity to use language within a technologically mediated environment and to use all kinds of symbol systems for persuasion. This is a prescription for learning how to find and display "definite, assignable reasons" with aesthetic skill so that we are better able to participate in decision-making processes and influence the course of sociopolitical affairs. Once again, these aesthetic skills cannot be limited to speech making but extend and apply to media production, design, architecture, and other areas in which aesthetics intersects with politics, law, and society.

Pragmatism seeks a sustained democratic culture constantly regenerated by meaningful rhetorical action. In so doing, it requires responsible agents of change who aim to bring about a brighter tomorrow. Such a project demands the practice of rhetoric in both its practical and productive capacities. Ihab Hassan gets it right when he says that pragmatism has "no rancorous urge to demystify all beliefs" but instead "invites us to reconstruct our discourse, to ground it even, not on some rock of the Absolute but on resilient concretions of human desire in their circumstance" (1987, 453). It is my contention that rhetoric, broadly construed as an intellectual tradition, and rhetorics, narrowly construed as sets of appropriate strategies and tactics, are the best available resources for making that possible.

By emphasizing both the skills necessary for making the world new and the practical application of knowledge for that task, pragmatism teaches us that rhetoric is the best available means for making our way as well as we can in a world marked by contingency, uncertainty, and plurality. Rhetoricians are waiting at the end of neopragmatism's focus on antifoundationalism. In order to carry on Fish's intellectual work (as well as the work of other neopragmatists such as Richard Rorty and Richard Bernstein), rhetoric must regain its place at the center of contemporary thought and move beyond classical preoccupations to develop multiple strategies fit to our contemporary predicament. From this perspective, pragmatism has facilitated a turn from the classical conception of rhetoric to a uniquely American conception of rhetoric. More broadly, pragmatism has demonstrated the need for and the centrality of rhetoric in human affairs.

Notes

Introduction

1. This story is recounted in John Patrick Diggins, *The Promise of Pragmatism: Modernism and the Crisis of Knowledge and Authority* (Chicago: University of Chicago Press, 1994), 1–4. The quotes from this lecture are taken from Diggins's account as well.

2. In *The Promise of Pragmatism,* Diggins uses Dewey's lecture as grounds for a critique of pragmatism that claims that Dewey and other pragmatists failed to live up to their own principles. Such a criticism is a justification for my interpretation. Without an appropriate and timely rhetoric to find persuasive expression for such principles, pragmatism was unable to have the success that Diggins demands of it, but that is only a warrant to find and practice a rhetoric capable of best employing pragmatic principles.

3. It is interesting to note that Cicero attributed two important transformations in human life to language: the translation of the survival instinct into the idea of the common good; and the conquest of physical force by persuasion. If pragmatism is designed to make it harder for us to be driven to violence by our ideas, the rhetorical tradition suggests that language and communication were also designed for that same task.

4. For a thorough account of Darwin's influence on pragmatism, see John Dewey, *Influence of Darwin on Philosophy and Other Essays in Contemporary Thought* (Bloomington: Indiana University Press, [1910] 1965); and Philip P. Wiener, *Evolution and the Founders of Pragmatism* (Gloucester, Mass.: P. Smith, [1949] 1969).

5. Louis Agassiz was the champion of the position that species were stable, general types that were not subject to change over time. In some sense Agassiz represents the antithesis of Darwinian thought. See Louis Menand, *The Metaphysical Club: A Story of Ideas in America* (New York: Farrar, Straus and Giroux, 2001), 97–116.

6. Albert Einstein's "theory of relativity" and Werner Heisenberg's "uncertainty principle" articulate similar perspectives on the indeterminacy of the natural world and use theories as tools for explaining that indeterminacy. On the influence of quantum mechanics on Dewey's philosophy, see Thomas Dalton, *Becoming John Dewey: Dilemmas of a Philosopher and Naturalist* (Bloomington: Indiana University Press, 2002), 149–74.

7. For a discussion of Wundt's influence on Dewey, see Dalton, *Becoming John Dewey,* 10–11, 44–57.

8. Ralph Barton Perry, *The Thought and Character of William James* (Nashville: Vanderbilt University Press, [1948] 1996) is the best account of James's depression and its influence on his intellectual development.

9. See Andrew Feffer's *The Chicago Pragmatists and American Progressivism* (Ithaca, N.Y.: Cornell University Press, 1993) for an account of the sociopolitical factors in Chicago that helped shape pragmatist thought.

10. For a description of Holmes's activities as a judge and their relationship to larger sociopolitical issues, see G. Edward White, *Justice Oliver Wendell Holmes: Law and the Inner Self* (New York: Oxford University Press, 1993).

11. See Menand, *Metaphysical Club,* 3–72.

12. See Ross Posnock, *Color & Culture: Black Writers and the Making of the Modern Intellectual* (Cambridge: Harvard University Press, 1998), for an account of Locke's role in the Harlem Renaissance.

13. For an account of the origins of rhetoric as a method capable of such tasks, see Thomas Cole, *The Origins of Rhetoric in Ancient Greece* (Baltimore: Johns Hopkins University Press, 1991).

14. For an account of the various interpretations of Protagoras's "human-measure" principle, as well as an interpretation of the significance of this principle for rhetorical theory, see Edward Schiappa, *Protagoras and Logos: A Study in Greek Philosophy and Rhetoric* (Columbia: University of South Carolina Press, 2003b), 117–33.

15. See Edward Schiappa, *The Beginnings of Rhetorical Theory in Classical Greece* (New Haven, Conn.: Yale University Press, 1999). Schiappa argues that Isocrates actually anticipates many of the basic philosophical tenets of American pragmatism. He suggests that Isocrates' "philosophy" shares a great deal with contemporary pragmatism and that Isocrates can serve as an inspiration and useful resource for contemporary pragmatism (an argument that I try to develop in greater detail): "That he found new ways to contribute to the political life of the community in which he found himself suggests, for contemporary Pragmatists, that the last message provided by Isocrates' texts is that our own roles in society are limited by our ingenuity" (184).

16. On Aristotle's place in the rhetorical tradition, see Friedrich Solmsen, "The Aristotelian Tradition in Ancient Rhetoric," in *Aristotle: The Classical Heritage of Rhetoric,* ed. Keith V. Erickson (Metuchen, N.J.: Scarecrow Press, Inc., 1974), 278–309. For general reflections on Aristotle's rhetoric, see Richard Leo Enos and Lois Peters Agnew, eds., *Landmark Essays on Aristotelian Rhetoric* (Mahwah, N.J.: Lawrence Erlbaum Associates, 1998).

17. For a contemporary interpretation of the connection between contingency and rhetoric (as well as an interpretation of Aristotle's perspective on that connection), see Dilip Gaonkar's entry on "Contingency" in *Encyclopedia of Rhetoric,* ed. Thomas Sloane (New York: Oxford University Press, 2001); as well as Thomas B. Farrell, *Norms of Rhetorical Culture* (New Haven, Conn.: Yale University Press, 1993), 27–28.

18. Interpreting rhetorical theory as a serious attempt to articulate a philosophy, or from my perspective "an orientation to the world," is not new. See G. B. Kerferd, *The Sophistic Movement* (New York: Cambridge University Press, 1981). Kerferd argues that Protagoras's beliefs are "intended" to be a serious "contribution to a serious philosophic problem" (93). Throughout *The Sophistic Movement,* Kerferd develops the philosophical positions of the sophists in relation to their attention to rhetoric. My analysis follows this kind of interpretation.

19. On the relationship between rhetoric as *techné* and rhetoric as *dynamis,* see Farrell, *Norms of Rhetorical Culture,* 62–68.

20. One could argue that any further extension of rhetoric is no longer needed. With such a variety of work concerned with the "rhetoric of X," one could argue that we have extended rhetoric's role too far. However, the warrant for the kind of extension I am making comes from the historical precedent set in classical Athens. This is not a study that claims that "X has a rhetoric because all things have a rhetoric." Instead, I argue that there are sound historical reasons for considering pragmatism as a philosophy of rhetoric, and these sound historical reasons provide a warrant for the extension of rhetoric to include pragmatism while many other "rhetoric of X" projects lack such historical warrant.

Chapter One: William James on Contingency, Plurality, and Belief

1. These lectures were delivered after James's retirement from Harvard, and James had been hesitant to accept the invitation to lecture because of health issues. In a way they mark the end of James's extraordinary career as a lecturer. He died two years later in 1910.

2. These quotes are taken from R. B. Perry, *Thought and Character of William James,* 328.

3. The phrase "public philosopher" is taken from George Cotkin, *William James, Public Philosopher* (Baltimore: Johns Hopkins University Press, 1990). Cotkin demonstrates how James's performances as a public lecturer were an integral part of his career as a philosopher, and how James's philosophical position was rooted in the timely and pressing issues of the day.

4. I consistently refer to the importance of uncertainty for James's pragmatism throughout this chapter. Several other sources corroborate the importance of uncertainty for James's philosophy. The primary example is James Kloppenberg, *Uncertain Victory: Social Democracy and Progressivism in European and American Thought, 1870–1920* (New York: Oxford University Press, 1986), especially chap. 1, "The Philosophy of the *Via Media,*" 15–63, and chap. 2, "The Radical Theory of Knowledge," 64–94.

5. Often James is criticized for his lack of logical rigor and his lack of concern for conceptual philosophical subtleties—he devotes a great deal of *The Meaning of Truth* to defending his position against such criticisms. It is not my intention to support that argument. Just because James did not attend to the careful logical and rational explication of his philosophical position in a manner befitting a professional philosopher did not mean that he did not have a serious and robust philosophy. Part of his philosophy is founded on ignoring overconceptualizations, and so any charge against his ability to "rationalize" seems to miss a very fundamental part of pragmatism. James tried to make this point throughout *The Meaning of Truth.*

6. I site these five works—*The Will to Believe: And Other Essays in Popular Philosophy* (New York: Dover Publications, Inc., [1897] 1956) (hereafter *WB*); *Pragmatism* (New York: Dover Publications, Inc., [1907] 1995) (hereafter *PR*); *A Pluralistic Universe* (Cambridge: Harvard University Press, [1909] 1977) (hereafter *PU*); *The Meaning of Truth* (Amherst, N.Y.: Prometheus Books, [1911] 1997) (hereafter *MT*); and *Some Problems in Philosophy: A Beginning of an Introduction to Philosophy* (Lincoln: University of Nebraska Press, [1911] 1996) (hereafter *SPP*)—because they represent James's major contributions to philosophy. However, James had several other significant interests, including religion, empirical science, and psychology. His religious views and his psychological and

scientific views are certainly intertwined with his pragmatism, although I do not address either of these in full and complete manner. Therefore, *Principles of Psychology* (New York: Dover Publications, Inc., [1890] 1950), *The Varieties of Religious Experience* (New York: Simon & Schuster Inc., [1902] 1997), and *Essays in Radical Empiricism* (Lincoln: University of Nebraska Press, [1912] 1996) do not have a central place in this chapter.

7. I use the word "vision" here intentionally. Richard Bernstein in his introduction to *A Pluralistic Universe* demonstrates the importance of the concept of vision for James's philosophy. In many ways philosophy was, for James, "a way of *seeing* and feeling the total push and pressure of the cosmos" (*PR*, 1, italics mine).

8. In many ways C. S. Peirce compensates for this oversight by articulating a provocative theory of signs. In addition, contemporary pragmatists such as Richard Rorty have linked James's work to the traditions of poststructuralism, where the emphasis on language is more clearly pronounced.

9. On the affectionate relationship between Schiller and James, see R. B. Perry, *Thought and Character of William James,* 301–5.

10. Mailloux's introductory essay "Sophistry and Rhetorical Pragmatism" focuses on the ways that pragmatism, sophistry, and rhetoric overlap in their theoretical implications. By tracing the presence of the sophists in the writings of some major pragmatists from both the beginning and the end of this century, Mailloux makes a convincing argument that there is a relevant and provocative intersection of ideas between sophistic rhetoric and American pragmatism.

11. William James, "Humanism," *Nation* 78 (March 3, 1904): 175–76; reprinted in William James, *Essays, Comments, and Reviews,* ed. Frederick Burkhardt, Fredson Bowers, and Ignas K. Skrupskelis (Cambridge: Harvard University Press, 1987), 552.

12. See also his discussion of *dissoi logoi* in F. C. S. Schiller, *Studies in Humanism* (New York: Macmillan, 1907), 112; his discussion of "The Ambiguity of Truth," in Schiller, *Studies in Humanism,* 144–46; and Schiller, *Plato or Protagoras?* (Oxford: Blackwell, 1908).

13. This is a reiteration of the key intellectual features of the philosophers of the "via media" that Kloppenberg describes in *Uncertain Victory.*

14. On James's conception of reality, see Ellen Kappy Suckiel, *The Pragmatic Philosophy of William James* (Notre Dame, Ind.: University of Notre Dame Press, 1982), 122–42.

15. For a more thorough explication of the roles that perception and reality play in James's psychology and philosophy, see Patrick Kiaran Dooley, *Pragmatism as Humanism: The Philosophy of William James* (Chicago: Nelson-Hall, 1974), 11–60.

16. James also makes this same point in the section on philosophy in *Varieties of Religious Experience:* "Philosophy lives in words, but truth and fact well up into our lives in ways that exceed verbal formulation" (356).

17. See also Gorgias's *Encomium of Helen* and *Defense on Behalf of Palamedes.* In the former, Gorgias points to the importance of language in determining the fate of Helen, and in the latter, Gorgias uses rhetorical techniques to demonstrate the uncertainty of the accusations against Palamedes.

18. In *A Pluralistic Universe,* James lists philosophers associated with the intellectualist and rationalist tradition, including Kant, Hegel, and F. H. Bradley.

19. On James's notion of experience and its connection to both radical empiricism and a pluralistic universe, see Dooley, *Pragmatism as Humanism,* 146–54.

20. If the world does stand fixed, its fixity is outside our perceptual/cognitive awareness; in short, it does not exist *for us*.

21. Plato's desire to refute this perspective stands as the inspiration for the kind of philosophy James is working against.

22. In this quote James refers to "truth" as a matter of degree, not kind. By claiming that some opinions are "truer" he implicitly refutes any notion of truth independent of human experience. In addition, he makes measuring the degree of truth in an opinion a central feature of epistemology.

23. There is some dispute over Isocrates' use of the word "philosophy." Although that is the term he uses to describe his educational program, many have interpreted "philosophy" to mean "rhetoric." See Edward Schiappa's essay "Isocrates' *Philosophia* and Contemporary Pragmatism," in *Rhetoric, Sophistry, Pragmatism,* ed. Steven Mailloux (New York: Cambridge University Press, 1995), for an account of this controversy and general insight into Isocrates' philosophy. Also, for further explication of Isocrates' practical rhetoric, see Takis Poulakos, *Speaking for the Polis: Isocrates' Rhetorical Education* (Columbia: University of South Carolina Press, 1997).

24. For a history of the lyceum movement in America at the end of the nineteenth century and the beginning of the twentieth century, see Carl Bode, *American Lyceum: Town Meeting of the Mind* (New York: Oxford University Press, 1956); or John Tapia, *Circuit Chautauqua: From Rural Education to Popular Entertainment in Early Twentieth Century America* (Jefferson, N.C.: McFarland & Co., 1997); or David S. Reynolds, *Walt Whitman's America: A Cultural Biography* (New York: Vintage Books, 1996), 166–76.

25. At this point one might ask why none of these figures explicitly linked the project of pragmatism to rhetorical theory. Why was it that William James did not see the benefits of the rhetorical tradition for his philosophy? The predominant conception of rhetoric in nineteenth-century American culture could not account for the radical claims James made. Adams Sherman Hill was the Boylston Professor of Rhetoric and Oratory at Harvard from 1876 until 1904 and therefore was a contemporary of James. According to Ronald Reid, in "The Boylston Professorship of Rhetoric and Oratory, 1806–1904: A Case Study in Changing Concepts of Rhetoric and Pedagogy," *Quarterly Journal of Speech* 45, no. 3 (1959), Hill's conception of rhetoric "was concerned not with oratory, but with written composition, expository and literary as well as persuasive, and made little direct reference to classical authors" (239). During this time rhetoric was incorporated into English departments, and eventually rhetoric courses were renamed "composition" courses. Perhaps more importantly, the study of rhetorical theory was almost completely abandoned for writing and literary criticism. The case of the Boylston professorship at Harvard represents a larger trend in the nineteenth century. Hill's turn to grammar at the end of the nineteenth century exemplifies a complete turn in the study of rhetoric to a formal art of composition. This was made possible by the influence of figures such as George Campbell and Hugh Blair. For example, Campbell tried to banish the role of invention in rhetoric in favor of the management of discourse, and Blair denied rhetoric's responsibility for providing the content of discourse and claimed that composition was rhetoric's only function. James asked questions about the individual's relationship to the community and to the natural world. In asking such questions he returned to the intellectual roots of rhetoric's birth in classical Athens and not the formal study of composition. See also James Berlin, "The Transformation of Invention in Nineteenth Century American Rhetoric," *Southern Speech Communication Journal* 46 (Spring 1981): 292–304.

26. One could argue that books such as Kenneth Burke's *Rhetoric of Motives* (Los Angeles: University of California Press, 1969) and Michael Billig's *Arguing and Thinking: A Rhetorical Approach to Social Psychology* (New York: Cambridge University Press, 1987) are anticipated in James's psychological writings. In other words, James reintroduces the important links between psychology and rhetoric, and those connections are made explicit in twentieth-century rhetorical theory.

27. One could also argue that books such as Thomas Kuhn's *Structure of Scientific Revolutions* (Chicago: University of Chicago Press, [1962] 1970), Bruno Latour and Steve Woolgar's *Laboratory Life: The Construction of Scientific Facts* (Princeton, N.J.: Princeton University Press, 1986), and Ian Hacking's *Representing and Intervening: Introductory Topics in the Philosophy of Natural Science* (New York: Cambridge University Press, 1983) are anticipated.

Chapter Two: John Dewey on Communication and the Practical Arts

1. In what follows, I quote extensively from four works by Dewey: *Reconstruction in Philosophy* (Boston: Beacon Press, [1920] 1957) (hereafter *RP*); *Experience and Nature* (New York: Dover Publications Inc., [1925] 1958) (hereafter *EN*); *The Public and Its Problems* (Athens: Swallow Press / Ohio University Press, [1927] 1954) (hereafter *PP*); and *The Quest for Certainty: A Study of the Relation of Knowledge and Action* (New York: Minton, Balch & Company, 1929) (hereafter *QC*).

2. In the spring of 1894 George Pullman cut wages at the Pullman Car Works but refused to cut rents, food prices, and service rates that he charged his workers in the model company town he had built for them just south of Chicago in the 1880s. After Pullman refused to respond to the workers' grievances and fired the workers who presented those grievances, there was a strike on May 11. Eventually the strike gained support from Eugene Debs, escalating it from a local dispute to a national struggle between classes. President Cleveland dispatched federal troops to Chicago to stop the strike and arrest Debs and others, ending the conflict. For a more detailed account of the strike, see Stanley Buder, *Pullman: An Experiment in Industrial Order and Community Planning, 1880–1930* (New York: Oxford University Press, 1967); and Almont Lindsey, *The Pullman Strike* (Chicago: University of Chicago Press, 1942).

3. See John Dewey to Alice Dewey, July 2, 1894, Dewey Papers (Southern Illinois University), quoted in Robert Westbrook, *John Dewey and American Democracy* (Ithaca, N.Y.: Cornell University Press, 1991), 86–87.

4. Robert Westbrook identifies the Hegelian preoccupations of Dewey's early intellectual career (*John Dewey,* 13–32). I rely on Westbrook's analysis at several points throughout this chapter because he provides a thorough overview of Dewey's intellectual development. See also Dalton, *Becoming John Dewey.* Dalton argues that Hegel remained an important preoccupation for Dewey's thought throughout his career, and his account is an excellent resource for understanding the importance of Hegel for Dewey. In addition, I use "the problems of men" in quotes because this is Dewey's own phrase. In 1946 he edited a collection of his own essays that he titled *The Problems of Men* (New York: Philosophical Library, Inc.).

5. Dewey confessed that "upon the whole the forces that have influenced me have come from persons and from situations more than from books." What he learned from books was merely "technical in comparison with what [he] had been forced to think upon

and about because of some experience in which [he] found [himself] entangled." See Dewey, "From Absolutism to Experimentalism," in *Contemporary American Philosophy,* ed. G. P. Adams and W. P. Montague (New York: Macmillan, 1930), 22.

6. At a celebration of his eightieth birthday Dewey debated the difference between an effort to "practicalize intelligence" and "intellectualize practice" with several of his colleagues. He contended that his career had been marked by an effort to "intellectualize practice," which marks the importance of taking practice as a starting point. For an excellent analysis of Dewey's lifelong effort to promote intelligent action, see Michael Eldridge, *Transforming Experience: John Dewey's Cultural Instrumentalism* (Nashville: Vanderbilt University Press, 1998). Eldridge argues that the effort to "intellectualize practice" is the most fundamental aspect of Dewey's instrumentalism and his pragmatism as a whole.

7. The idea of a "philosophy of action" has been commented on extensively in the secondary literature on Dewey. The case is almost always made that pragmatism represents a philosophy of action, and then in the subsequent interpretation of that term competing perspectives develop. See R. W. Sleeper, *The Necessity of Pragmatism: John Dewey's Conception of Philosophy* (New Haven, Conn.: Yale University Press, 1986); and S. G. Sathaye, *Instrumentalism: A Methodological Exposition of the Philosophy of John Dewey* (Bombay: Popular Prakashan, 1972). Both works begin with that assumption, and both explicate the ways in which philosophy, according to Dewey, can and should have an impact on the social world. My interpretation differs from these others by claiming that a philosophy of action implies the necessity of rhetoric.

8. Despite a great deal of secondary literature that attends to Dewey's rejection of classical philosophy, no one, that I am aware of, makes an explicit link between this rejection and the possibility of an American rhetoric. See, for example, J. J. Chambliss, *The Influence of Plato and Aristotle on John Dewey's Philosophy* (Lewiston, N.Y.: Edwin Mellen Press, 1963). Despite Chambliss's attempt to "provide a comprehensive account of the thought of the ancient Greeks and that of Dewey," he fails to address the importance of rhetoric for such a project.

9. This phrase, "the practical arts," appears repeatedly in Dewey's discussions of the history of philosophy. For my purposes, I assume that rhetoric is one of the foundational practical arts.

10. In the introduction to *Reconstruction in Philosophy,* Dewey discusses the possibility that his philosophy could be identified with the work of "reformers." Although he welcomes the comparison between his work and such socially active figures as the progressives, he does claim that his pursuit is a theoretical attempt to introduce the importance of practice to democracy.

11. Whether or not Plato actually did have the influence that Dewey describes is, of course, an open question. In fact, it seems that Plato did not have any such influence.

12. Dewey seems to conflate "matter of fact knowledge" and "purely intellectual knowledge," at some points intimating that "purely intellectual knowledge" was a result of "matter of fact knowledge." Plato clearly advocated "purely intellectual knowledge," and both Plato and the sophists assigned "matter of fact knowledge" an inferior status to their respective projects. Regardless, from Dewey's perspective the history of philosophy began with a pursuit of "matter of fact knowledge" and eventually became an obsession with "purely intellectual knowledge"—two different descriptions of the same process.

13. Dewey's position here does not differentiate between Plato and Aristotle, when perhaps there is justification for such a distinction.

14. Such a link could also provide rhetoric (as well as other practical arts) with the philosophical means to improve itself, and the practical arts could provide philosophy with the means to improve as well. In other words, we can achieve an advanced understanding of rhetoric through philosophical investigation, and we can improve our ability to do philosophy by attention to practical arts.

15. J. J. Chambliss, in *Influence of Plato and Aristotle on John Dewey's Philosophy,* demonstrates that Dewey's interpretation of Aristotle relied on a close connection between the classical notion of *phronesis* and Dewey's experimental method—both are methods of linking action and intelligence. According to Chambliss, Dewey was influenced by Aristotle's understanding of *phronesis.* Westbrook also links Aristotle's notion of *phronesis* to Dewey's understanding of science (*John Dewey,* 187).

16. For a more complete account of Isocrates' conception of *phronesis,* see Takis Poulakos, "Isocrates' Civic Education and the Question of *Doxa,*" in *Isocrates and Civic Education,* ed. Takis Poulakos and David Depew (Austin: University of Texas Press, 2004), 44–68.

17. On the relationship between the sophists and the possible, see John Poulakos, "Rhetoric, the Sophists, and the Possible," *Communication Monographs* 51, no. 3 (September 1984): 215–26.

18. It is also Aristotle's focus in the *Rhetoric* and the *Ethics.*

19. For a further discussion of the connection between ethics and rhetoric, see Richard Weaver, *The Ethics of Rhetoric* (Davis, Calif.: Hermagoras Press, 1985).

20. There are two other significant places where Dewey discusses the relationship between the sophists and Plato. In *Democracy and Education: An Introduction to the Philosophy of Education* (New York: Free Press, [1916] 1944), 329–30, Dewey claims that the sophists introduced questions about the relationship between reason and action. As early educators they claimed that there was a connection between action and virtue. Unfortunately, shortly after the sophists gained fame, the central questions about the relationship between reason and action and virtue and action were ignored by philosophy. Philosophers instead sought a separate branch of inquiry. Also, *Experience and Nature* (126–28) mentions the debate between Plato and the sophists as over the question whether practical activity or philosophical wisdom should secure control.

21. See James Mackin, "Rhetoric, Pragmatism, and Practical Wisdom," in *Rhetoric and Philosophy,* ed. Richard Cherwitz (Hillsdale, N.J.: Lawrence Erlbaum Associates, 1990). Mackin argues that the impetus behind Bitzer's essay was Dewey's focus on situations and problems.

22. Aristotle also describes the role that contingency plays in human affairs. More specifically, he claims that because "individual cases are so infinitely various . . . no systematic knowledge of them is possible" (1356b35). Dilip Gaonkar's essay "Contingency and Probability" in *Encyclopedia of Rhetoric* cites Aristotle as the source for placing rhetoric in the realm of the contingent. By virtue of its concern with contingency, rhetoric attends to issues of public or social knowledge, as well as prudence or practical wisdom. Gaonkar also cites Thomas Farrell's *Norms of Rhetorical Culture* and the introduction to *Contemporary Rhetorical Theory* as examples of contingency's place in contemporary rhetoric. When Dewey claims that practical activity must always attend to contingency, he is working directly in line with the rhetorical tradition.

23. Here, Dewey recounts a similar position to that advanced by Protagoras in Plato's dialogue *Protogoras* (320d–329d), again reworking a key theme in the rhetorical tradition.

24. In *Becoming John Dewey,* Dalton explains the relationship between Heisenberg's "uncertainty principle" and Dewey's claims about knowing (172–74). Dalton emphasizes the process "of exercising human judgment under conditions of uncertainty" throughout his work as a critical factor in Dewey's thought.

25. Dewey's vision of the marriage of science and social reform has been widely critiqued from many different perspectives, including early analyses by Randolph Bourne, Max Horkheimer, and even philosophers of science such as Hans Reichenbach. See Westbrook, *John Dewey,* 138–47, 149, 170, 187, 322–23, 350–57, 489–99.

26. Dewey is an important resource for contemporary students of the rhetoric of science, social epistemology, or the sociology of science—all of which play explicitly on rhetorical themes implied in Dewey's thought. For example, Steve Fuller's *Social Epistemology* (Bloomington: Indiana University Press, 1988) uses rhetorical theory to show how science is related to social issues. In part, such work picks up on the tradition begun by Kuhn's *Structure of Scientific Revolutions.* I would argue that Dewey makes a first step in that tradition and begins to lay the groundwork for a concern with "science communication" or "the rhetoric of science." Kuhn's book is directly influenced by the pragmatist tradition; his whole understanding of language communities and the relativity of ontologies is taken from W. V. O. Quine (clearly a pragmatist) and the later Ludwig Wittgenstein (arguably also a pragmatist).

27. See James Carey, *Communication as Culture* (New York: Routledge, 1988). Carey uses Dewey's insights to develop a "ritual model of communication" that is based on ideas of association, participation, and fellowship.

28. See Jerome Nathanson, *John Dewey: The Reconstruction of Democratic Life* (New York: Charles Scribner's Sons, 1951). Nathanson demonstrates the connections between democracy as a way of life and philosophy as a tool for realizing the possibilities of "human nature." Nathanson begins with an analysis of the relationship between human problems and philosophy and proceeds to show how philosophy can make the community better. In many ways my argument parallels his, but I try to show that philosophy needs a complementary rhetoric in order to achieve the kind of democracy that Nathanson describes.

29. It seems that *Art as Experience* may be an excellent place to begin to look for hints or suggestions as to how one could craft an art of rhetoric to match the pressing concerns of contemporary American life. By trying to describe art in its most general sense, Dewey may make useful suggestions for considering rhetoric as a special kind of art.

Chapter Three: Jane Addams and the Practice of Deliberation

1. Cassandra was the daughter of Priam, leader of Troy. She predicted that the Greeks would destroy her father's city, but the Trojan warriors laughed at her prophecy. The text of Addams's speech is recorded in *The Jane Addams Reader,* ed. Jean Bethke Elshtain (New York: Basic Books, 2002). In what follows I rely extensively on four collections of essays: *The Jane Addams Reader* (hereafter *JAR*); *Democracy and Social Ethics* (Cambridge: Harvard University Press, 1964) (hereafter *DSE*); *Jane Addams on Education,* ed. Ellen Condliff Lagemann (New Brunswick, N.J.: Transaction, Inc., 1994) (hereafter *JOE*); and *The Social Thought of Jane Addams,* ed. Christopher Lasch (New York: Bobbs-Merrill Company, Inc., 1965) (hereafter *STJ*). In each case I cite the work, the original

date of publication for the particular essay, and the page number. I also rely on *Twenty Years at Hull-House* (New York: Signet Classic, [1910] 1961) (hereafter *TYH*).

2. On the right of the speaker to be heard, see Peter Brown, *Power and Persuasion in Late Antiquity: Towards a Christian Empire* (Madison: University of Wisconsin Press, 1992).

3. By "voice" I mean the rhetorical authority to be heard, not the literal ability to speak.

4. I use the word "modern" to describe American democracy throughout. However, "modern" is meant to highlight the differences between ancient Athens and U.S. culture in the nineteenth and twentieth centuries. "Modern" is not meant to evoke all of the arguments and the language surrounding philosophical or literary "modernism." In addition, there are two senses of democracy at work throughout this chapter. The first is "Athenian democracy," which is marked by the participation of all citizens in the decision-making process, and which further implies that politics is a process in which competing voices try to guide the course of the city-state. In contrast, the second sense of democracy is the one that Addams considers "a form of public action making possible the doing of simple tasks in peace" (Jean Bethke Elshtain, *Jane Addams and the Dream of American Democracy* [New York: Basic Books, 2002], 249). Furthermore, Addams argues that "politics was the realm of the best possible" (186). Addams's primary concern was to create or develop a new sense of democracy that was tied to the social life of the community, and therefore, politics implicated a vast array of activities used to secure the best possible life for all in the community. It is the meaning and significance of these two kinds of democracy that this chapter explores and that the word "modern" is meant to highlight.

5. See Westbrook, *John Dewey*, 80–81, 88–90. Dewey also named his daughter Jane.

6. Louise Knight's new biography recounting the early years of Addams's life, *Citizen: Jane Addams and the Struggle for Democracy* (Chicago: University of Chicago Press, 2005), further attests to this fact. In addition, on Addams's ability to successfully solve social problems and make the community better, see Allen Davis, *American Heroine: The Life and Legend of Jane Addams* (Chicago: Ivan Dee, 2000); James Weber Linn, *Jane Addams: A Biography* (Urbana: University of Illinois Press, 2000); Cornelia Meigs, *Jane Addams: Pioneer of Social Justice: A Biography* (Boston: Little, Brown, 1970); and Winnifred Wise, *Jane Addams of Hull-House: A Biography* (New York: Harcourt, Brace, 1935).

7. This is a serious oversight, considering that Diggins argues that pragmatism fails, on its own terms, to effectively ground action on knowledge and effect the course of social affairs. Addams's lifework would seem to be an obvious counterargument to Diggins's main criticism.

8. Peter Simonson, in "Varieties of Pragmatism and Communication: Visions and Revisions from Peirce to Peters," does cite Jane Addams as one of a group of "important defenders not always recognized as pragmatists" but does not treat Addams's pragmatism in any substantive way; see David Perry, ed., *American Pragmatism and Communication Research* (Mahwah, N.J.: Lawrence Erlbaum Associates, 2001), 2.

9. For a description of the organization and operation of Athenian democracy, see David Stockton, *The Classical Athenian Democracy* (New York: Oxford University Press, 1990). I use the word "citizen" in quotes here because in Athenian democracy citizenship meant just the adult male members of the population with full and equal legal and political privileges.

10. For a detailed account of citizen participation in Athenian democracy, see Cynthia Farrar, *The Origins of Democratic Thinking: The Invention of Politics in Classical Athens* (New York: Cambridge University Press, 1988); or A. H. M. Jones, *Athenian Democracy* (Baltimore: Johns Hopkins University Press, 1986). Both illustrate the complex workings of democratic politics in Athens by attending to specific constitutional and sociocultural issues. In some ways the image of Athenian politics I present is too simple. To claim that all citizens could participate in politics through the practice of rhetoric may have been a regulative ideal of democracy in Athens, but it did not necessarily function that way. Regardless, both accounts do show the role of oratory in the Athenian Assembly in making decisions, with added descriptions of all of the other political mechanisms in place for deciding who became an orator, how issues were brought up, and why some citizens had more power than others.

11. For an account of Addams's role in Progressive Party politics, see Dorothy Schneider and Carl Schneider, *American Women in the Progressive Era, 1900–1920* (New York: Facts on File, Inc., 1993), 195–98, 200–204; and Ellen Fitzpatrick, *Endless Crusade: Women Social Scientists and Progressive Reform* (New York: Oxford University Press, 1990), 146–50.

12. Town-hall meetings are an exception to this claim. In such local forms of government, public address does play a role, but federal and state governments exclude the possibility of direct participation.

13. This was the case with the Progressive Party for Addams. In *The Second Twenty Years at Hull-House,* Addams traces her connection to Teddy Roosevelt and the Progressive Party: "We were, first and foremost, faced with the necessity of selecting from our many righteous principles those that might be advocated at the moment, and deciding which must still wait for a more propitious season" (34). Here we see the classical concern with *kairos.* However, we also see Addams struggling to convince herself to support Roosevelt even though he refused to advocate specific policies that Addams believed were important. Addams, then, accepted the Progressive Party platform in order to help the party gain wider acceptance and because she knew that deliberation required the voices of many people organized together.

14. Addams does not specify who these "French Philosophers" were, but it seems safe to assume that she meant primarily Rousseau and Montesquieu. In an essay entitled "Survivals of Militarism in City Government," Addams develops the idea of a "first phase of democracy" further: "The philosophers and the statesmen of the eighteenth century believed that the universal franchise would cure all ills; that liberty and equality rested only upon constitutional rights and privileges; that to obtain these two and to throw off all government oppression constituted the full duty of the progressive patriot. We still keep this formalization because the philosophers of this generation give us nothing newer. We ignore the fact that world-wide problems can no longer be solved by a political constitution assuring us against opposition, but that we must frankly face the proposition that the whole situation is more industrial than political" (*JAR* 1907, 152). It seems clear from this quote that "the first phase of democracy" established a constitution that was meant to secure freedom and the right to vote.

15. According to Addams, political parties did not fulfill these functions. Instead, she pursued the progressive ideal of education outside of partisanship because corrupt political machines had a bad influence. On the progressive belief that party politics were corrupt, see

Richard Hofstadter, *The Age of Reform: From Bryan to F.D.R.* (New York: Vintage Books, 1955), 5–6.

16. This may seem like a counterintuitive argument. One might assume that the American Congress provides the most obvious comparison to the Athenian Assembly. However, the Congress is designed to exclude the participation of many for the wisdom of the elected few. I would argue that settlement houses can be compared to the Assembly more accurately because of the question of access and possibility for participation.

17. Elshtain describes Addams's emphasis on citizenship further: "All of Hull-House's many activities pointed toward one goal: the building up of a social culture of democracy. Addams insisted that the residents were neither philanthropists nor charity visitors nor social workers. Rather, they were citizens—although most of them, being women, did not have the right to vote. Hull-House's objective value lay in its capacity to help create strong citizens through a variety of means, methods, and media" (*Jane Addams and the Dream,* 100–101).

18. The home can even become a site for deliberative rhetoric. According to Elshtain, Addams "helped create what might be called a countertradition, another way of doing and thinking, which one day bore fruit. In lecture after lecture, newspaper article after newspaper article, interview after interview she stressed the theme of municipal housekeeping as a type of applied morals (her characterization) and as a mode of analysis" (*Jane Addams and the Dream,* 162–63).

19. According to Addams, it is imperative that "women's sense of obligation" be "modified and enlarged as the social conditions changed, so that" women "might naturally and almost imperceptibly have inaugurated the movements for social amelioration in the line of factory legislation and shop sanitation" (*JAR* 1908, 255).

20. For an explanation of Addams's understanding of identity and selfhood and how it differs from contemporary notions of identity, see Herbert Leibowitz, *Fabricating Lives: Explorations in American Autobiography* (New York: Alfred A. Knopf, 1989), 130.

21. See Werner Jaeger, *Paideia: The Ideals of Greek Culture,* 3 vols., trans. G. Norlin and L. Van Hook (New York: Oxford University Press, 1971); and Nicole Loraux, *The Invention of Athens: Funeral Orations in the Classical City,* trans. A. Sheridan (Cambridge: Harvard University Press, 1986).

22. For a more complete account of Protagoras's "Great Speech" and its relationship to rhetorical theory and notions of democratic citizenship, see Schiappa, *Protagoras and Logos,* 168–87.

23. In "The Objective Value of a Social Settlement," Addams claims that "the chief value of a Settlement to its neighborhood, certainly to the newly arrived foreigner, is its office as an information and interpretation bureau" (*JAR* 1893, 39).

24. Addams's essay "A Function of the Social Settlement" begins by citing both William James and John Dewey as advocates of restructuring and reorganizing philosophy's approach to knowledge. Addams understands the function of the settlement in terms of the kinds of changes that both James and Dewey sought for philosophy: "The ideal and developed settlement would attempt to test the value of human knowledge by action, and realization. . . . The settlement stands for application as opposed to research; for emotion as opposed to abstraction, for universal interest as opposed to specialization" (*JOE* 1899, 78).

25. According to Addams, "the labor movement must include all men in its hopes. It must have the communion of universal fellowship" (*JAR* 1907, 160). The labor union,

then, begins to act as the classical rhetor, but instead of one voice, it embodies as many voices as possible.

26. In *Twenty Years at Hull-House,* Addams describes how the Pullman Strike led to a "cleavage of society" and not to the further integration of the interests of both sides (142–46).

27. For an extended discussion of Plato's "Phaedrus" and its connection with rhetoric, see Weaver, *Ethics of Rhetoric,* 3–26.

28. See Mary Jo Deegan, *Jane Addams and the Men of the Chicago School, 1892–1918* (New Brunswick, N.J.: Transaction, Inc., 1988). Deegan offers a thorough account of Addams's influence on Chicago sociology and her connection with feminism and critical pragmatism.

29. See Norman Clark, "The Critical Servant: An Isocratean Contribution to Critical Rhetoric," *Quarterly Journal of Speech* 82 (1996): 111–24.

30. See T. Poulakos, *Speaking for the Polis,* 27–34.

Chapter Four: Oliver Wendell Holmes Jr. and Legal Rhetoric

1. In what follows I cite two anthologies: Max Lerner, ed., *The Mind and Faith of Justice Holmes: His Speeches, Essays, Letters, and Judicial Opinions* (New York: Modern Library, 1943) (hereafter *MFJH*); and Richard A. Posner, *The Essential Holmes: Selections from the Letters, Speeches, Judicial Opinions, and Other Writings of Oliver Wendell Holmes, Jr.* (Chicago: University of Chicago Press, 1992) (hereafter *EH*). For particular speeches, letters, or opinions drawn from these works, I cite the anthology, the date of original publication of the specific work (unless that is clear from the text), and the page number in the anthology. "The Path of the Law" and key parts of *The Common Law* are also recorded in the two anthologies. When relying on quotes not from these two sources, I use footnotes to cite the origins of the quotes.

2. Holmes was injured three times during the war, once just above the heart at Ball's Bluff, once in the neck at the Battle of Antietam, and once in the foot at the Second Battle of Fredericksburg. Menand offers an excellent account of Holmes's part in these battles (*Metaphysical Club,* 23–69).

3. Several sources point to the impact of the war on Holmes, including, most recently, Menand. Menand's work builds on more extensive and authoritative biographies of Holmes, most notably: Mark DeWolfe Howe, *Justice Oliver Wendell Holmes: The Shaping Years, 1841–1870* (Cambridge: Harvard University Press, 1957) and *Justice Oliver Wendell Holmes: The Proving Years, 1870–1882* (Cambridge: Harvard University Press, 1963); Liva Baker, *The Justice from Beacon Hill: The Life and Times of Oliver Wendell Holmes* (New York: HarperCollins, 1991); and G. E. White, *Justice Oliver Wendell Holmes.*

4. For Holmes, "faith" refers to the belief that people have in their own capacity for right action, not some religious notion of supernatural faith. As he put this sentiment elsewhere: "I know of no true measure of men except the total of human energy which they embody—counting everything, with due allowance for quality, from Nansen's power to digest blubber or to resist cold, up to his courage, or to Wordsworth's power to express the unutterable, or to Kant's speculative reach. The final test of this energy is battle in some form—actual war—the crush of Arctic ice—the fight for mastery in the market or the court. Many of those who are remembered have spared themselves this supreme trial, and have fostered a faculty at the expense of their total life. It is one thing to utter a happy

phrase from a protected cloister; another to think under fire—to think for action upon which great things depend. The most powerful men are apt to go into the melee and fall or come out generals. The great problems are here and now" (*EH* 1897, 97).

5. According to Menand, after returning from his duty in the war, Holmes went to Concord to visit Emerson. He wanted "to see whether he should try to make a career like Emerson's, as a writer of philosophy. He concluded that he should not, and that fall he enrolled at Harvard Law School. But he had not given up the idea of doing philosophy. He had only given up the idea of doing it in the way Emerson and his father had done it—by synthesis and introspection. He thought it could be done better by scholarship and analysis" (*Metaphysical Club,* 57).

6. On the affectionate, yet strained friendship between Holmes and James, see R. B. Perry, *Thought and Character of William James,* 112–19, 125–29, 216–17; and Lerner's editorial comments in *Mind and Faith of Justice Holmes* (403–5).

7. Holmes had a more favorable impression of John Dewey, calling *Experience and Nature* a "great book" and claiming that Dewey "seemed to me to have more of our cosmos in his head than I ever found in a book before" (*MFJH* 1927, 433). In addition, in a letter to Harold Laski, Holmes claimed that "I read John Dewey, *Human Nature and Conduct,* a book that I find it hard to characterize. It is like shavings of jade—subtle—sometimes epigrammatic—emancipated—seeing the world and man as fluid—an immense advance upon any book there was when I was younger—yet somehow not quite seeming to arrive anywhere—and not feeling to me quite as new as it is civilized" (*EH* 1922, 71).

8. In *Vegelahn v. Guntner* (1896) the majority opinion upheld an injunction that prohibited even peaceful picketing by strikers, on the grounds that threats of violence might be implied as well as actual and that there were such things as moral intimidation and constraint that were outside of allowable competition. Holmes dissented by arguing that combinations of interests happen all the time and that any such organization should have the capacity to engage in "organized persuasion or argument" and that this is part of the "free struggle for life" just as much as the struggle between individuals or different classes (*MFJH,* 112, 115).

9. Expanding on this proposition, Holmes wrote, "When I say that a thing is true, I mean that I cannot help believing it. I am stating an experience as to which there is no choice. But as there are many things that I cannot help doing that the universe can, I do not venture to assume that my inabilities in the way of thought are inabilities of the universe. I therefore define the truth as the system of my limitations, and leave absolute truth for those who are better equipped. With absolute truth I leave absolute ideas of conduct equally on one side" (*MFJH* 1915, 392).

10. See Holmes to Lewis Einstein, November 9, 1913, in *The Holmes-Einstein Letters: Correspondence of Mr. Justice Holmes and Lewis Einstein 1903–1935,* ed. James Bishop Peabody (New York: St. Martin's, 1964), 82.

11. For a broader account of the political implications of Holmes's work, see David Burton, *Political Ideas of Justice Holmes* (Cranbury, N.J.: Associated University Presses, 1992).

12. Holmes asserted that all thought is social and that pluralism is indelibly part of the human world: "We live by symbols, and what shall be symbolized by any image of the sight depends upon the mind of him who sees it. . . . This day marks the fact that all thought is social, is on its way to action" (*MFJH* 1913, 385). The first part of this quote

is clearly aligned with James's pragmatism, while the second is clearly aligned with Dewey's pragmatism.

13. See Max Fisch, "Justice Holmes, the Prediction Theory of Law, and Pragmatism," *Journal of Philosophy* 39 (1942); and Morton White, *Social Thought in America: The Revolt against Formalism* (New York: Viking Press, 1949).

14. See Thomas C. Grey, "Holmes and Legal Pragmatism," *Stanford Law Review* 41 (1989): 787–870.

15. See Richard Posner, *Law, Pragmatism, and Democracy* (Cambridge: Harvard University Press, 2003).

16. Others have argued that Holmes is not fully a pragmatist; see Albert Alschuler, *Law without Values: The Life, Work, and Legacy of Justice Holmes* (Chicago: University of Chicago Press, 2000), 100–103.

17. Lerner also states that Holmes's "triumph in American jurisprudence was thus linked with the same social forces that brought the triumph of William James and John Dewey in American philosophy and education" (*MFJH,* 369).

18. See, for example, Michael Brint and William Weaver, eds., *Pragmatism in Law and Society* (Boulder, Colo.: Westview Press, 1991).

19. For a more complete account of Thrasymachus's argument in the first book of the *Republic,* see Kerferd, *Sophistic Movement,* 120–23.

20. On the connection between Thrasymachus and Holmes, see also Alschuler, *Law without Values,* 8, 60.

21. This, of course, leaves open the question of to what "strength" actually refers. Socrates takes advantage of this ambiguity by associating strength with skill at leadership. This causes another shift in Thrasymachus's definition of justice. During a long speech he claims that justice is acting for another's good while injustice is acting in one's own interest. However, at the end of this speech he abruptly juxtaposes this definition with his earlier claim that justice is the interest of the stronger (344c). It is clear that Plato is trying to make Thrasymachus's position seem contradictory. Instead, however, Thrasymachus demonstrates that "strength" differs based on the perspective of the ruler or the ruled.

22. On the function of law and the courts in Athens, see Richard Garner, *Law and Society in Classical Athens* (London: Croom Helm, 1987); Douglass MacDowell, *The Law in Classical Athens* (Ithaca, N.Y.: Cornell University Press, 1978); and R. Osborne, "Law in Action in Classical Athens," *Journal of Hellenic Studies* 105 (1985): 40–58.

23. See Chaim Perelman and L. Olbrechts-Tyteca, *The New Rhetoric: A Treatise on Argumentation* (Notre Dame, Ind.: University of Notre Dame Press, 1969), 31–35.

24. Quoted in Baker, *Justice from Beacon Hill,* 172–73.

25. Quoted in Menand, *Metaphysical Club,* 344.

26. On Holmes's foresight-based liability, see Alschuler, *Law without Values,* 111–25; and H. L. Pohlman, *Justice Oliver Wendell Holmes: Free Speech and the Living Constitution* (New York: New York University Press, 1991), 20–52.

27. Quoted in Menand, *Metaphysical Club,* 346.

28. Quoted in Sheldon Novick, *Honorable Justice: The Life of Oliver Wendell Holmes* (Boston: Little, Brown, 1989), 216.

29. Ibid.

30. See Oliver Wendell Holmes, Jr., "Speech to the Twentieth Regiment, Massachusetts Volunteers," December 1892, and "Remarks at a Tavern Club Dinner for Paul Bourget," December 4, 1893, both in *The Collected Works of Justice Holmes: Complete Public*

Writings and Selected Judicial Opinions of Oliver Wendell Holmes, ed. Sheldon Novick (Chicago: University of Chicago Press, 1995), 3:512–14.

31. Quoted in Alschuler, *Law without Values,* 23.

32. Holmes to John Gray, September 3, 1905, quoted in Novick, *Honorable Justice,* 283.

33. From "Address of Chief Justice Holmes at the Dedication of the Northwestern University Law School Building," in *Collected Works of Justice Holmes,* 3:530.

34. The four quotes in the text concerning natural rights and equality are from *Holmes-Laski Letters: The Correspondence of Mr. Justice Holmes and Harold J. Laski, 1916–1935,* ed. Mark DeWolfe Howe (Cambridge: Harvard University Press, 1953), 1:768–69, 2:941–42, 2:948, 1:20–21.

35. On these notions of conversation, eloquence, and Holmes's style, see Peter Gibian, "Opening and Closing the Conversation: Style and Stance from Holmes Senior to Holmes Junior," in *The Legacy of Oliver Wendell Holmes, Jr.,* ed. Robert Gordon (Stanford, Calif.: Stanford University Press, 1992), 186–215.

36. For an extended discussion of *Lochner,* see G. E. White, *Justice Oliver Wendell Holmes,* 324–33.

37. As Holmes put it elsewhere: "As law embodies beliefs that have triumphed in the battle of ideas and then have translated them into action, while there still is doubt, while opposite convictions still keep a battle front against each other, the time for law has not come; the notion destined to prevail is not yet entitled to the field. It is a misfortune if a judge reads his conscious or unconscious sympathy with one side or the other prematurely into the law, and forgets that what seem to him to be first principles are believed by half his fellow men to be wrong. I think that we have suffered from this misfortune, in State courts at least, and that this is another and very important truth to be extracted from the popular discontent" (*MFJH* 1913, 390).

38. In a letter to a young law student Holmes wrote, "Probably you will also find as I do, that ideas are not difficult, that the trouble is in the words in which they are expressed. Every group, and even almost every individual when he has acquired a definite mode of thought, gets a more or less special terminology which it takes time for an outsider to live into. Having to listen to arguments, now about railroad business, now about a patient, now about an admiralty case, now about mining law and so on, a thousand times I have thought that I was hopelessly stupid and as many have found that when I got hold of the language there was no such thing as a difficult case" (*MFJH* 1923, 421). On another occasion Holmes wrote, "I was amused by a question of taste yesterday. In one of my opinions I give a short account of a statute and say that there are amplifications 'to stop rat holes' that need to be stated as the plaintiffs admit that they are within the statute. The C.J. criticised. I said our reports were dull because we had the notion that judicial dignity required solemn fluffy speeches, as when I grew up, everybody wore black frock coats and black cravats" (*EH* 1924, 40). In both of these quotes we see Holmes's sensitivity to the function of language in law and his desire to develop a legal style less focused on dry, logical phrases.

Chapter Five: Alain Locke and Epideictic Rhetoric

1. In what follows I rely extensively on four works by Locke: *The Critical Temper of Alain Locke: A Selection of His Essays on Art and Culture,* ed. Jeffrey C. Stewart (New York: Garland Publishing, Inc., 1983) (hereafter *CTAL*); *The Philosophy of Alain Locke:*

Harlem Renaissance and Beyond, ed. Leonard Harris (Philadelphia: Temple University Press, 1989) (hereafter, *PAL*); *Race Contacts and Interracial Relations* (Washington, D.C.: Howard University Press, 1992) (hereafter, *RCIR*); and *The New Negro: An Interpretation* (New York: Arno Press, Inc., [1925] 1968 (hereafter, *NN*). For particular essays drawn from these works I cite the work, the date of original publication for the essay, and the page number in the book. In addition, I rely on Leonard Harris, ed., *The Critical Pragmatism of Alain Locke: A Reader on Value Theory, Aesthetics, Community, Culture, Race, and Education* (New York: Rowman & Littlefield Publishers, Inc., 1999) (hereafter *CP*), for several important interpretations of Locke's work.

2. For an extended discussion of the Harlem Renaissance as well as Locke's specific connections to that larger movement, see George Hutchinson, *The Harlem Renaissance in Black and White* (Cambridge: Harvard University Press, 1995); and Mark Helbling, *The Harlem Renaissance: The One and the Many* (Westport, Conn.: Greenwood Press, 1999). Although Locke did not live in Harlem and was not an artist, he participated in the Harlem Renaissance by finding ways of displaying and gaining public recognition for particular artists and their work. In addition, he interpreted this work by identifying the larger themes that connected different artists to one another, and therefore he was, in part, responsible for giving voice to the collective project of the Harlem Renaissance as well as the unique projects of particular artists.

3. Locke attended Harvard as an undergraduate from 1904 to 1907. While there, he was a student in courses taught by Josiah Royce, George Herbert Palmer, Ralph Barton Perry, and Hugo Munsterberg. After spending time at Oxford on a Rhodes Scholarship and teaching philosophy at Howard University, Locke returned to Harvard in 1916 and 1917 to complete his doctoral dissertation. Originally he intended on working under Josiah Royce, but Royce had died. Instead he studied under, and submitted his dissertation to, Ralph Barton Perry and was awarded his doctoral degree in the spring of 1918. Although he never studied directly with James, Locke developed a passion for James's thinking through Perry and other members of the Harvard faculty.

4. The most general and authoritative account of Locke's philosophy is Johnny Washington, *Alain Locke and Philosophy: A Quest for Cultural Pluralism* (New York: Greenwood Press, 1986).

5. Locke has been called the "philosophical midwife" of the Harlem Renaissance for his role as master of ceremonies, editor, and art critic; see Verner Mitchell, "Alain Locke: Philosophical 'Midwife' of the Harlem Renaissance" (*CP*, 191–98).

6. See Yun Lee Too's article "Epideictic Genre," in *Encyclopedia of Rhetoric,* 251–57.

7. Locke, in fact, wrote his doctoral dissertation, "Problems of Classification in Theory of Value," on value theory, and much of his subsequent philosophical work derived from questions he struggled with in his dissertation.

8. The word "culture" implicated in the phrase "cultural pluralism" appears again and again in Locke's writings, and I use it as well to interpret his arguments. According to Locke, culture is "the capacity for understanding the best and most representative forms of human expression, and of expressing oneself, if not in similar creativeness, at least in appreciative reactions and in progressively responsive refinements of tastes and interests. Culture proceeds from personality to personality. To paraphrase Bacon, it is that, and only that, which can be inwardly assimilated. It follows, then, that, like wisdom, it is that which cannot be taught, but can only be learned. . . . The man of culture is the man of trained sensibilities, whose mind expresses itself in keenness of discrimination and, therefore, in

cultivated interests and taste" (*PAL* 1923, 177–78). Here, Locke's definition comes close to Matthew Arnold's. Locke is undoubtedly an elitist, but he is the kind of elitist who acknowledges the possibility of many forms of elitism. In other words, culture is the best artistic expressions of individuals and communities, and cultural pluralism is the recognition that the best differs from community to community. In cultivating cultural pluralism, we cultivate the best from different groups, and we are then in a position to learn from the best of each. Culture, for Locke, is clearly tied to cultivation of the best artistic expressions, and as part of the Harlem Renaissance he was interested in cultivating the best artists as an indication of the excellence and cultured status of African Americans.

9. For an excellent account of life in Harlem in the 1920s, as a site for artistic expression and for social and political action, see David Levering Lewis, *When Harlem Was in Vogue* (New York: Alfred A. Knopf, 1981).

10. In 1908 Locke got a chance to see James in England because he was studying at Oxford, as the first black Rhodes Scholar.

11. For an account of the connections between Dewey's aesthetics and Locke's, see Richard Shusterman, "Pragmatist Aesthetics: Roots and Radicalism" (*CP,* 97–110).

12. For an account of Kallen's notion of cultural pluralism, as well as his friendship with Locke and his intellectual debt to James, see Menand, *Metaphysical Club,* 388–400; and Hutchinson, *Harlem Renaissance,* 78–90.

13. There are subtle and significant differences between Du Bois's pragmatism and Locke's that are beyond the scope of this project. Posnock carefully explains these differences throughout *Color & Culture,* or for another explanation of the differences, see Menand, *Metaphysical Club,* 394–97.

14. Schiappa, in *Beginnings of Rhetorical Theory,* argues that the political dimension of early epideictic practices gets downplayed in Aristotle (185–206). This may be the case, but several contemporary scholars (beginning with Perelman and Olbrechts-Tyteca and including T. Poulakos, Hauser, Vickers, Ochs, and others) continue to suggest that epideictic rhetoric did have a significant civic function in classical Athens and that it continues to serve an important civic function in contemporary democracies.

15. For a description of the role of the epideictic genre in classical Athens, see also E. L. Bowie, "Early Greek Elegy: Symposium and Public Festival," *Journal of Hellenic Studies* 106 (1986): 13–35; Loraux, *Invention of Athens;* and Laurence Rosenfield, "The Practical Celebration of Epideictic," in *Rhetoric in Transition,* ed. Eugene White (University Park: Pennsylvania State University Press, 1980), 131–56.

16. Beginning in 1928 Locke wrote a yearly "retrospective review" of Negro literature for the magazine *Opportunity.* In these reviews he struggled to identify the singular artistic talents of various writers and the general trend represented by the different writers (*CTAL,* 201–85).

17. For a more extended account of Locke's philosophy of value, see Ernest Mason, "Alain Locke's Philosophy of Value," in *Alain Locke: Reflections on a Modern Renaissance Man,* ed. Russell Linnemann (Baton Rouge: Louisiana State University Press, 1982), 1–16.

18. This essay, simply called "Value" by Leonard Harris, was not published before its appearance in *The Philosophy of Alain Locke* and has no date of original composition.

19. See especially book three ("Principles of a New Valuation") of Friedrich Nietzsche's *Will to Power,* trans. Walter Kaufmann and R. J. Hollingdale (New York: Vintage Books,

1967), as well as his *Thus Spoke Zarathustra,* trans. Thomas Common (New York: Random House, 1967) for a more complete account of Nietzsche's conception of "transvaluation" and its connection to art and language.

20. Here again Locke reiterates a specifically Nietzschean position that regards all claims to truth as powerful fictions and artistic representations.

21. By current standards Locke's account of imperialism is rudimentary. According to Nancy Fraser, "elaborated chiefly in terms of Third World markets, it says little about the extraction of primary resources or the exploitation of labor power" (*CP,* 10–11). Regardless, establishing such an international frame for criticism is an insightful move, given the time period.

22. The term "melting pot" is a reference to Israel Zangwill's popular play from 1908 called *The Melting Pot.* It was a term used to describe and explain the effects of the massive influx of immigrants into the United States between 1900 and 1920. (Specifically, these twenty years witnessed the immigration of 14,531,197 people, mostly from southern and eastern Europe.)

23. Two essays in *The Critical Pragmatism of Alain Locke* ("Alain Locke, Essentialism, and the Notion of a Black Aesthetic" and "Aesthetics and the Issue of Identity") offer excellent, detailed explanations of the connection between art and group identity. In both cases the authors point to a pragmatic, strategic essentialism as the product of Locke's aesthetics and as a complicated topos for African American artists to negotiate.

24. Such an identity is also tied to the legacy of African art that operates as a useful resource for artists in Harlem. In *The New Negro,* Locke included an essay, "The Legacy of the Ancestral Arts," that attempts to account for both the disjunction between New Negro art and the "African spirit" and the continuities between the two. Locke is careful to suggest that the "Ancestral arts" offer useful resources for New Negro art, but he also argues that New Negro art cannot be reduced to more traditional African art (254–67). In addition, in a 1924 essay titled "A Note on African Art," Locke argues that "nothing is more galvanizing than the sense of a cultural past. This at least the intelligent presentation of African art will supply to us"; such a past provides "incentives toward fresher and bolder forms of artistic expression and a lessening of that timid imitativeness which at present hampers all but our very best artists" (*CTAL,* 135). In other words, the celebration of instances of African art from the past can serve a useful function in inspiring present artists to develop a new style.

25. This is also the theme of a 1937 essay called "Spiritual Truancy," in which Locke argues that artists have the ability to describe the spirit of an entire community. In reference to the latest Negro artists, he claims that "the task confronting the younger generation of Negro writers and artists is to approach the home scene and the folk with high seriousness, deep loyalty, racial reverence of the unspectacular, unmelodramatic sort, and when necessary, sacrificial devotion" because the "program of the Negro Renaissance was to interpret the folk to itself, to vitalize it from within" (*CTAL* 1937, 66). Locke celebrates the "real spokesman and representative character" who accepts "some group loyalty" and has the "ability to express mass sentiment" (63).

26. Six essays in *Alain Locke: Reflections on a Modern Renaissance Man* reflect on specific aspects of Locke's aesthetic theory by considering such issues as black folk expression, beauty, jazz, and African music (77–132). These essays offer a more detailed account of Locke's interpretation of technical style in African American art.

27. Hutchinson, in *Harlem Renaissance,* offers an excellent explanation of pragmatist aesthetics and its relation to experience, social reconstruction, and the Harlem Renaissance (42–50).

28. By way of contrast, the civil rights movement operated in and through already existing political institutions with much clearer goals in mind.

Conclusion

1. Burke's notion of "entitlement" also works to demonstrate this kind of constitutive approach to language. In *Language as Symbolic Action: Essays on Life, Literature, and Method* (Berkeley: University of California Press, 1966), he argues that instead of understanding words as signs of things, we should understand things as signs of words. This leads to the belief that "language derives its materials from the cooperative acts of men in sociopolitical orders, which are themselves held together by a vast network of verbally perfected meanings" (378). This demonstrates the pragmatic tendencies of Burke's approach to rhetoric.

2. See also Steven Toulmin, "The Recovery of Practical Philosophy," *American Scholar,* 57, no. 3 (1988): 337–52.

3. To attest to this variety of neopragmatisms and contemporary rhetorics further, I could choose to discuss Steven Mailloux's *Rhetorical Power* (1989) or Robert Scott's "rhetoric as epistemic" line of work (1967). Mailloux's work is clearly influenced by the pragmatists and draws on both classical and contemporary rhetorical theory to advance his claims about hermeneutics. Scott draws heavily on Stephen Toulmin and the sophists to advance a distinctly pragmatic argument concerning the epistemological function of rhetoric. Again, these are just examples of the rich variety of work at the intersection of rhetoric and pragmatism.

4. For example, James Kloppenberg accuses Stanley Fish of having the attitude that "anything goes" in "Pragmatism: An Old Name for Some New Ways of Thinking?," in *The Revival of Pragmatism: New Essays on Social Thought, Law, and Culture,* ed. Morris Dickstein (Durham, N.C.: Duke University Press, 1998), 125.

5. On Aristotle's classification of language and knowledge into the theoretical, practical, and productive, see Richard McKeon, "Aristotle's Conception of Language," *Classical Philology* 41 (October 1946): 193–206; and John Poulakos and Takis Poulakos, *Classical Rhetorical Theory* (Boston: Houghton Mifflin, 1999), 110–17, 141–46.

6. See Richard Rorty, *Philosophy and the Mirror of Nature* (Princeton, N.J.: Princeton University Press, 1979).

Bibliography

Adams, G. P., and W. P. Montague, eds. 1930. *Contemporary American Philosophy.* New York: Macmillan.

Addams, Jane, ed. 1895. *Hull-House Maps and Papers.* New York: T. Y. Crowell & Co.

———. [1902] 1964. *Democracy and Social Ethics.* Cambridge: Harvard University Press.

———. 1906. *Newer Ideals of Peace.* New York: Macmillan.

———. 1910. *The Spirit of Youth and the City Streets.* New York: Macmillan.

———. [1910] 1961. *Twenty Years at Hull-House.* New York: Signet Classic.

———. 1922. *Peace and Bread in Time of War.* New York: Macmillan.

———. 1930. *Second Twenty Years at Hull-House.* New York: Macmillan.

———.1994. *Jane Addams on Education.* Ed. Ellen Condliff Lagemann. New Brunswick, N.J.: Transaction, Inc.

———. 2002. *The Jane Addams Reader.* Ed. Jean Bethke Elshtain. New York: Basic Books.

Alschuler, Albert. 2000. *Law without Values: The Life, Work, and Legacy of Justice Holmes.* Chicago: University of Chicago Press.

Annas, Julia. 1981. *An Introduction to Plato's Republic.* New York: Oxford University Press.

Antczak, Frederick. 1985. *Thought and Character: The Rhetoric of Democratic Education.* Ames: Iowa State University Press.

Atwill, Janet. 1998. *Rhetoric Reclaimed: Aristotle and the Liberal Arts Tradition.* Ithaca, N.Y.: Cornell University Press.

Backman, Mark. 1991. *Sophistication: Rhetoric and the Rise of Self-Consciousness.* Woodbridge, Conn.: Ox Bow Press.

Baker, Liva. 1991. *The Justice from Beacon Hill: The Life and Times of Oliver Wendell Holmes.* New York: HarperCollins.

Barnes, Jonathan, ed. 1984. *The Complete Works of Aristotle.* Princeton, N.J.: Princeton University Press.

Benoit, William. 1990. "Isocrates and Aristotle on Rhetoric." *Rhetoric Society Quarterly* 20, no. 3:251–59.

———. 1991. "Isocrates and Plato on Rhetoric and Rhetorical Education." *Rhetoric Society Quarterly* 21, no. 1:60–71.

Berlin, James. 1981. "The Transformation of Invention in Nineteenth Century American Rhetoric." *Southern Speech Communication Journal* 46:292–304.

Billig, Michael. 1987. *Arguing and Thinking: A Rhetorical Approach to Social Psychology.* New York: Cambridge University Press.

Bitzer, Lloyd. 1968. "The Rhetorical Situation." *Philosophy and Rhetoric* 1:1–14.

Blair, Hugh. 1965. *Lectures on Rhetoric and Belles Lettres.* Carbondale: Southern Illinois University Press.

Bode, Carl. 1956. *American Lyceum: Town Meeting of the Mind.* New York: Oxford University Press.

Booth, Wayne. 1974. *Modern Dogma and the Rhetoric of Assent.* Notre Dame, Ind.: University of Notre Dame Press.

———. 1979. *Critical Understanding: The Powers and Limits of Pluralism.* Chicago: University of Chicago Press.

Bowie, E. L. 1986. "Early Greek Elegy: Symposium and Public Festival." *Journal of Hellenic Studies* 106:13–35.

Brint, Michael, and William Weaver, eds. 1991. *Pragmatism in Law and Society.* Boulder, Colo.: Westview Press.

Brown, Peter. 1992. *Power and Persuasion in Late Antiquity: Towards a Christian Empire.* Madison: University of Wisconsin Press.

Bryant, Donald. 1958. *The Rhetorical Idiom: Essays in Rhetoric, Oratory, Language, and Drama.* Ithaca, N.Y.: Cornell University Press.

Buder, Stanley. 1967. *Pullman: An Experiment in Industrial Order and Community Planning, 1880–1930.* New York: Oxford University Press.

Burke, Kenneth. 1945. *A Grammar of Motives.* New York: Prentice Hall.

———. 1966. *Language as Symbolic Action: Essays on Life, Literature, and Method.* Berkeley: University of California Press.

———. 1969. *A Rhetoric of Motives.* Los Angeles: University of California Press.

Burton, David. 1992. *Political Ideas of Justice Holmes.* Cranbury, N.J.: Associated University Presses.

Campbell, George. 1963. *The Philosophy of Rhetoric.* Carbondale: Southern Illinois University Press.

Carey, James. 1988. *Communication as Culture.* New York: Routledge.

Chambliss, J. J. 1990. *The Influence of Plato and Aristotle on John Dewey's Philosophy.* Lewiston, N.Y.: Edwin Mellen Press.

Cherwitz, Richard, ed. 1990. *Rhetoric and Philosophy.* Hillsdale, N.J.: Lawrence Erlbaum Associates.

Clark, Norman. 1996. "The Critical Servant: An Isocratean Contribution to Critical Rhetoric." *Quarterly Journal of Speech* 82, no. 2: 111–24.

Cmiel, Kenneth. 1990. *Democratic Eloquence: The Fight over Popular Speech in Nineteenth-Century America.* New York: William Morrow and Company, Inc.

Cole, Thomas. 1991. *The Origins of Rhetoric in Ancient Greece.* Baltimore: Johns Hopkins University Press.

Consigny, Scott. 1974. "Rhetoric and Its Situations." *Philosophy and Rhetoric* 7, no. 3: 175–86.

———. 2001. *Gorgias: Sophist and Artist.* Columbia: University of South Carolina Press.

Cotkin, George. 1990. *William James, Public Philosopher.* Baltimore: Johns Hopkins University Press.

Crusius, Timothy. 1999. *Kenneth Burke and the Conversation after Philosophy.* Carbondale: Southern Illinois University Press.

Dalton, Thomas. 2002. *Becoming John Dewey: Dilemmas of a Philosopher and Naturalist.* Bloomington: Indiana University Press.

Darwin, Charles. [1859] 1985. *The Origin of the Species by Means of Natural Selection.* New York: Penguin Books.

Davis, Allen. 2000. *American Heroine: The Life and Legend of Jane Addams.* Chicago: Ivan Dee.

Deegan, Mary Jo. 1988. *Jane Addams and the Men of the Chicago School, 1892–1918.* New Brunswick, N.J.: Transaction, Inc.

Dewey, John. [1910] 1965. *Influence of Darwin on Philosophy and Other Essays in Contemporary Thought.* Bloomington: Indiana University Press.

———. [1911] 1997. *How We Think.* New York: Dover Publications Inc.

———. [1916] 1944. *Democracy and Education: An Introduction to the Philosophy of Education.* New York: Free Press.

———. [1920] 1957. *Reconstruction in Philosophy.* Boston: Beacon Press. (Enlarged edition with a new forty-page introduction by the author.)

———. 1922. *Human Nature and Conduct: An Introduction to Social Psychology.* New York: Henry Holt and Company.

———. [1925] 1958. *Experience and Nature.* New York: Dover Publications Inc.

———. [1927] 1954. *The Public and Its Problems.* Athens: Swallow Press/Ohio University Press.

———. 1929. *The Quest for Certainty: A Study of the Relation of Knowledge and Action.* New York: Minton, Balch & Company.

———. 1934. *Art as Experience.* New York: Perigee Books.

———. 1946. *The Problems of Men.* New York: Philosophical Library, Inc.

Dickstein, Morris, ed. 1998. *The Revival of Pragmatism: New Essays on Social Thought, Law, and Culture.* Durham, N.C.: Duke University Press.

Diggins, John Patrick. 1994. *The Promise of Pragmatism: Modernism and the Crisis of Knowledge and Authority.* Chicago: University of Chicago Press.

Diliberto, Gioia. 1999. *A Useful Woman: The Early Life of Jane Addams.* New York: Simon & Schuster Inc.

Dooley, Patrick Kiaran. 1974. *Pragmatism as Humanism: The Philosophy of William James.* Chicago: Nelson-Hall Co.

Dyck, A. R. 2004. *A Commentary on Cicero, De legibus.* Ann Arbor: University of Michigan Press.

Dykhuizen, George. 1973. *The Life and Mind of John Dewey.* Carbondale: Southern Illinois University Press.

Eldridge, Michael. 1998. *Transforming Experience: John Dewey's Cultural Instrumentalism.* Nashville: Vanderbilt University Press.

Elshtain, Jean Bethke. 2002. *Jane Addams and the Dream of American Democracy.* New York: Basic Books.

Emerson, Edward Waldo, ed. 1903. *The Complete Works of Ralph Waldo Emerson.* 12 vols. Boston: Houghton Mifflin.

Enos, Richard Leo, and Lois Peters Agnew, eds. 1998. *Landmark Essays on Aristotelian Rhetoric.* Mahwah, N.J.: Lawrence Erlbaum Associates.

Erickson, Keith V., ed. 1974. *Aristotle: The Classical Heritage of Rhetoric.* Metuchen, N.J.: Scarecrow Press, Inc.

Farrar, Cynthia. 1988. *The Origins of Democratic Thinking: The Invention of Politics in Classical Athens.* New York: Cambridge University Press.

Farrell, Thomas B. 1993. *Norms of Rhetorical Culture.* New Haven, Conn.: Yale University Press.

Feffer, Andrew. 1993. *The Chicago Pragmatists and American Progressivism.* Ithaca, N.Y.: Cornell University Press.

Festenstein, Matthew. 1997. *Pragmatism and Political Theory: From Dewey to Rorty.* Chicago: University of Chicago Press.

Fisch, Max. 1942. "Justice Holmes, the Prediction Theory of Law, and Pragmatism." *Journal of Philosophy* 39.

Fish, Stanley. 1989. *Doing What Comes Naturally: Change, Rhetoric, and the Practice of Theory in Literary and Legal Studies.* Durham, N.C.: Duke University Press.

Fitzpatrick, Ellen. 1990. *Endless Crusade: Women Social Scientists and Progressive Reform.* New York: Oxford University Press.

Fuller, Steve. 1988. *Social Epistemology.* Bloomington: Indiana University Press.

Garner, Richard. 1987. *Law and Society in Classical Athens.* London: Croom Helm.

Garrison, Jim. 1995. *The New Scholarship on Dewey.* Boston: Kluwer Academic Publishers.

Gordon, Robert, ed. 1992. *The Legacy of Oliver Wendell Holmes, Jr.* Stanford, Calif.: Stanford University Press.

Gouinlock, James. 1972. *John Dewey's Philosophy of Value.* New York: Humanities Press.

Grey, Thomas C. 1989. "Holmes and Legal Pragmatism." *Stanford Law Review* 41: 787–870.

Gross, Allan. [1990] 1996. *The Rhetoric of Science.* Cambridge: Harvard University Press.

Gross, Allan, and William Keith, eds., *Rhetorical Hermeneutics: Invention and Interpretation in the Age of Science.* Albany, N.Y.: SUNY Press.

Guthrie, W. K. C. 1971. *The Sophists.* New York: Cambridge University Press.

Hacking, Ian. 1983. *Representing and Intervening: Introductory Topics in the Philosophy of Natural Science.* New York: Cambridge University Press.

Halloran, Michael. 1982. "Rhetoric in the American College Curriculum: The Decline of Public Discourse." *Pre/Text* 3, no. 3:245–69.

Hamilton, Edith, and Huntington Cairns, eds. 1989. *The Collected Dialogues of Plato.* Princeton, N.J.: Princeton University Press.

Harris, Leonard, ed. 1999. *The Critical Pragmatism of Alain Locke: A Reader on Value Theory, Aesthetics, Community, Culture, Race, and Education.* New York: Rowman & Littlefield Publishers, Inc.

Hassan, Ihab. 1987. "Making Sense: The Trials of Postmodern Discourse." *New Literary History* 18, no. 2: 437–59.

Hauser, Gerard. 1999a. "Aristotle on Epideictic: The Formation of Public Morality." *Rhetoric Society Quarterly* 29:5–20.

———. 1999b. *Vernacular Voices: The Rhetoric of Publics and Public Spheres.* Columbia: University of South Carolina Press.

———. 2002. *Introduction to Rhetorical Theory.* Prospect Heights, Ill.: Waveland Press.

Heilbrunn, Gunther. 1975. "Isocrates on Rhetoric and Power." *Hermes* 103: 154–78.

Helbling, Mark. 1999. *The Harlem Renaissance: The One and the Many.* Westport, Conn.: Greenwood Press.

Herrick, James. 1998. *The History and Theory of Rhetoric: An Introduction.* Boston: Allyn and Bacon.

Hofstadter, Richard. 1955. *The Age of Reform: From Bryant to F.D.R.* New York: Vintage Books.

Holmes, Oliver Wendell Jr. 1953. *Holmes-Laski Letters: The Correspondence of Mr. Justice Holmes and Harold J. Laski, 1916–1935.* 2 vols. Ed. Mark DeWolfe Howe. Cambridge: Harvard University Press.

———. 1964. *The Holmes-Einstein Letters: Correspondence of Mr. Justice Holmes and Lewis Einstein 1903–1935.* Ed. James Bishop Peabody. New York: St. Martin's.

———. 1995. *The Collected Works of Justice Holmes: Complete Public Writings and Selected Judicial Opinions of Oliver Wendell Holmes.* Ed. Sheldon Novick. Chicago: University of Chicago Press.

Howe, Mark DeWolfe. 1957. *Justice Oliver Wendell Holmes: The Shaping Years, 1841–1870.* Cambridge: Harvard University Press.

———. 1963. *Justice Oliver Wendell Holmes: The Proving Years, 1870–1882.* Cambridge: Harvard University Press.

Hutchinson, George. 1995. *The Harlem Renaissance in Black and White.* Cambridge: Harvard University Press.

Jaeger, Verner. 1971. *Paideia: The Ideals of Greek Culture.* 8 vols. Trans. G. Norlin and L. van Hook. New York: Oxford University Presss.

James, William. [1890] 1950. *Principles of Psychology.* New York: Dover Publications, Inc.

———. [1897] 1956. *The Will to Believe: And Other Essays in Popular Philosophy.* New York: Dover Publications, Inc.

———. [1902] 1997. *The Varieties of Religious Experience.* New York: Simon & Schuster Inc.

———. [1907] 1995. *Pragmatism.* New York: Dover Publications, Inc.

———. [1909] 1977. *A Pluralistic Universe.* Cambridge: Harvard University Press.

———. [1911] 1996. *Some Problems in Philosophy: A Beginning of an Introduction to Philosophy.* Lincoln: University of Nebraska Press.

———. [1911] 1997. *The Meaning of Truth.* Amherst, N.Y.: Prometheus Books.

———. [1912] 1996. *Essays in Radical Empiricism.* Lincoln: University of Nebraska Press.

———. 1948. *Essays in Pragmatism.* New York: Hafner Press.

———. 1987. *Essays, Comments, and Reviews.* Ed. Frederick Burkhardt, Fredson Bowers, and Ignas K. Skrupskelis. Cambridge: Harvard University Press.

Johnson, Nan. 1991. *Nineteenth-Century Rhetoric in North America.* Carbondale: Southern Illinois University Press.

Jones, A. H. M. 1986. *Athenian Democracy.* Baltimore: Johns Hopkins University Press.

Kennedy, George. 1972. *The Art of Rhetoric in the Roman World, 300 B.C.–A.D. 300.* Princeton, N.J.: Princeton University Press.

———. 1980. *Classical Rhetoric and Its Christian and Secular Traditions from Ancient to Modern Times.* Chapel Hill: University of North Carolina Press.

Kerferd, G. B. 1981. *The Sophistic Movement.* New York: Cambridge University Press.

Kimball, Bruce A. 1995. *Orators and Philosophers: A History of the Idea of Liberal Education.* New York: College Examination Board.

Kitzhaber, Albert. 1990. *Rhetoric in American Colleges, 1850–1900.* Dallas: Southern Methodist University Press.

Kloppenberg, James. 1986. *Uncertain Victory: Social Democracy and Progressivism in European and American Thought, 1870–1920.* New York: Oxford University Press.

Knight, Louisa. 2005. *Citizen: Jane Addams and the Struggle for Democracy.* Chicago: University of Chicago Press.

Kuhn, Thomas. [1962] 1970. *The Structure of Scientific Revolutions.* Chicago: University of Chicago Press.

Kuklick, Bruce. 1977. *The Rise of American Philosophy: Cambridge, Massachusetts 1860–1930.* New Haven, Conn.: Yale University Press.

Langsdorf, Lenore, and Andrew Smith, eds. 1995. *Recovering Pragmatism's Voice: The Classical Tradition, Rorty, and the Philosophy of Communication.* Albany: State University of New York Press.

Lasch, Christopher, ed. 1965. *The Social Thought of Jane Addams.* New York: Bobbs-Merrill Company, Inc.

Latour, Bruno, and Steve Woolgar. 1986. *Laboratory Life: The Construction of Scientific Facts.* Princeton, N.J.: Princeton University Press.

Leibowitz, Herbert. 1989. *Fabricating Lives: Explorations in American Autobiography.* New York: Alfred A. Knopf.

Lerner, Max, ed. 1943. *The Mind and Faith of Justice Holmes: His Speeches, Essays, Letters, and Judicial Opinions.* New York: Modern Library.

Lewis, David Levering. 1981. *When Harlem Was in Vogue.* New York: Alfred A. Knopf.

Lindsey, Almont. 1942. *The Pullman Strike.* Chicago: University of Chicago Press.

Linn, James Weber. 2000. *Jane Addams: A Biography.* Urbana: University of Illinois Press.

Linnemann, Russell, ed. 1982. *Alain Locke: Reflections on a Modern Renaissance Man.* Baton Rouge: Louisiana State University Press.

Locke, Alain Leroy, ed. [1925] 1968. *The New Negro: An Interpretation.* New York: Arno Press, Inc.

———. 1983. *The Critical Temper of Alain Locke: A Selection of His Essays on Art and Culture.* Ed. Jeffrey C. Stewart. New York: Garland Publishing, Inc.

———. 1989. *The Philosophy of Alain Locke: Harlem Renaissance and Beyond.* Ed. Leonard Harris. Philadelphia: Temple University Press.

———. 1992. *Race Contacts and Interracial Relations.* Washington, D.C.: Howard University Press.

Loraux, Nicole. 1986. *The Invention of Athens: Funeral Orations in the Classical City.* Trans. A. Sheridan. Cambridge: Harvard University Press.

Lucaites, John, Celeste Michelle Condit, and Sally Caudill, eds. 1999. *Contemporary Rhetorical Theory: A Reader.* New York: Guilford Press.

MacDowell, Douglass. 1978. *The Law in Classical Athens.* Ithaca, N.Y.: Cornell University Press.

Mailloux, Steven. 1989. *Rhetorical Power.* Ithaca, N.Y.: Cornell University Press.

Mailloux, Steven, ed. 1995. *Rhetoric, Sophistry, Pragmatism.* New York: Cambridge University Press.

Mattson, Kevin. 1998. *Creating a Democratic Public: The Struggle for Urban Participatory Democracy during the Progressive Era.* University Park: Pennsylvania State University Press.

McComiskey, Bruce. 2002. *Gorgias and the New Sophistic Rhetoric.* Carbondale: Southern Illinois University Press.

McKeon, Richard. 1946. "Aristotle's Conception of Language." *Classical Philology* 41, no. 4:193–206.

Meigs, Cornelia. 1970. *Jane Addams: Pioneer of Social Justice; A Biography.* Boston: Little, Brown.

Menand, Louis. 2001. *The Metaphysical Club: A Story of Ideas in America.* New York: Farrar, Straus and Giroux.

Morris, Charles. 1970. *The Pragmatic Movement in American Philosophy.* New York: George Braziller, Inc.

Nathanson, Jerome. 1951. *John Dewey: The Reconstruction of Democratic Life.* New York: Charles Scribner's Sons.

Nelson, John, Allan Megill, and Deirdre McCloskey. 1987. *The Rhetoric of the Human Sciences: Language and Argument in Scholarship and Public Affairs.* Madison: University of Wisconsin Press.

Nietzsche, Friedrich. 1967a. *Thus Spoke Zarathustra.* Trans. Thomas Common. New York: Random House.

———. 1967b. *The Will to Power.* Trans. Walter Kaufmann and R. J. Hollingdale. New York: Vintage Books.

Novick, Sheldon. 1989. *Honorable Justice: The Life of Oliver Wendell Holmes.* Boston: Little, Brown.

Oakeshott, Michael. 1975. *On Human Conduct.* Oxford: Clarendon Press.

Ober, Josiah. 1989. *Mass and Elite in Democratic Athens: Rhetoric, Ideology, and the Power of the People.* Princeton, N.J.: Princeton University Press.

Ochs, Donovan. 1993. *Consolatory Rhetoric: Grief, Symbol, and Ritual in the Greco-Roman Era.* Columbia: University of South Carolina Press.

Oravec, Christine. 1976. "Observation in Aristotle's Theory of Epideictic." *Philosophy and Rhetoric* 9:162–74.

Osborne, R. 1985. "Law in Action in Classical Athens." *Journal of Hellenic Studies* 105:40–58.

Perelman, Chaim, and L. Olbrechts-Tyteca. 1969. *The New Rhetoric: A Treatise on Argumentation.* Notre Dame, Ind.: University of Notre Dame Press.

Perry, David, ed. 2001. *American Pragmatism and Communication Research.* Mahwah, N.J.: Lawrence Erlbaum Associates.

Perry, Ralph Barton. [1948] 1996. *The Thought and Character of William James.* Nashville: Vanderbilt University Press.

Peterson, Forrest. 1987. *John Dewey's Reconstruction in Philosophy.* New York: Philosophical Library, Inc.

Pohlman, H. L. 1984. *Justice Oliver Wendell Holmes and Utilitarian Jurisprudence.* Cambridge: Harvard University Press.

———. 1991. *Justice Oliver Wendell Holmes: Free Speech and the Living Constitution.* New York: New York University Press.

Posner, Richard A. 1992. *The Essential Holmes: Selections from the Letters, Speeches, Judicial Opinions, and Other Writings of Oliver Wendell Holmes, Jr.* Chicago: University of Chicago Press.

———. 2003. *Law, Pragmatism, and Democracy.* Cambridge: Harvard University Press.

Posnock, Ross. 1998. *Color & Culture: Black Writers and the Making of the Modern Intellectual.* Cambridge: Harvard University Press.

Poulakos, John. 1984. "Rhetoric, the Sophists, and the Possible." *Communication Monographs* 51, no. 3:215–26.

———. 1995. *Sophistical Rhetoric in Classical Greece.* Columbia: University of South Carolina Press.

Poulakos, John, and Takis Poulakos. 1999. *Classical Rhetorical Theory.* Boston: Houghton Mifflin.

Poulakos, Takis. 1988. "Toward a Cultural Understanding of Classical Epideictic Oratory." *Pre/Text* 9:147–66.

———. 1997. *Speaking for the Polis: Isocrates' Rhetorical Education.* Columbia: University of South Carolina Press.

Poulakos, Takis, and David Depew, eds. 2004. *Isocrates and Civic Education.* Austin: University of Texas Press.

Pratt, Scott. 2002. *Native Pragmatism: Rethinking the Roots of American Philosophy.* Bloomington: Indiana University Press.

Reid, Ronald. 1959. "The Boylston Professorship of Rhetoric and Oratory, 1806–1904: A Case Study in Changing Concepts of Rhetoric and Pedagogy." *Quarterly Journal of Speech* xlv, no. 3:239–57.

Reynolds, David S. 1996. *Walt Whitman's America: A Cultural Biography.* New York: Vintage Books.

Robinson, David. 1982. *Apostle of Culture: Emerson as Preacher and Lecturer.* Philadelphia: University of Pennsylvania Press.

Rorty, Richard. 1979. *Philosophy and the Mirror of Nature.* Princeton, N.J.: Princeton University Press.

Rosenfield, Laurence. 1980. "The Practical Celebration of Epideictic." In *Rhetoric in Transition,* ed. Eugene White. University Park: Pennsylvania State University Press.

Rosenthal, Sandra, Carl Hausman, and Douglas Anderson, eds. 1999. *Classical American Pragmatism: Its Contemporary Vitality.* Chicago: University of Illinois Press.

Roth, Robert. 1962. *John Dewey and Self-Realization.* Englewood Cliffs, N.J.: Prentice-Hall, Inc.

Sathaye, S. G. 1972. *Instrumentalism: A Methodological Exposition of the Philosophy of John Dewey.* Bombay: Popular Prakashan.

Schiappa, Edward, ed. 1994. *Landmark Essays on Classical Greek Rhetoric.* Davis, Calif.: Hermagoras Press.

———. 1999. *The Beginnings of Rhetorical Theory in Classical Greece.* New Haven, Conn.: Yale University Press.

———. 2003a. *Defining Reality: Definitions and the Politics of Meaning.* Carbondale: Southern Illinois University Press.

———. 2003b. *Protagoras and Logos: A Study in Greek Philosophy and Rhetoric.* Columbia: University of South Carolina Press.

Schiller, F. C. S. 1903. *Humanism: Philosophical Essays.* New York: Macmillan.

———. 1907. *Studies in Humanism.* New York: Macmillan.

Schneider, Dorothy, and Carl Schneider. 1993. *American Women in the Progressive Era, 1900–1920.* New York: Facts on File, Inc.

Schollmeier, Paul. 2002. "The Pragmatic Method and Its Rhetorical Lineage." *Philosophy and Rhetoric* 35, no. 4:368–81.

Schudson, Michael. 1998. *The Good Citizen: A History of American Civic Life.* Cambridge: Harvard University Press.

Scott, Donald. 1980. "The Popular Lecture and the Creation of a Public in Mid-Nineteenth Century America." *Journal of American History* 66, no. 4:791–809.

———. 1983. "Print and the Public Lecture System, 1840–1860." In *Printing and Society in Early America,* ed. William Joyce, David Hall, Richard Brown, and John Hench. Worcester, Mass.: American Antiquarian Society.

Scott, Robert. 1967. "On Viewing Rhetoric as Epistemic." *Central States Speech Journal* 18:9–17.

Seigfried, Charlene Haddock. 1990. *William James's Radical Reconstruction of Philosophy.* Albany: State University of New York Press.

———. 1996. *Pragmatism and Feminism: Reweaving the Social Fabric.* Chicago: University of Chicago Press.

Shook, John. 2000. *Dewey's Empirical Theory of Knowledge and Reality.* Nashville: Vanderbilt University Press.

Shusterman, Richard. [1992] 2000. *Pragmatist Aesthetics: Living Beauty, Rethinking Art.* New York: Rowman & Littlefield Publishers, Inc.

———. 1997. *Practicing Philosophy: Pragmatism and the Philosophical Life.* New York: Routledge.

Singer, Beth. 1999. *Pragmatism, Rights, and Democracy.* New York: Fordham University Press.

Sleeper, R. W. 1986. *The Necessity of Pragmatism: John Dewey's Conception of Philosophy.* New Haven, Conn.: Yale University Press.

Sloane, Thomas, ed. 2001. *Encyclopedia of Rhetoric.* New York: Oxford University Press.

Stockton, David. 1990. *The Classical Athenian Democracy.* New York: Oxford University Press.

Suckiel, Ellen Kappy. 1982. *The Pragmatic Philosophy of William James.* Notre Dame, Ind.: University of Notre Dame Press.

Sullivan, Dale. 1993. "The Ethos of the Epideictic Encounter." *Philosophy and Rhetoric* 26:113–33.

Tapia, John. 1997. *Circuit Chautauqua: From Rural Education to Popular Entertainment in Early Twentieth Century America.* Jefferson, N.C.: McFarland & Co.

Thayer, H. S. 1981. *Meaning and Action: A Critical History of Pragmatism.* Indianapolis: Hackett Publishing Company.

Tiles, J. E. 1988. *Dewey.* New York: Routledge.

Too, Yun Lee. 1995. *The Rhetoric of Identity in Isocrates: Text, Power, and Pedagogy.* New York: Cambridge University Press.

Toulmin, Stephen. 1964. *The Uses of Argument.* Cambridge: Cambridge University Press.

Toulmin, Stephen, and R. Jonsen. 1988. *The Abuse of Casuistry.* Berkeley: University of California Press.

Tuggle, Melvin. 1997. *The Evolution of John Dewey's Conception of Philosophy and His Notion of Truth.* New York: University Press of America, Inc.

Vickers, Brian. 1988. *In Defense of Rhetoric.* New York: Oxford University Press.

Warren, James Perrin. 1999. *Culture of Eloquence: Oratory and Reform in Antebellum America.* University Park: Pennsylvania State University Press.

Washington, Johnny. 1986. *Alain Locke and Philosophy: A Quest for Cultural Pluralism.* New York: Greenwood Press.

Watson, Steven. 1995. *The Harlem Renaissance* New York: Pantheon.

Weaver, Richard. 1985. *The Ethics of Rhetoric.* Davis, Calif.: Hermagoras Press.

West, Cornel. 1989. *The American Evasion of Philosophy: A Genealogy of Pragmatism.* Madison: University of Wisconsin Press.

Westbrook, Robert. 1991. *John Dewey and American Democracy.* Ithaca, N.Y.: Cornell University Press.

White, G. Edward. 1993. *Justice Oliver Wendell Holmes: Law and the Inner Self.* New York: Oxford University Press.

White, James Boyd. 1985. *Heracles' Bow: Essays on the Rhetoric and Poetics of the Law.* Madison: University of Wisconsin Press.

White, Morton. 1949. *Social Thought in America: The Revolt against Formalism.* New York: Viking Press.

Whitehead, Alfred North. 1929. *Process and Reality: An Essay in Cosmology.* New York: Macmillan.

Wiener, Philip P. [1949] 1969. *Evolution and the Founders of Pragmatism.* Gloucester, Mass.: P. Smith.

Wiley, Mark. 1992. "Reading and Writing in an American Grain." *Rhetoric Review* 2, no. 1:133–45.

Wise, Winnifred. 1935. *Jane Addams of Hull-House: A Biography.* New York: Harcourt, Brace & Co.

Wood, Neal. 1988. *Cicero's Social and Political Thought.* Berkeley: University of California Press.

Yunis, Harvey. 1996. *Taming Democracy: Models of Political Rhetoric in Classical Athens.* Ithaca, N.Y.: Cornell University Press.

Index

About the Author

Robert Danisch received his Ph.D. in communication from the University of Pittsburgh and a B.A. in philosophy and in history from the University of Virginia, where he was an Echols Scholar.